SCREEN VIOLENCE

To Fiona

SCREEN VIOLENCE

edited by KARL FRENCH

BLOOMSBURY

ACKNOWLEDGEMENT

I thank my film-obsessed family and my friends (especially Dixie Linder) for their help, advice and encouragement. Also everyone at Bloomsbury, particularly Michael Jones and Penny Phillips, and Matthew Hamilton whose contribution was invaluable.

First published 1996

This paperback edition published 1997

This anthology © 1996 by Bloomsbury Publishing

The copyright of the individual contributors remains
with the respective authors.

The moral right of the authors have been asserted

Bloomsbury Publishing PLC, 38 Soho Square, London W1V 5DF

A CIP catalogue record for this book
is available from the British Library

ISBN 0 7475 3093 9

10 9 8 7 6 5 4 3 2 1

Typeset by Hewer Text Composition Services, Edinburgh
Printed in England by Clays Ltd, St Ives plc

CONTENTS

Contents

Introduction

KARL FRENCH

Let me come clean. I like violent films. Invariably, in debates on the subject I add several redundant qualifications – 'But I don't like real violence', 'I'm not at all violent myself', 'Well, that is, I like *good* violent films'. Of course, few people enjoy in a conventional sense the violence in certain great films – whether or not you enjoy what is on the screen, how you experience and react to it is the key to this subject. Often the film-maker's intention is to prevent the viewer from enjoying the event.

Going to the cinema, sitting down in the dark to be transported to a separate place, is a peculiar experience, intimate and shared, of a world recognisable and at the same time exotic and magical. At the beginning of Martin Scorsese's *Goodfellas*, the narrator Henry Hill says, 'As far back as I can remember, I always wanted to be a gangster.' In the safety of your seat, you silently nod and agree vicariously to live this life of exhilaration, sudden, random brutality, drugs and sordidness. The viewer is in a position of power and vulnerability. Films like *Blue Velvet* and *Peeping Tom* have exploited and investigated the essentially voyeuristic nature of cinema-going. Sitting safely in your seat, you are made complicit in what is happening on the screen. Hitchcock was supremely aware of this relationship between audience and film. He knew, for instance, that after the painstaking, even dull, establishment of milieu and characters at the beginning of *The Birds*, the audience would be almost crying out

2 for something dramatic to happen, effectively bringing on the action themselves. This dramatic device is a staple of the action thriller; films like *Aliens* and *The Wages of Fear* are constructed by the clock with the real thrills emerging roughly on the hour. This is closely connected to the offensiveness of violence. One can object not only to being forced (if one is ever *forced*) to see the dark and violent events on the screen but by implication to being made to feel responsible for them as a member of the audience.

Quentin Tarantino, who has been equally lionised and condemned as a creator of chic and insidious screen violence, is well aware of this idea of being trapped and constrained. Characters tied down awaiting torture or death are a recurrent feature in his work and such scenes in *Reservoir Dogs*, *True Romance* and *Pulp Fiction* became instant classics of cinematic sadism. Tarantino has said of his own work that violence is 'simply one of the things that you can do in cinema that's interesting to watch'. His hero, Jean-Luc Godard, was once asked by a critic why there was so much blood in *Pierrot le Fou*. He replied, 'That's not blood, that's red.'

My ever-growing list of favourite violent scenes and films includes perhaps the classic example of an eruption that just has to happen. In John Sturges's *Bad Day at Black Rock* (1955), Spencer Tracy is a one-armed war veteran, arriving at a small Western town in 1945 to deliver a medal to the family of a Japanese-American who died saving his life. The community harbours a dark secret; Tracy is constantly harassed until, long after the audience has not only silently granted him permission but begun urging him to take revenge, he is confronted by Ernest Borgnine. Pushed even further by this xenophobic bully, he gets to deliver the knock-out line, 'You're not only wrong, you're wrong at the top of your voice', before pulverising him with some fancy, one-armed karate.

Another acknowledged classic is *The Godfather*, which features as its climax the christening of Michael Corleone's nephew, cross-cut (particularly memorably as Michael renounces Satan and all his ways) with the four murders that wipe away his enemies and rivals. Rarely has the potential grandeur of screen violence been better realised. Brian De Palma, too, is a great one for the big shot, the grand effect. The end of his *Blow Out* possibly marks the zenith of nasty, unexpected violence, and what Pauline Kael calls the 'Mack Sennet chainsaw sequence' in *Scarface* is groundbreaking. But his greatest moment is the slow-motion climax of *The Untouchables* (film action, like basketball, was designed for slo-mo) at the Chicago railway station when a pram goes down the steps as a gunfight takes place between Kevin Costner, Andy Garcia and assorted gangsters. You can even impress your friends by commenting on how wittily it refers to Eisenstein's *Battleship Potemkin*.

There are many great, bloody climaxes (see Leone, Kurosawa) but one I must mention is the end of *Bonnie and Clyde* (1967). Some of the film's impact has been diluted by what has succeeded it. Still, you can take nothing away from the finale. In real life, Bonnie Parker and Clyde Barrow were shot a ridiculous number of times, and you can feel the film-makers' sense of freedom and possibility – one of the first sado-masochistic slow-motion orgies of squibs as the camera lingeringly records the young couple twitching from countless bullets.

While working on this list, I feel myself curiously pulled away from what I really like and drawn into a litany of filmic butchery. My mind fills with images and scenes from good, bad and ugly films: impalement (Dracula films *passim*, *Death Wish II*, *Friday the Thirteenth* parts I to VIII); bodies sliced in two (*Catch 22*, *Blind Fury*); rape (*A Clockwork Orange*, *The Accused*, *Straw Dogs*, *Death Wish* series *passim*); head injuries by gun (*Miller's Crossing*, *The Last Boy Scout*), baseball bat (*The Untouchables*); vice (*Casino*); psychic explosion (*The Fury*, *Scanners*). I could go on and it is all personal. These images remain, linger in the imagination, often uncomfortably but they exist in a separate realm from reality.

4   Whether this means we are ultimately safe from their effects is
a question that forms a connecting strand in this book.

Throughout the preparation of this anthology, I have continually asked people the question 'What do you think of screen
violence?'. What does it mean to you? *The Great Train Robbery*,
Bonnie and Clyde, *Psycho*, *The Blue Dahlia*, *Scarface*, *The Wild Bunch*,
A Clockwork Orange, *Blue Velvet*, video nasties, explosions, gunfire,
covering your eyes, walking out, fun, poetry, Clint Eastwood,
Tarantino, censorship versus freedom of expression, Chucky
the devil doll? The people I approached for contributions
responded in very different ways, with passion, disdain, concern,
confusion. Quentin Tarantino himself explained, bizarrely, that
he didn't want to be associated with violent films.

Since the turn of the century, violence (closely followed by
sex) has been the most controversial and emotive aspect of
the movies. Virtually every week it is the subject of attacks and
occasionally defence in the media. I am writing this just a few
days after a man shot and killed sixteen young children and their
teacher in a primary school gymnasium in the Scottish town of
Dunblane. This act will remain ultimately incomprehensible.
But there is now an almost routine agenda of healing, and one
element of this is apportioning blame. So, before the Queen,
John Major, Tony Blair or the grief and trauma counsellors
could reach the town, in fact just a few hours after the slaughter,
violence in films and videos was held partly responsible. By the
following morning, Warner Brothers announced that the video
release of Oliver Stone's *Natural Born Killers* would be delayed.
There is no evidence whatever that videos had played any role
in the crime.

In the same way, after the murder of the infant Jamie Bulger
by two young boys in Liverpool in 1993, there was a serious
attempt by some intelligent people (including the trial judge)
to blame this appalling crime on an inconsequential horror
film called *Child's Play III*. The boys had probably never seen

the film (although the parents of one owned a copy), but in 5
the atmosphere of moral panic that follows shocking events,
politicians, journalists, moralists and censors must be seen to
be doing something in reaction.

This has been the case for a hundred years. From the
start, film-makers were drawn to subjects involving action and
violence, and, as Will Self mentions, it is possible to say that
film is an inherently violent medium.

Throughout its history, the cinema has been accused of
being a medium of dangerous, subversive influence. Crudely
expressed, the argument is that if films are influential, then
the violence they portray will incite the audience and make
the world more violent.

The Great Train Robbery (1903), the first sustained narrative
film to receive worldwide distribution, contains the famous and
potent image of a gun being turned towards the camera and fired
straight at the audience. Not only is this perhaps the first great
unforgettable moment of screen violence, it is, incidentally, also
the cinema's first example of truly gratuitous brutality. When the
prints were sent out to cinemas, this scene was on a separate reel
with the instruction to the cinema owner that it could be shown
either at the beginning or at the end of the film.

Again, from the beginning, sociologists, politicians and
religious pressure groups have examined, been suspicious
of and tried to control violent images in films. Surveys
and commissions have explored the amount of violence in
films and the effect it has on the audience (usually with an
emphasis on children). These efforts have generally failed
to come up with evidence establishing a causal link between
cinematic and real violence. For example, in their influential
The Popular Arts (1964), Stuart Hall and Paddy Whannel
quote various reports on the effects of television violence,
and conclude that 'only the child who is already emotionally disturbed will actually *learn* violence [from a particular
programme]'.

6   But Hall and Whannel, having virtually dismissed the possibility of the direct link, almost immediately move on to the vague (and very common) warning that 'we gradually become habituated to certain attitudes and situations *if they are repeated often enough*' [their italics]. A similar conclusion is reached by John Trevelyan in *What the Censor Saw*, his memoir of his time as Director of the British Board of Film Censorship: 'Yet, except possibly in rare cases, there is no evidence that the fantasy violence in films and television begets or stimulates real violence. What I think it may do, if there is enough of it, is to desensitise people so that they find violence both normal and acceptable.' The present Chair of the BBFC (the 'C' now stands for Classification), James Ferman – who admits 'There's no doubt, I suppose, I do act like a Big Brother' – operates in a similarly idiosyncratic atmosphere. He will not, for instance, allow the martial arts weapons known as nunchakus to be seen in use on screen, and refuses *The Exorcist* a video certificate because of what he has described as its strange effect on adolescent girls. He is guided by the rule that 'There are certain kinds of images and certain kinds of contexts for images which are worrying.' This, while generally applied to the subject of sexual violence, is the rationale for censoring films that might lead to so-called copycat crimes. Back to *Natural Born Killers*. The cinema release of Stone's film was also delayed in this country pending the results of a BBFC investigation into accusations that it had incited imitation. 'We found media hype but no substance,' Ferman reported. The film was eventually released with the 150 cuts that had been made in America. Now, as we see in John Grisham's piece and Oliver Stone's response, the film and its producers may be subject to unprecedented litigation.

   The nub of the arguments of Mary Whitehouse and Michael Medved is their very real belief in the direct influence of the violent moving image. Medved talks of the possible effects of violent images in relation to the power of advertising – can violent films be said to be advertisements for violence? Mary

Whitehouse cites a case from the early seventies in which a tramp was bottled by a young man who had seen *A Clockwork Orange*. Martin Amis contends that this is chiefly a matter of style. Despite tremendous media coverage of imitative violence (mostly free publicity and often not discouraged by distributors) following films like *A Clockwork Orange* and *The Warriors*, it seems most likely that these films don't make peaceful people violent, but sometimes make violent people dress differently while they beat people up. However, it would surely take a pedantic mugging victim to complain of the indignity of being beaten up by men wearing bowler hats, white flares and fake eyelashes. Likewise, when news stories appear concerning the fights that have taken place during screenings of, say, John Singleton's *Boyz N the Hood* or, indeed, *Rock around the Clock*, surely it's just a matter of a cinema offering gangs a nice warm place to have a fight.

Alexander Walker talks of his resentment at being restricted in his viewing: because parliamentary legislation and the BBFC see their principal role as protecting children from the harmful effects of film, the whole audience is effectively treated like children. This can lead to a a target-market type of censorship. In the case of Richard Fleischer's *The Boston Strangler* (1968), John Trevelyan recalls that '. . . on specialist advice from psychiatrists we required a number of cuts to be made in order to avoid the risk of stimulation to potential psychopathic killers who might see the film.'

Trevelyan sums up his basic stance quite simply: 'Violence offended me personally.' This, I think, gets close to the heart of the matter. Screen violence is a complex affair, and the central issue of the relationship between film and viewer has possibly become more intricate in the last thirty years.

Films have certainly become more explicitly violent since the early sixties and their presentation of violence has changed significantly. In the Golden Age of Hollywood (Hollywood is largely what we mean by cinema, and Hollywood films provide the focus for most of the pieces in this collection), Westerns and

8 crime films (largely) took place in a world of moral certainty. The Western hero used his fists and revolver as tools of justice, and however glamorous the gangsters portrayed by Edward G. Robinson, James Cagney and Paul Muni, the audience knew that they would in the end be destroyed by the forces of law or their own hubris. But since McCarthyism, the Vietnam War (extensively witnessed throughout the world on newsreel film) and the exposure of political corruption, cinema audiences have become progressively more cynical and sophisticated and film-makers must be aware of this shift. (Although it's true that we *do* still go to the cinema for fantasy and escape, i.e. to be told stories, to be lied to.)

In 1960 in *Psycho*, it was deemed necessary to have a *deus ex machina* psychiatrist appear after the slaughter, to explain to the audience the nature of what they had just witnessed. Maybe, almost certainly, this was a Hitchcockian joke in which he mocked psychological explanations. In the nineties, it is assumed (by the film-makers if not the censors) not only that an audience is responsible enough to draw its own conclusions about the actions in *Henry: Portrait of a Serial Killer* (a film whose most violent, shocking and cut sequence was, in this post-modern, film-literate world, based not on any real events but on the scene of the family being killed in *Manhunter*), but that in *The Silence of the Lambs* a psychopathic serial killer should become the hero. Or was it just in the packed cinema where I saw it that the climactic prospect of Hannibal Lecter (who famously recalls having eaten a census-taker's liver) cannibalising a vindictive psychiatrist was greeted with cheers and laughter. Nigel Andrews touches on this unusual aspect of present-day cinema, where the biggest laugh relieves the greatest brutality.

Violence has become an increasingly complex tool – no longer just used by the bad guys to create an imbalance of justice which will be rectified by the good guys. But there is, I think, in tandem with this loss of innocence, another and simpler reason why screen violence has become more shocking, visceral and unsettling. It is often pointed out that in classical Greek drama, following the dictates of Aristotle, acts of violence take place off-stage and the audience is confronted with the shocking, bloody aftermath (blind Oedipus, butchered Agamemnon etc.). This is still an effective device, as shown in David Fincher's *Seven* which features almost no overt violence but is, as Nicci Gerrard observes in her essay, in its own way deeply and violently disturbing.

I suspect the Greek dramatists' restraint was not solely in the cause of maintaining an abstract dramatic purity. They simply didn't *have* blood squibs or swords with sprung blades. If you can't do violence well it is better not to do it at all. For example, the emasculation scene at the end of *Ai No Corrida* has obviously (and mercifully) not been achieved with the obsessive realism of the sex scenes. By the end of the film you are intimately familiar with the hero's penis, and it is patently clear that what the heroine has excised and is carrying around in her little bag is of different proportions.

With greater expectations of realism, with a greater knowledge of what real violence is like and with the increased sophistication of special effects, the look of cinematic violence has changed beyond recognition. *The Wild Bunch* is a watershed film. It is memorable as a great fable about the death of the West and for a superb, macho cast, but most of all for its glorious climactic, slow-motion blood-fest. In Sam Peckinpah's hands, the Western moved decisively away from the world of *The Lone Ranger* where men killed not only without drawing blood but without damaging clothes. In fact it travelled quite far in the other direction. It is not the occasional bullet but *every* bullet which penetrates the body, traverses the flesh and pulls a spurt of crimson viscera after it through the exit wound. This is a magnificent, heroic, tragic, satisfyingly and necessarily bloody sequence. This film is revered by many, among them Harry McCallion who writes here about its central, mythical place in his violent life.

10   This trend of escalation has continued to the present through films like *A Clockwork Orange* and *Straw Dogs*, the Vietnam cycle and the work of Coppola and Scorsese down to Tarantino and John Woo. I believe that the graphic depiction of conflict is the central concern for those who hate, dislike, fear or are disturbed by violent films. Will Self, a writer whose fiction many readers find offensively violent, dislikes and increasingly cannot watch violence on the screen. Nicci Gerrard and Ptolemy Tompkins are concerned about the impact of cinema on children's imaginations. Part of this worry derives from not knowing precisely what effect these films and images will have on young minds. But beyond that, and crucially, there is the simple offence (as expressed by John Trevelyan). Many viewers feel abused by being forced to confront violence. Gilbert Adair, for example, has compared the explicit modern cinematic killing as exemplified in the casual, shocking but semi-humorous scene in *Pulp Fiction* in which a young man is accidentally shot in the back seat of a car to the killing in the bowling alley in *Scarface* (1932). Where-as *Scarface* achieves its power through symbolism, he felt assaulted by the literalness and realism of the Tarantino film.

That these scenes are capable of giving offence is undeniable. But how dangerous are they? Are they dangerous at all? However apparently realistic films become, they are never truly real. I exclude of course 'snuff movies', if they actually exist, the death documentaries discussed (and on the whole enjoyed) by Poppy Z. Brite, and possibly *JFK* which must be the first and so far only mainstream Hollywood snuff movie, featuring in the Zapruder footage a real, famous exploding head. Surely the central aspect of screen violence, the central importance of films and art in general, is the relationship between the work and the audience. Why was it made? How does it make you feel? What does it make you think? Naturally one ought to acknowledge the fact that some people are offended, but the point is often to shock and surprise as much as to excite and exhilarate. Indeed Salman Rushdie has argued that he is delighted to cause offence – and he should know. Yet should one legislate or tailor works to accommodate this reaction? This offensiveness is certainly part of the appeal of violent films.

It is perhaps strange that so many (myself included) enjoy on the big screen what is repellent in real life. Vietnam War – bad: *Apocalypse Now!* –good. One can hardly overstate the importance, the sheer fun of screen violence. Many great films, virtually the whole careers of several top film directors (Lang, Kurosawa, Leone, Peckinpah) and stars (John Wayne, Clint Eastwood, Robert De Niro, Al Pacino) and entire genres (Westerns, crime/police/gangster films) have relied on the portrayal of action and violence.

There is a thread of violence running through the history of cinema that continues to fascinate and appal. In *Adventures in the Screen Trade*, William Goldman famously summed up what he had learned from his considerable experience in Hollywood: 'Nobody knows anything.' This golden rule applies here. James Trevelyan quoted a 1961 UNESCO report on 'The Influence of Cinema on Children and Adolescents' which tellingly concluded, 'The only thing we know for certain about the cinema is that we don't know anything for certain.'

It is claimed that we live in the most violent century in mankind's history and that the situation is getting steadily worse. This is arguable and it is ironic that what is often referred to as cinema's golden age of innocence coincided with millions dying in two world wars. What is certain is that we live in a world where violence constantly threatens to rip through the thin veneer of civilisation. The extent to which films reflect, exploit or influence this menacing undercurrent is unclear. In this book there are twenty-three highly personal pieces sometimes funny, serious or moving but always deeply felt – that examine the aesthetic, moral and political aspects of this controversial subject. I hope that, singly and collectively, they may throw some new light on it.

Blown Away

MARTIN AMIS

In the cinema, if not elsewhere, violence started getting violent in 1966. The films that marked the escalation, in my memory, were Arthur Penn's *Bonnie and Clyde* (1967) and Sam Peckinpah's *The Wild Bunch* (1969). And I was delighted to see it, all this violence. I found it voluptuous, intense, and (even then) disquietingly humorous; it felt subversive and counter-cultural. Violence had arrived. There was also, I noticed, a sudden flowering of sex and swearing. The future looked bright.

Before then, violence wasn't violent. People often talk, usually disapprovingly, about the way violence has become 'stylised' on film. But the old violence was stylised, too; it simply wore the soft gloves of much gentler conventions. Writing in the Fifties, Nabokov noted the ineffectuality of the 'ox-stunning fisticuffs' of an average cinematic rumble, and remarked on the speed with which the hero invariably recovered from 'a plethora of pain that would have hospitalised a Hercules'. Few of us are in a position to say which style is the more lifelike: the cartoonish invulnerability of the old violence or the cartoonish besplatterings of the new. We imagine that reality lies somewhere in between – that it is less dramatic, less balletic, and, above all, quicker. In life, the average fistfight, for instance, lasts about a second and consists of one blow. The loser gets a broken nose, the winner gets a broken hand, and they both trudge off to the outpatient clinic. Thus the great Stallone joins the queue at the trauma unit, while Chuck Norris fumbles with his first-aid kit. It just wouldn't play.

What happens, now, if you drag out the old movies and look again at even their most violent violence? I gained my first solid apprehension of earthly mortality not from the death of a relative or a pet but from the death of Jim Bowie in *The Alamo* (1960). Richard Widmark's skirling death cry haunts me still. I also remember my audible 'Jesus!' when I saw Paul Newman smash his rifle butt into the raised glass of the saloon Okie, in *Hombre* (1967). And who can forget the various torments meted out to Marlon Brando in *On the Waterfront* (1954), *One Eyed Jacks* (1961), and *The Chase* (1966)? (Brando, always well known for having his artistic 'say', definitely has a thing about getting beaten up.) Look again at such scenes and you marvel at your earlier susceptibility. They seem tame partly because they *are* tame (not dramatically but technically tame), and also because, in the interim, you have yawned and blinked your way through a thirty-year Passchendaele of slaughter. You have become, in other words, irreversibly desensitised. Macbeth – and let's make that Polanski's Macbeth – speaks for you when he says:

> I am in blood
> Stepp'd in so far, that, should I wade no more,
> Returning were as tedious as go o'er.

In real life, interestingly, desensitisation is precisely the quality that empowers the violent; empowers them to beat it away. In the moments leading up to violence, the nonviolent enter a world drenched with unfamiliar revulsions. The violent know this. Essentially, they are taking you to where they feel at home. You are leaving your place and going over to their place.

Screen violence, we might notice, has close affinities with the weapons business, and, to borrow an ageing phrase from the nuclear-arms community, is often technology-led. *Bullitt* (1968) is justly remembered for its car chase, which, astonishingly,

14 remains unsurpassed, despite bigger budgets, bigger engines, and the existence of furiously literal-minded actors willing to spend years of their lives bonding with racing drivers and crash dummies. But there was another standard-setting scene in *Bullitt*: the shotgun slaying of the underground witness, which entrains the incomprehensible plot. Suddenly, the door of the murky hotel room is kicked open; the police guard is shot in the thigh; the camera glances at this wound and then turns on the swarthy stoolie, who retreats with his hands raised, clambering up onto the foot of the low bed. As the gun is fired he is lifted off his feet and jerked through the air, smashing back-first into the wall in a nebula of blood. Soon after the film appeared, I happened to meet its director, Peter Yates, and when I asked him about this scene he took me through the mechanics of it – the blood pouch, the steel wires; in the old days, an actor who stopped a bullet would merely crush a ketchup sachet to the supposed entry wound and look indignant. If he was a bad guy, he would roll to the floor and decorously close his eyes. If he was a good guy, he would get really mad, then later assure the gasping blonde at his side that the bullet hole was just a 'scratch' or, better, a 'flesh wound'. Well, after 1968 there were no more scratches, no more flesh wounds. With the electronically ignited plasma-brimmed sandwich Baggie, the lurch cables and jolt harnesses, and so on, death by shotgun ceased to look like something you could quickly recover from.

In this context, the recent *Schindler's List* marks a progression or maybe a retrogression. Here the point-blank pistol shot to the head results in a tubular spout of blood followed by a tragic curtsy to the ground almost as girlish and theatrical as Uma Thurman's swoon in *Dangerous Liaisons*. One feels sure that this rendition was the result of close research, part of the carapace of verisimilitude that Spielberg needed to allow him artistic passage to the Holocaust. (Nearing the Holocaust, a trespasser finds that his imagination is decently absenting itself, and reaches for documentation and technique. The last thing he wants to do, once there, is make anything up.) In general, the escalation of violence in war films is not much questioned. Even the squeamish accept that a mechanised heartlessness forms the natural background – a civilian obedience, perhaps, to the hawkish axiom 'What did you expect? This is *war*.' We know more and more about the horror and pity of war, but we still seem to need persuading about the horror and pity of, for example, bank robbing, drug trafficking, serial murders, and chainsaw massacres.

To the extent that screen violence is technology-led, a specialised value system will tend to assert itself. As in the weapons industry, you will get no moral guidance from the specialist, the salaried expert. What you will get is the explanation 'Everyone *else* does it,' because, when up against can-do, don't-do will always finish second. Still, the prop-shop eggheads at places like Praxis and Visual Concept Engineering, the morphers and animators at Industrial Light & Magic or Dream Quest Images are mere hirelings; somebody has to *want* that particular splat or splatter, that cute decapitation, that ginchy evisceration. There is this half-formed view of Hollywood as an acropolis of conglomerates, or marketers and targeters, unsmilingly supplying the public with what it has come to want and need: more violence. But it doesn't work like that. 'Projects' swim around the movie community until someone with power gets connected to them. Then they get 'developed' by writers, producers and directors, and then get sent upstairs to the 'suits' – these supposedly pitiless bottom-liners. But what happens up there remains a mystery to everyone, the suits included. Some projects go ahead, and some don't. 'The only films they make,' a director once told me, 'are the films they can't get out of making.' The final decision, then, is the result of fatalism, embarrassment, or inertia – office politics, maybe, but not policy. So violence is director-led or auteur-led. Films are violent because the talent wants it that way.

Who else does, apart from me? One of the few points that survives the battering of Michael Medved's beleaguered

16   monograph *Hollywood vs. America* is that the moviegoing public *doesn't* like violence. In his introduction to the paperback edition Medved writes in heroic cadences about 'the passionate intensity of the public response to my work'; yes, he has taken his share of 'intemperate anger' and 'personal abuse', but on the whole, says Medved, 'I am grateful for whatever contribution my arguments have made to facilitating this discussion.' Certainly, *Hollywood vs. America* got Hollywood thinking, at least for a weekend or two (late nights in the dens of the Moorish mansions). And it got America thinking, too, and the controversy that gathered around it managed to trickle up as high as Janet Reno and Bill Clinton. It was a book, and a mood, whose time had come; the feeling that Hollywood – that faceless monolith – loved everything that America hated (violence, sex, swearing, drugging, drinking and smoking), and hated everything that Americans loved (religion, parents, marriage and monogamy, plus the military; policemen, businessmen and America). Now, I'm sure that Mr Medved seldom, if ever, gets into fights, which is just as well. After three hundred pages of his pedantry and sarcasm, I imagine him tooled up like he loathed Schwarzenegger, and spray-firing from either hip. His argumentative style is so strident that even his own intelligence, you suspect, is cowed and deafened by it. Why, oh, why, he typically asks, is Hollywood so obsessed by Vietnam and so unmoved by the struggle in Kuwait, which, 'amazingly enough', has yet to be celebrated on film? If Dan Quayle were a lot brighter, this is what he would sound like.

Despite its contemporary attire, Medved's theme, or plaint, is as old as time. It is *Ubi sunt!?* all over again. Where are they now, the great simplicities of yesterday?

In years past, in the heyday of Gary Cooper and Greta Garbo, Jimmy Stewart and Katharine Hepburn, the movie business drew considerable criticism for manufacturing personalities who were larger than life, impossibly noble and

appealing individuals who could never exist in the real world.
Today, the industry consistently comes up with characters
who are *smaller* than life – less decent, less intelligent, and
less likeable than our own friends and neighbors.

Medved's 'beat is the entertainment industry'. He knows about
the entertainment industry, but does he know about art – about
literature, for example, which has been following exactly the
same graph line for two thousand years? If art has an arrow,
then that is the way it points; straight downward, from demigod
to demirep.

Cinema is a young form, and has been obliged to make this
same journey in less than a century. I said earlier that violence got
violent in 1966, because that was the year the Hays Production
Code was revised, and film edged closer to being a director's
medium, freer to go where the talent pushed it. As we now know,
the talent pushed it away from the mainstream of America and
towards the mainstream of contemporary art, while playing to its
own strengths – action, immediacy, effect. So the great current
debate is caught in a confusion of categories. If cinema is just
mass entertainment, then Medved is an eloquent awakener. If
cinema is art, then Medved is just a noisy philistine.

We now enter a world of closed circles. By 1966, movie audiences halved, and they have stayed that way. Proportionately,
auteurism did more damage to the industry than the arrival
of television. Medved, with his polls and his content analysis,
gathers plenty of evidence to confirm what he wants to believe:
that Americans don't like violence – and violent themes and
violent language – and won't pay money to see it. (A final
analogy with weaponry; Americans have always been avowedly
pro-gun-control but somehow never pro enough to make any
difference.) Americans don't want violence. They probably
don't want art either. What Americans want is escape – escape
from American violence. American violence 'travels', it's said,
and enthralls audiences all over the planet, but Americans have

18   to live in America, where all the violence is. Does screen violence
provide a window or a mirror? Is it an effect or is it a cause, an
encouragement, a facilitation? Fairly representatively, I think,
I happen to like screen violence while steadily deploring its
real-life counterpart. Moreover, I can tell the difference between
the two. One is happening, one is not. One is earnest, one is play.
But we inhabit the postmodern age, an age of mass suggestibility,
in which image and reality strangely interact. This is now perhaps
the most vulnerable area in the common mind. There is a hole
in the credulity layer, and it is getting wider.

In Britain, in recent months, two of the most sensational
murder trials of the century have involved discussion of the
same rental video; namely, *Child's Play 3*. The first case was
that of James Bulger, a toddler who was beaten to death by
two ten-year-olds; the second case was that of Suzanne Capper,
a teenager who was kidnapped, strenuously tortured, and finally
set alight by a clique of young acquaintances. *Child's Play 3*
has therefore been much in the news, and therefore much
in demand. It, too, has been set alight, semi-ritualistically, by
public-spirited managers of video-rental stores. When my two
children (aged seven and nine) noticed *Child's Play 3* in its
package, up on a high shelf, they regarded it with reverent dread.
In their schoolyard voodoo, *Child's Play 3* was considered potent,
venomous, toxic. It was like angel dust – a ticket to frenzy.

So one afternoon I duly settled down to watch a routine little
horror film about a children's doll called Chucky that comes
to life and starts killing people. The modicum of horror it
inspires can be traced back to Freud's definition of the uncanny:
ambiguity about the extent to which something is, or is not, alive.
Equally conventionally, such frights and shrieks as the film elicits
have to do not with very scary things happening but with mildly
scary things happening very suddenly. As the credits rolled on
Child's Play 3, I felt no urge or prompting to go out and kill
somebody. And I knew why, too. It's nothing to boast about,
but there is too much going on in my head for Chucky to gain

sway in there. Probably the worst that Chucky could do to me is to create an appetite to see more Chucky, or more things like Chucky.

What we have to imagine is a mind that, on exposure to Chucky, is already brimful of Chucky and things like Chucky. Then, even if you mix in psychopathology, stupidity, moral deformation, dreams of omnipotence and sadism, and whatever else, Chucky is unlikely to affect anything but the *style* of your subsequent atrocities. Murderers have to have something to haunt them; they need their internal pandemonium. A century ago, it might have been the Devil. Now it's Chucky. When the killers tortured Suzanne Capper, they chanted the catchphrase, 'I'm Chucky. Wanna play?' When the ten-year-old boy began to throw bricks, James Bulger fell down and stood up again. 'Just stand there,' said the killer, 'and we'll get you a plaster.' And then he threw another brick. This is Chucky's way: the worthless joke, the worthless swagger. Here was a mind that had seen a lot of things like Chucky, and had nothing much in prospect but more things like Chucky. Perhaps, also, the child didn't understand the meaning of earnest. As a result, he was all too ready to play.

from *The New Yorker*, 1995.

Hollywood's Four Big Lies

MICHAEL MEDVED

On November 25, 1995, unidentified thugs perpetrated an especially pointless and sadistic act of violence against an innocent employee of the New York City subway system.

Squirting a huge quantity of flammable liquid into a Brooklyn token booth, they then lit a match and blew it to pieces, burning toll-taker Harry Kaufman, aged 50, over most of his body. After remaining for two weeks in critical condition, Kaufman died of his injuries, leaving behind the two children he had been working overtime to support through college.

This horrible incident might have been ignored as just another example of random urban cruelty except for the eerie resemblance between the attack and scenes in a movie that had been released just four days earlier. In *Money Train*, a mindlessly violent 'action film' in which Wesley Snipes and Woody Harrelson play New York City transit cops, a vicious pyromaniac executes two fiery assaults on toll booths that are identical in virtually every detail to the episode that killed Harry Kaufman.

The unusually close connection, in terms of both substance and timing, between these movie images and correspondingly violent realities seemed to offer an unmistakable instance of life imitating art – if one chooses to dignify *Money Train* with a designation as art. The incident also presented a particularly potent challenge to those Hollywood apologists who continue to deny the increasingly obvious (and in fact unmistakable) connection between violence on screen and violence in the streets.

In the aftermath of the much-discussed toll-booth attack, those apologists resorted to the four well-rehearsed, endlessly repeated arguments which for many years have characterised the entertainment industry's defence of its own bloody excesses. Those arguments are:

1 – There is no conclusive scientific proof that media violence encourages real world violence in any way, or is anything more than harmless entertainment. Moreover, the fact that tens of millions of people watch television and motion picture brutality without ever imitating what they see suggests that such imagery exerts less of an influence than critics suggest.

2 – Hollywood just reflects reality, rather than shaping it. Don't blame the entertainment industry, blame society at large.

3 – The potentates of the popular culture merely give the public what it wants, following the profit motive in the manner of all other businessmen. Consumers are at fault with the emphasis on violence, not producers.

4 – If people don't like brutal films and television programmes, they can always choose to ignore them and to support more innocent alternatives. Meanwhile, they should stop complaining and attempting to interfere with the sort of entertainment preferred by their neighbours and fellow citizens.

Each of these familiar and superficially plausible arguments is so profoundly misleading that it properly could be called a lie. Reviewing and rebutting these four big lies is the first essential step to any honest or enlightening discussion of the deeper issues of violence in the media.

To reconsider these arguments in turn:

22   **Lie Number 1 – 'It's just harmless entertainment, with no solid proof that it influences the public.'**

Not even the most short-sighted and self-absorbed Hollywood executive believes this absurd proposition.

About two years ago I appeared on a panel which included officers of three major film studios. After I criticised what I considered the irresponsible behaviour of the entertainment industry, one of these executives angrily observed that while Hollywood is always blamed for the damage it does, it's never given credit for its positive impact. 'You don't acknowledge that a movie like *Lethal Weapon III* saved thousands of lives,' he declared.

Though I had reviewed the film, I couldn't recall any life-giving messages in this blood-spattered thriller. So during my allotted rebuttal period I asked what he had in mind.

'It's very simple,' he explained. 'In that movie, right before a big chase scene, there was an intense three-second close-up showing Mel Gibson and Danny Glover fastening their seat belts.'

Just consider for a moment the blatant contradiction and hypocrisy in his suggestion. He seems to be arguing that the mass audience would immediately imitate the socially constructive messages of a three-second scene, but that the rest of the movie's ultra-violent 118 minutes would have no influence at all. The same stupidity is involved with the entertainment industry's self-congratulations regarding the responsible messages about condoms or recycling or saving the rain forest that are inserted occasionally in films and TV programmes. How can we think that such fleeting images will have a positive impact on society, but the irresponsible sex or unrestrained violence that often accompany them will have no negative impact?

The same contradiction is built into the very structure of the commercial television industry.

That industry exists based on its ability to persuade hard-headed corporate chiefs that thirty seconds of advertising time can influence the public on the widest possible range of products. No one in the television business even questions the notion that a well-crafted commercial can help to sell anything, from pet food to politicians – and even some politicians who resemble pet food. Yet television and movie executives stubbornly deny that the thirty minutes that surround the thirty seconds will in any way sell behaviour or values. Are we supposed to believe that the public watches most television shows in a semi-conscious stupor, too inattentive to be influenced in any way, but then when the commercials come on the average viewer snaps smartly to attention?

Beyond the illogic in this notion, there's a wealth of academic research to disprove it. Despite the insistence of industry apologists that no definitive connection exists between pop culture violence and real world crime, more than two hundred recent studies show that prolonged exposure to brutal imagery in the media leads to more hostile, violent and aggressive attitudes and behaviour on the part of those who consume such material. For instance, Professors Leonard Eron and Rowell Huesmann of the University of Michigan completed a twenty-two-year study following children from age eight through adulthood. They found that the single best predictor of later aggression – more than poverty, school performance, family structure or exposure to real violence – was a heavy childhood diet of television bloodshed. 'Of course not every youngster is affected,' says Eron. 'Not everyone who gets lung cancer smoked cigarettes. And not everyone who smokes cigarettes gets lung cancer. But nobody outside the tobacco industry denies that smoking causes lung cancer. The size of the correlation is the same.'

Epidemiologist Brando Centerwall of the University of Washington has made exhaustive studies for the American Medical Association of the statistical impact of the introduction of television on various communities around the world. Adjusting for all other factors, he still concludes that televised violence contributes mightily to the high rate of crime. He asserts that

24   without TV there would be 10,000 fewer murders per year in the United States, 70,000 fewer rapes and 700,000 fewer assaults.

Leaders of the entertainment industry remain unpersuaded by such research, countering this data with the irrefutable observation that many people watch violent imagery without any demonstrable change in their behaviour. For instance, movie critics do not have a measurably higher incidence of violent crime – despite the fact that we see more violent films than nearly anyone else. Jack Valenti, president of the Motion Picture Association of America, made this same argument in a televised debate with me in 1994, triumphantly citing the example of his own two children who seemed addicted to violent entertainment as they were growing up, but now have reached adulthood without ever entering a life of crime. According to Mr Valenti's thinking, this homely example disproved the notion that media violence exerts any destructive influence.

Such logic is, of course, absurd.

Consider again the example of television advertising. Hundreds of millions of people around the world may see a commercial for a luxury motor car, for instance. Does the fact that the overwhelming majority of those who watch the ad will never buy the car prove that the commercial has exerted no influence?

Of course not. The automobile company knows that if they sell their product to only a tiny fraction of those who see their ad then they have enjoyed a spectacular success.

The fact that a piece of violent entertainment doesn't influence *everybody*, doesn't mean that it doesn't influence *anybody*. But like a commercial for any product, if it touches the lives of only a small portion of the audience then it can significantly change the social reality. The problem of crime in western society isn't that everyone behaves violently, but that a relatively tiny number of us behave violently again and again. Studies indicate that media imagery is one of the significant factors driving this small but dangerous group.

At the same time, brutal films and television programmes affect even those who never imitate what they see, in the same way that the aforementioned automobile commercial will serve to change the attitudes of even those who never buy the car. Those who watch that advertisement may come away, after repeated viewings, with the unspoken impression that the car in question represents some new standard of elegance – it's chic, sexy, fashionable and desirable. In the same way, repeated exposure to hyper-violent entertainment redefines brutal behaviour as the ultimate standard of manliness. By associating such behaviour with some of the most attractive stars in the world, Hollywood inevitably glamorises violence.

This is the fundamental power of the entertainment industry: its ability to redefine normal conduct and to shape new standards of desirable behaviour. In this way, the popular culture can not only change our ideas of what is accepted, but alter our notions of what is expected.

This brings us to the second of Hollywood's Four Big Lies, which suggests:

Lie Number 2 – 'We don't shape reality, we just reflect the world as it is.'

Paul Verhoeven, director of such glittering ornaments to our civilisation as *Robocop*, *Basic Instinct* and *Show Girls*, makes this point whenever he discusses these issues. 'Art is a reflection of the world. If the world is horrible, the reflection in the mirror is horrible.' In other words, Verhoeven argues, Hollywood's contributions to the pop culture of the world are saturated with violence and horror only because the society that gives birth to these visions is similarly saturated with violence and horror.

I actually enjoy testing this hypothesis whenever I have the opportunity to lecture before a large group. First, I'll ask for a show of hands from all those who have ever experienced the tragedy of witnessing a murder in real life; only very rarely will

26 a hand go up. Then, I'll ask a follow-up question, asking how many people present have recently witnessed a murder – or a dramatisation of a murder – on television; invariably, everyone in the hall raises a hand.

This simple demonstration reflects the fact that the most violent ghetto in American life isn't South Central Los Angeles or Southeastern Washington, D.C. – it's prime-time television. The overstatement of violence is appalling and inexcusable. Studies at the Annenberg School of Communication at the University of Pennsylvania indicate that an average of 350 characters appear every night on all prime-time shows on all major networks, and that seven of these people are murdered each night. If this murder rate applied in reality, Americans wouldn't need to argue about 'Zero Population Growth' because we would very quickly have zero population; within some fifty days, all Americans would have been murdered, and the last one left alive could turn off the TV.

The overstatement of violence leads to other distortions in Hollywood's reflection of reality. Authoritative statistics compiled by the Screen Actors Guild show that 70.9 per cent of all roles in feature films – and 64.6 per cent of all TV roles – go to men. In the face of these well-advertised numbers it's hard to imagine how leaders of the entertainment industry can still claim that they merely portray the world as it is. Thank God we don't live in a world that's 71 per cent male!

Of course, the princes of the popular culture will argue that such alterations of actuality are nothing more than harmless dramatic licence with no negative impact on the audience. This assertion is contradicted, however, by many academic studies of the impact of media. Professor George Gerbner of the University of Pennsylvania writes about the 'mean world syndrome' which TV and movies encourage, leading to fearful and anti-social behaviour particularly among children. In a similar vein, criminologist James Q. Wilson of the University of California at Los Angeles (UCLA) writes about the 'broken windows effect' and its impact on crime. He notes studies performed on four different continents that show that on city streets where broken windows remain unrepaired, the crime rate immediately soars. These streets will register significantly higher rates of violence than other largely identical blocks in the same neighbourhood, with no broken windows. Why? How can we explain the odd fact that broken windows – or uncollected trash, or prominent graffiti – should apparently cause crime?

The answer is that the broken windows make a powerful statement to the public. They shout out the idea that here, chaos reigns. Here, standards have broken down, and no authority applies. Law-abiding citizens are encouraged to leave the neighbourhood, or else to huddle, terrified, behind the locked doors and windows of their homes. Meanwhile, the shattered glass serves as an invitation to the most destructive criminal elements, urging them to come and do as they please, without consequences.

Today, television and movies have become a huge broken window to the entire society. The portrayal of life without standards and violence without consequences sends the message that it's potential victims, not potential criminals, who should be most fearful.

In any event, the blood-soaked imagery of American entertainment may display elements of a self-fulfilling prophecy, but it can hardly be justified as an accurate reflection of reality.

When forced to concede that obvious point, defenders of the entertainment establishment inevitably regroup behind the next line of defence, insisting that these violent fantasies are needed in order to attract an audience, and advancing the third of Hollywood's big lies:

Lie Number 3 – 'We just give the public what it wants.'

This contention carries the force of common sense; after all, everyone knows that the major entertainment conglomerates are ruthless in their pursuit of profit. One might therefore

28   automatically assume that the mere fact that they feature carnage so prominently in their entertainment menu demonstrates that the public craves and demands such material.

The only problem with this assumption is that it's flatly contradicted by data from the box office. For the last twenty years, relatively non-violent 'family fare' has consistently outperformed blood-soaked shockers among motion picture releases, while television ratings from the United States and around the world show little appetite for the most brutal material. Consider the leading money-makers of 1995, including *Apollo 13*, *Toy Story*, *Casper* and *Pocahontas*. None of them could be described as hyper-violent. Along similar lines, *The Lion King*, *Forrest Gump*, *Aladdin*, *Driving Miss Daisy*, *Mrs Doubtfire*, *Four Weddings and a Funeral*, and countless other films have achieved spectacular commercial success without emphasising blood and guts.

In my book, *Hollywood vs. America*, I analysed the box office performance of all films released in the United States since 1980 according to their rating by the Motion Picture Association. This computer study produced startling results, as those titles rated 'G' and 'PG', and aimed at family audiences, consistently outperformed 'R' rated films with their emphasis on graphic sex and violence. In fact, during the entire period under study (1980 through 1992) the 'G' and 'PG' titles earned more than twice as much on average at the domestic box office as the 'R' films – and yet the percentage of 'R' titles continued to soar beyond the level of 60 per cent of the total release schedule.

This is not to say that no audience exists for graphically violent 'action' films; of course, some moviegoers in every country enjoy this sort of material and will eagerly pay their money to see it. But no evidence suggests that this is the only audience for feature films, or even the largest audience. The idea that Hollywood can only make major profits out of movies dramatising murder and mayhem is only a convenient fiction, utterly unsupported by statistics or experience.

This conclusion doesn't argue that the entertainment industry is evil or conspiratorial, but it does suggest that it is profoundly dysfunctional. Hollywood continues to emphasise violent material for several reasons – it is always easy to write and produce, and many film-makers (who harbour deep insecurities as sensitive intellectuals) enjoy the aura of manliness and machismo that cutting-edge action fare helps to confer. There's also the problem of the industry's tendency to hand out prestige and recognition based on the dubious notion that artistry and shock value are roughly equivalent.

In 1994, *The Lion King* made three times the money worldwide that *Pulp Fiction* made, but everyone who follows films knows – and praises – the director of *Pulp Fiction* (Quentin Tarantino) while no one could even name the directors of *The Lion King* (Rob Minkoff and Roger Allers). By the time most writers, directors and stars get to the point where they can personally 'green light' a picture, they don't have to worry about where their next meal is coming from – or where their next Jaguar is coming from, for that matter. They crave acceptance and respect from their peers even more than they crave money, and that respect is often granted to the most violent and disturbing fare.

It's become a commonplace to condemn greed in Hollywood, but a bit more intelligent greed would probably be a good thing in the movie business. It would never lead to the total elimination of violent material (nor should it), but it would almost certainly result in a reduction of such fare.

And meanwhile, as we wait for changes in the movie business, Hollywood's leading spokesmen attempt to soothe an increasingly restive public by intoning the fourth, and final, of the industry's big lies:

Lie Number 4 – 'If you don't like it, you can always turn it off.'

This reassuring platitude turns up in different forms whenever the entertainment establishment hears pleas from the public for

30   greater media accountability. 'Nobody's holding a gun to your
head and forcing you to see destructive entertainment,' industry
leaders will argue. Or, as Jack Valenti once declared, 'When
people say, I don't like that kind of film, I say, you have the
most effective weapon known to man – don't go to see it.'

A personal experience in 1993 helped to teach me the
misleading and dishonest nature of this line of reasoning. On
that occasion I had the chance to talk about movies and media
with a classroom full of bright children between the ages of ten
and twelve. To my surprise, the film that most provoked their
interest was *Indecent Proposal* – the inane melodrama in which
billionaire Robert Redford offers struggling architect Woody
Harrelson $1,000,000 in return for spending just one night with
Harrelson's adoring wife, Demi Moore. Several kids felt that this
film raised particularly important issues, and speculated before
their classmates that their own mothers would gladly take such
payment for similar services. This entire discussion surprised me,
because *Indecent Proposal*, with its adults-only 'R' rating, should
have been hard to see for these ten, eleven and twelve-year-olds
– and, in fact, none of the children in the class had actually seen
the film. Nevertheless, they knew all about its plot, its steamy
scenes, and even its resolution.

The source of such information wasn't parents – it was
the implacable promotional machine that creates the widest
possible public awareness concerning new films, television
programmes and popular songs. Even if you don't pay money
to see a motion picture yourself, you can learn about its
contents from magazines, chat shows, television commercials,
newspapers, billboards, the Internet, newspaper reviews, and
the daily buzz at the water cooler in your office, or on
the playground at your school. Very few Americans actually
witnessed the notorious 'lap dancing' scene in the wretched
film *Showgirls* – the picture proved to be a major box office
bomb. Nevertheless, due to the intense public discussion
that the movie inspired, tens of millions of people for the

first time became familiar with the concept of lap dancing.

On a similar note, even those who have never attended a
Michael Jackson concert, never bought one of his tapes or CDs,
and never chosen to watch one of his TV specials, surely know
who Michael Jackson is – and probably know more than they
care to know about some of his personal idiosyncrasies. Like it
or not, Mr Jackson and other leading figures of the pop culture
are part of the air we breathe; you can no more escape them
than you can escape pollutants in the atmosphere.

That's why the statement that 'if you don't like it, you can
just turn it off' makes about as much sense as the assertion that
'if you don't like the smog, you can stop breathing'.

The influence of the media is pervasive, invasive and, ultimately, inescapable. Even if, through some miracle, you can
isolate your own family from the influence of TV and movie
messages, you can't protect the children who live next door –
and it is those children who may at some point hit yours over
the head or pull a knife on them in a school lavatory.

The question of media influence is properly understood as
an environmental issue. At a time when we are demanding that
leading corporations take more responsibility for their pollution
of our air and our water, it's entirely appropriate to insist
that huge entertainment conglomerates demonstrate greater
accountability for their pollution of the cultural atmosphere
we all breathe.

Understanding the four lies that Hollywood inevitably mobi-
lises in its own behalf is essential for a balanced discussion of the
current state of the entertainment industry. It's also appropriate
to begin answering those lies with the truth – knowing the truth,
speaking and writing the truth and, as far as possible, living
the truth.

This means that the first lie, arguing that violent entertainment actually influences no one, deserves an affirmation of the
simple but profound idea that 'messages matter'. This doesn't

32 mean that governmental censorship is an appropriate response, but it does suggest that television viewers should become more discerning consumers, considering the underlying values and influence of the entertainment they choose to support, as well as responding to the glamour of its stars or the excitement of its action scenes. The notion that 'messages matter' doesn't mean that exposure to one vile and violent movie, or one example of trash TV, will instantly change your life or reshape your personality – any more than a single indulgence in a hot fudge sundae will alter your cholesterol level. Repeated consumption of ice cream delights will, however, exert a cumulative impact on your health (and your waist line) and by the same token consistent indulgence in the worst aspects of the popular culture will exert a slow, subtle influence on your home and your family.

As to the second lie, the suggestion that popular culture merely reflects reality, it's essential to educate ourselves and our children to understand media distortions and to rely less on this source of information in drawing conclusions about the world around us. This education should take place not only at home but, where possible, in our schools. Among children, the tendency to unthinkingly accept Hollywood's often brutal and dysfunctional vision of society greatly encourages the sour, apathetic, cynical and self-pitying mood that afflicts too many young people in western society. We should lose no opportunity to affirm that the opportunities enjoyed by most people make the world a far more hopeful place than might be inferred from the dark fantasies of the American entertainment industry.

The third lie – that Hollywood merely gives the public what it wants – highlights the enormous difficulties in pushing the entertainment establishment to adopt a more responsible attitude towards media violence. If the public has already displayed a clear preference for less brutal, more family-oriented fare (as it unequivocally has), then the industry's reluctance to respond suggests that changing the consumption patterns of the public isn't enough to alter the emphasis of the show business elite. A comprehensive approach to the problem involves changing the stubbornly insular culture of the show business community, as well as adjusting the consumption patterns of the public. Part of this change requires a more sceptical view from critics and industry insiders of the latest examples of 'artistic' gore from Scorsese or Tarantino, and a less dismissive attitude towards the finest achievements in family friendly entertainment. The leaders of the pop culture, like chronically insecure creative people in every field, crave the respect of their peers even more than they yearn for purely commercial success. This means that Hollywood needs an attitude adjustment not only towards what constitutes good business, but towards what amounts to worthy art.

Finally, the fourth lie presents the most personal challenge – no, it's not possible simply to 'turn off' the popular culture in our lives, but it is possible to turn it down. The messages of the entertainment industry may be inescapable, but it's still within our grasp to reduce the amount of time we waste on show business fantasies. In the United States, the average citizen devotes an appalling twenty-six hours per week to watching TV. In Great Britain, the pattern is somewhat less alarming (with most estimates showing an average of twenty weekly hours spent with the small screen) but still involves an immense distraction from the more important and fulfilling business of life. Someone who averages twenty hours a week on television will, at the conclusion of an average life span, have given a total of nine uninterrupted years to his television set. This total involves twenty-four-hour days, seven-day weeks, fifty-two-week years. The most significant problem in the popular culture isn't too much violence; it's too much TV, period.

Would anyone wish for an inscription on a gravestone that declared, 'Here Lies Our Beloved Husband and Father, Who Selflessly Devoted Nine Years of His Life to His Television Set'?

34 That television set doesn't need your time, but your family does, your community does, your society does.

In devising strategies for dealing with media violence the most important priority is to encourage personal action to reduce TV consumption. Ultimately, the only television schedule you can control, the only movie release line-up you can definitively influence, involves the material that you choose to watch. At the moment, we need less attention to supply-side solutions, and more attention to a demand-side response; less focus on what Hollywood makes, and more focus on what the world takes. On this basis, we can each move swiftly and decisively to make a difference, taking powerful, private steps to shape our own more responsible media environments.

Interview with Karl French – June 1996

CAMILLE PAGLIA

KF: What do you think about the use of women characters, women actors, in violent films?

CP: Let me just make a general statement of my attitude towards screen violence. The largest ideas in my writing are these: that modern popular culture represents an eruption of the buried paganism in western culture, and part of my thesis is that Judaeo-Christianity never did defeat paganism at the end of the Roman Empire, but rather it went underground and has erupted at three key points – paganism at the Renaissance, at Romanticism, and now in what I call, 'The Age of Hollywood', (the twentieth century). The very first chapter of my first book has the phrase, 'sex and violence' in it because I regard the principle themes of paganism as sex and violence. So, when people deplore, especially in America, the pornographic sexuality or the excess of violence in the media, I always say that these are the energising principles, in point of fact, of mass media. Mass media to me is a pagan form, and Judaeo-Christianity has never been able to deal honestly with these great principles of sex and violence.

Secondly, there is a huge and very moralistic argument that has been going on in America now for twenty years: there is a kind of unholy alliance of Christian conservatives and feminists on the question of violence and its influence on actual behaviour.

36   I am one of those who do not believe that there is any direct
relationship between violence in fiction, in any representation
– whether it's a play, or the movies, or television – and actual
behaviour in real life. Evidence for this is merely anecdotal. In
America the overwhelming sentiment, with hundreds of studies
claiming to prove this, attributes the violence on the streets of
inner-city America to excessive television violence, excessive
violence in movies, and so on. I think that is ludicrous! I
follow the view that watching violence is cathartic – that
where you have examples of people imitating violence on
the screen, you already have a violent personality, who in
would not have needed that kind of model. We look through
history, and we see that violence and atrocities have occurred
in every era without the aid of movies or television. So, with
that out of the way, I view the violence of the twentieth century
as in fact an attempt to search for *nature* which has been lost
after the Industrial Revolution. In the last one-hundred years in
America anyway, we have gone from this agricultural country,
where eighty percent of the people lived on the land, to where
they now live in the cities in a very bland middle-class life, very
much removed from the elemental energies of nature. For me,
all screen violence ultimately has to do with a kind of religious
ritual – a pagan contemplation – of these forces that are out
there and that also erupt in storms and tornadoes and so on.
So, there is my theoretical position on. I do not follow the
puritanical and extreme feminist view that watching violence
on screen is bad for you, makes you a bad person. That is the
didactic, eighteenth century view of literature – that art has an
obligation to teach you a better way to behave.

I also make an analogy with sports. For me, the dominance
of sports in the world is part of this pagan eruption of popular
culture, and I think that when we talk about screen violence,
we have to talk about the controlled aggression in sport, which
I take very seriously as well. The second volume of *Sexual
Personae*, which has been sitting in a box since 1981, goes,

'Movies, television, sports, rock music'. We all know the way the Greeks viewed sport as a kind of sacred exercise. I believe it is impossible to talk about violence on the screen without talking about what's going on in sport because it all has a lot to do with choreography – that is, the choreography of the body. When we watch violence on screen, we are not only watching the body pushed to its literal limits but even every kind of mutilation or distortion or amputation or decapitation. Everything that we are seeing on screen is in fact an attempt to rediscover the lost sensual physical truths about the body that are completely removed from us, sitting in these sanitised offices with a computer.

KF: What do you think about the use and portrayal of women in violent films – like the portrayal of rape? Were you ever personally offended by these?

CP: You're talking about movies where women are the victims of violence . . .?

KF: Where women are used as victims of violence for entertainment.

CP: You're not talking about the great *film noir* style with the femme fatale – the vampy figure who actually deals the violence, who actually is holding the pistol? You're talking about cases where you see women as victims?

KF: Exactly.

CP: I personally believe that if someone undertook an accurate survey of violence in the movies from the beginning, from the nickelodeon period on, and really computed the number of victims, male and female, that there are, you would find, I believe, that the male victims far exceed the female victims. The obsession with the female victims in film is, I think, very moralistic and Victorian. Ultimately, I think it is a kind of testament to woman's power, as people remember the one woman who is victimised, not the twenty or forty male victims that may be piling up in any given Sylvester Stallone film. I think that this obsession with female victims is a form of hysteria and

38 that it has very little to do with reality. Are you referring to some specific film?

KF: Well, I was thinking of films like *The Accused*, which is one example, or *Straw Dogs*, where it's ostensibly an entertainment film, where part of the entertainment is derived from –

CP: Yes, I know exactly what you're talking about now. There seems to me – it has been going on now for several decades, and it's very strong on American TV – of great interest in watching a woman in peril. It goes all the way back to the beginning of silent films where you have the villain kidnapping the fair maiden and tying her down to the train tracks. Audiences derive some tremendous pleasure, a kind of combination of fear and pity, from watching a woman in peril. I don't believe in the usual conventional feminist view that what is going on is a sadistic desire to dominate the woman. On the contrary, I think that it has to do with woman's emotional importance, her centrality to everyone's lives. Every single individual, male or female, staggers out from the shadow of a mother goddess. So we are obsessed with the image of woman. I believe that woman is not the victim of the universe, in the normal feminist way, but the dominatrix of the universe.

Anyway, there is an entire genre of American TV docu-dramas, that has been going on for twenty years here, just night after night after night, not quite so much now, but consisting of some woman, a valiant woman played by Jaclyn Smith or Cheryl Ladd or someone like this, who would be put in danger. Sometimes these stories are based on real-life. She would be put in some terrible danger, perhaps raped, abused by a husband, whatever, and she fights back, and by the end she triumphs over her victimiser. There was just an incredible obsession with the story – a very structurally based, identical storyline, time after time after time after time. It's obvious that there is some sort of strange erotic pornography in this – a kind of delectation in identifying with her. The audience identifies itself with the travails of the heroine. I just do not accept the feminist party line thing that it's all about. '*Yes, well, we're going to put woman in her place now*'. I think that that's ridiculous!

As for the idea of taking voyeuristic pleasure in the suffering of male or female, I have constantly talked about this in terms of the iconography of Italian Catholicism, of Latin Catholicism, where you have tortured saints of both genders *everywhere*. If you want to talk about the biggest image in the history of the West – perhaps the history of the world – of sadomasochistic voyeurism, you must talk about the crucified Christ. I mean, many more millions of people have meditated on the crucified body of Christ the male than they have on victimized woman. So again I think that this is going into the history of mass media and picking out this one thing and interpreting it in a very flat and quite unimaginative feminist way. I have never been convinced by this. I always enjoy, myself, scenes where a woman is being pursued, she's being stalked, and there's like a slight rape innuendo, and so on. For some reason, I understand it. I don't know how I understand it – it's part of the diversity of my responses. I'm a lesbian, you have to remember. I'm looking at things often perhaps from the viewpoint of the male. But there are just so many movies like this. *Straw Dogs*, as a matter of fact, I think is less singular for the rape scene than for the fact that it was made at a period, like *Bonnie and Clyde*, where you suddenly began to get a very raw, rough and unedited version of screen violence. I think it's more *that* that we remember that film for. *Straw Dogs* didn't make that much of an impact over here. It's really *Bonnie and Clyde*, where there are two victims, male and female, who are being riddled with bullets.

KF: Yeah, but briefly going back to the idea of films from say *Psycho*, through the . . .

CP: *Psycho*! Oh, a masterpiece, yes of course. Yes, I *adore* *Psycho*. Of course, what I adore is the first forty minutes. I *love* the entire thing, the whole thing! Whenever that film is on, I watch it. To me it's like a Brahms' symphony or something, that first forty minutes, where Hitchcock goes through the whole

40   scene – where she steals the money, and then flees and she's
going along the highway, and then the shower scene, and so
on. Now there is absolutely no doubt that we are taking some
voyeuristic pleasure in watching it. I mean, Hitchcock goes to
great lengths to enhance the eroticism of that scene. I talked
about the parallels, in my first book, *Sexual Personae*, between the
great *Psycho* shower scene and the scene in the Balzac story, *The
Girl with the Golden Eyes*, where you have a lesbian woman who is
cutting to pieces, with a knife, the body of her lover for having
been unfaithful with a man. It's very, very similar. Both male
authors, Hitchcock and Balzac, go to great lengths to eroticise
that object, and then you have this slashing of the object to
ribbons, which deconstructs the object, and so on. Again, I
suppose the conventional feminist view would be to look at this
as some sort of sexism. That's not the way I look at it. I look at it
as, well, of *course* the female body is more fragile, more delicate,
more beautiful than the male body. The male body is beautiful
in art, in history, for its strength, for its muscular articulation,
but the female body, just by virtue of biology, has a softness and
vulnerability. Therefore when we see it being torn to ribbons,
we have this sense of a barbaric kind of splendour. I've also
made the parallel to Delacroix's great painting of *The Death of
Sardanapalus*, where you have the same thing happening, where
there's a swirl of destruction around the king Sardanapalus.
You have his horse being slaughtered, its throat is being cut,
you have his odalisques having their throats cut, you have all
of his possessions and his gold going up in flames and so on,
just as the fall of Troy is portrayed in Virgil, this kind of orgy
of destruction. So, again, I look at the history of film, and I
have to stress that people are really focusing too much on the
destruction of female images. Look at the way men are killed
– again and again and again.

KR: What about 'slasher' films like *Friday the Thirteenth*?

CP: The 'slasher' films are not my cup-of-tea! I've criticised
them. I've said, for example, that a film like Catherine Deneuve

in *The Hunger* – here you have an example, by the way, where the person doing the violence is a woman, okay? Why aren't people obsessed with this? – that I think that movie is really over the top. I complain in *Sexual Personae* that Catherine Deneuve on her hands and knees slavering over cut throats is just absolutely excessive. I prefer a vampirism that has to do with tasteful blood-sucking, with a lot of erotic settings and so on. No, I thought the 'slasher' movies, compared to Hitchcock, are very sloppy. But what has happened, in general, with the increase in the technical quality of the special effects is there has been an escalation in the savagery of the violence. There's a cartoon kind of violence, so that the children today, when they look at a film like *The Birds*, which terrorised my generation when we were in high-school – I know that my best friend's children laugh at us and say, 'The Birds?'. I mean, there is absolutely nothing that scares them in it at all, just a bunch of crows chasing some kids and getting their feet tangled in their hair! The kids today, I think, are really very jaded, because they look at films in the same way they look at video games – there is a sort of penny arcade look.

So I think that violence has indeed used to excess. But I *don't* look at it in moral terms. I don't say, 'Oh! There's too much violence. This is terrible! Look what it's doing to our society! I think, in point of fact, that a lot of violence in films *jades* people. It doesn't at all inspire them to violence. I think that it is an *artistic* error when you have explosions of violence which should be used minimally. I mean, we know that in the Greek theatre all violence, all physical action was narrated. There's all these long messenger speeches, and you're asked to *imagine* violence rather than see it portrayed in front of you. Shakespeare's having actual action on stage was regarded as a critical error by people who were trying to invoke the classical codes. Obviously, to the neo-classicists Shakespeare was vulgar, for his combat scenes on stage and so on. So, yes, there has been an increase in violence which has to do with a speed up

42 of culture in general in that period of the 1960s. But again, I don't draw any moral conclusions from it. I think there is an artistic deadening from it. On the whole, film has fallen off in artistic quality from the high point of European art film in the late fifties and sixties. Those great art films had very little violence in them, in fact I meaning Ingmar Bergman's *Persona* where you have the explosion at the end where the women start slapping each other and biting each other's wrists, it's like, 'Whoa!'. It's amazing because there has been no violence whatever in the film.

But I think that the body in action and the body in assertion and in suffering is one of the great themes of the movies, one of the great themes of modern popular culture. Christianity cannot deal with it. Christianity cannot deal with aggression, and so we get this spilling over into films. I fail to see how film is any less realistic than life. I mean, in a century where you have had two enormous world wars, okay, with fascism and Nazism and everything else, and the barbarities in the news – what's going on in Africa this very moment, in Liberia and Rwanda – for heavens sake, this just is the human condition. I do not think that movies lie. I think that movies are showing us the reality of history.

KF: Do you think that recent mainstream commercial successes like *Basic Instinct, Silence of the Lambs* and *Fatal Attraction* show us reality?

CP: I *love Basic Instinct,* and I defended it, okay? It was being constantly picketed over here by feminists and gay activists because something was a wrong way to show a woman or a lesbian.

KF: Even while it was being made.

CP: Yeah, even while it was being made. And then when it first came out, the protests were quite stupid. *I love* the film but I felt it was a bit excessive. The actual violence scenes were a little bit more than I would prefer, but on the other hand I think that it's very minimal when you actually compute the number of minutes, literally, in *Basic Instinct*, that are violent. Most of it is Sharon Stone vamping around, looking fabulous. Either she's sitting on her patio over the rocky shore, or she's engaging in that fantastic interrogation scene with the policeman, or she's mixing a drink for Michael Douglas and dropping ice on the floor. What made that movie great and made it indelible and made it a masterpiece, in my view, is Sharon Stone's vampy performance. Towards the end there's a big slaughter as well. I mean, I don't like that kind of thing. I love the great Hitchcock period where violence is done in a very skilful way. I think that was a high point, where you get violence integrated with eroticism. But Hitchcock was a genius, and it's very difficult for other people to imitate him. The moment you start getting imitations, you know, De Palma imitating Hitchcock, you can see that they are not able to do it, to treat violence in an economical way.

Now, *Fatal Attraction*, I think, is one of those great films that came out of nowhere, no one expected it to do well, it just struck a chord with the popular imagination. It is one of the most *abused* films, of course, by the feminist establishment. Susan Faludi, who knows nothing about popular culture and who has no feeling for art whatsoever and who had a very expensive and flawed Harvard education, okay, treats *Fatal Attraction* as some sort of a conspiracy in her book *Backlash*, by the Hollywood, white male, heterosexist establishment to set feminism back. In point of fact, that movie struck a chord – the people voted with their dollars for that film, and it really appealed to them. Now, in terms of the violence in it, I cannot *bear* any kind of scenes where animals are abused. That is where I draw the line! (laughs) I dislike the scene with the rabbit, I think that's pathos and has nothing to do with adult art forms. But as far as the violent scenes – it's so beautifully choreographed, where you have Glenn Close and Michael Douglas slamming each other around, first in the apartment where he goes to warn her – there's this great scene where they smash each other back and forth and she grabs the knife for the first time – and then that scene at the end where

44 she invades the house and it ends with her being drowned in the bathtub – those are brilliantly done scenes. Both of them are absolutely mind-boggling. I think that they really stand up, they hold up, they are imaginative, and it makes you feel that the man is fighting for his life against this woman who seems paranormally energised. She seems like Ligeia, like something out of an Edgar Allan Poe story. I think that it's a wonderful film. And the third one you asked about was *Silence of the Lambs*. Well, it's a little queasy for me, that kind of stuff. I don't think that we absolutely need to be contemplating body parts in films. You see things starting to go wrong a tiny bit in Hitchcock's *Frenzy*, where the movie opens with a body being fished out of the river.

KF: Yeah – and Anna Massie ends up dead in a potato van.

CP: Oh, yeah, that is wonderfully done, by the way. I think that's amusingly done, where you have (laughs) a nude body being tossed around with all the dust from the potatoes. But I think something started to happen. Historically, at the moment that Hitchcock was doing *Frenzy*, Anglo-American culture was starting to go haywire. Because reality was starting to overwhelming film at that point. From the moment of the assassination of John Kennedy in 1963, all hell breaks out. You've got every kind of mass murder, assassination, riot. I mean, for instance, the Manson murders, the Richard Speck killing of eight student nurses in Chicago. You see, that's what happened, and so one cannot keep on looking to film and blaming film for these things, when films was pedalling furiously and still not coming anywhere near the horrors of what actually was happening. My God, you had the President of the United States with his skull exploded, at the side of his wife. His wife has to try to get up on the back of the moving limousine to catch a piece of his skull as it flies out – come on – his brains splattered all over the car, we're talking about the leader of the free world. So movies at that point in the sixties began to lose the balance between the suggestion of violence and the actual representation of violence and became sort of

nauseating. I don't like to be nauseated So I am critical but for
artistic reasons. I am absolutely totally opposed to the idea that
movies or any form of art have an obligation to show us a better
life. And I also reject the idea that life imitates art – that there's
an absolute, slavish connection between a person who goes into
a theatre and is brainwashed by what he or she sees and then
copies it. That is an absurd argument and always has been.

KF: A couple of things. One, briefly about Hitchcock. I
agree that he was a great director, but he was nakedly
misogynistic . . .

CP: I don't accept this. This business – which is very current
and has been going on for fifteen years at least – where people
attack artists of the rank of Hitchcock – whether you have Albert
Goldman talking about Elvis Presley or John Lennon, or you
have the feminists dismissing Picasso and Degas as misogynists.
I do not accept this, that Hitchcock was a misogynist. That is an
absurd argument that is indeed current. Good God, what are
we talking about? We're talking about a man who made films
in which are some of the most beautiful and magnetic images
of women that have ever been created. I mean, for heaven's
sake, to call that misogynistic, when we think of Grace Kelly
in *To Catch a Thief*, when we think how fabulous Janet Leigh
is in that shower scene, we think of Kim Novak in *Vertigo*, and
Eva-Marie Saint in *North by Northwest*. That is absolute madness.
I mean, Tippi Hedren is so fabulous in *The Birds* and *Marnie*.
They say, 'Oh, well. He has to punish them at the end. He wants
to see them suffer.' Give me a break!

What I'm saying in my work about all of the great artists
from Michelangelo and Botticelli to everyone else is that in the
fascination with these goddess-like figures of women there is an
ambivalence, a push-pull in it, a complexity of response, but no
stress the negative in Hicthcock, to say that he was dreaming,
dreaming, dreaming always about women, and that he was
paralysed in his imagination between adulation and fear? I
think you need far more complex terminology to deal with

people who achieve at the level Hicthcock did. My favourite Hitchcock is from exactly that period – he period where the women come forward in this dreamy way. I admire but don't particularly care for the earlier Hitchcock, in black and white. It's the Technicolor Hitchcock, where these women come out The women he created, for heaven's sake, absolutely have dominated the imagination of late twentieth century cinema. Everyone's imitating it, everywhere, to this day.

So, I reject the word 'misogyny' when applied to Hitchcock. I reject the word 'misogyny' when applied to anyone, in point of fact. I think that that is a stupid word. 'Misogyny' means literally, 'hatred of woman', okay? Now and then, I have met misogynists, some doctrinarian gay activists, for example, I am aware of certain misogynists in the literary establishment in America towards me, for example. In other words, if I were a Jewish male, I would not necessarily have gotten the abuse I have gotten, as an Italian-American woman. I know that perfectly well. But I think that it is utterly inappropriate when we are talking about imaginative artists of this level. Don't ever, ever, ever, listen to any artist talking about his or her work. I mean, everyone knows this. Okay, not everyone. It's like saying to bob Dylan about something in a song, 'Oh, what, huh, huh, huh . . .', Imean, please. Artists are under obligation to create, but you cannot ask them to explain, that is the function of critics. You can never, ever trust an artist talking about his own films. The artist is usually lying, about his work and about other people's work.

KF: What do you think about women taking control in violent films? I'm thinking of the heroines in James Cameron movies and the director Kathryn Bigelow.

CP: Well, I don't know much about Bigelow. As for *Aliens*, people hailed it as some big feminist thing at the time. I suppose that is good in its own way. I like the idea of putting guns in women's hands, but you know Bette Davis was doing it – playing murder scenes, early on. It is good to have women that are superheroines, but I don't think that a woman's power in the world is primarily as a superhero. I cast myself as a superhero on the front of my last book, *Vamps and Tramps*. Look there I'm posing as Diana Rigg in *The Avengers*, with a knife stuck to my hip, and I'm in a guerilla mode. I think that is one model of womanhood. I think it is an extreme model – it's the Amazon model, alright? But I think that from the beginning of time to the end of time, woman's greatest power is in the sexual realm. It will always be that, and most art is going to be contemplating that. You have brief periods where, you know, the career woman comes in – Joan Crawford or Katharine Hepburn, and so on – and I love that, but I don't think that the world's obsession is going to be with women actually acting in that way. I think that it's important for women to have that option for life, to actually have a career, to make social changes in the world, to rise in their profession, but I think that so much of world art is focused, is obsessed with, woman's dominance of the sexual realm. So I think that great movies will continue to be entranced by that, and most artists are inspired by that. I think cinema is a mode of dreaming, really, dreaming in public.

KF: You've probably heard that John Grisham is blaming *Natural Born Killers* for two recent murders and is encouraging the families of the victims to take Oliver Stone to court.

CP: Well, I respect Oliver Stone, but I thought *Natural Born Killers* was an awful film. It's sometimes stupid beyond belief. Almost an impossible plot. First of all, my problem with that film is that it is not realistic. I feel that if violence is going to be used in a film, it's either going to be some sort of a wild, futuristic, science-fiction fantasy of some sort where clearly we are living in another realm, but if you're dealing with contemporary life, I think that violence gains by being surrounded by a very ordinary, realistic context. The plot of *Natural Born Killers* makes no sense whatever. In term of, especially, its treatment of television, the television news, I mean, this was a great opportunity to really do a scathing critique of television news. I don't think it succeeded

48 because I don't think it shows much familiarity television. It's the creation of a movie mind, someone who's been watching movies, not someone who's been watching television. Television has quite different rhythms than are shown in that film. The film is just totally over the top, out of control. At a certain point, violence used too much becomes a kind of caricature. If you were suing any artist – I mean, Ozzie Osborne was dragged into the courts, in Utah or Nevada, for some album that supposedly caused a kid to commit suicide. I mean, it's ludicrous. In fact, Ozzie Osbourne's wife said very pungently to the American media, something like, 'Good thing Shakespeare isn't around, he'd probably be sued. Heaven knows how many people have been inspired to violence by the *Hamlet*'. I've said this many times – there are a lot corpses piled up by the end of *Hamlet* and we don't have any examples of people rushing out into the street and committing murder because of it.

But Tarantino, well, I *loved Pulp Fiction*. I thought it was absolutely wonderful, but I thought *Reservoir Dogs* was way too violent. In *Pulp Fiction*, there's this balance between comedy and character development and full-fleshed performances and the violence. Many people detested *Pulp Fiction*. People either love a cult film here or they loathe it and find the violence absolutely unbearable. I did not find the violence off-putting at all. I found it very well integrated with the whole. It's a very difficult balancing act, very difficult indeed. I absolutely take the position that no artist in any medium has the obligation to elevate the audience, okay? Every artist must follow his or her instinct. If Oliver Stone felt like doing that movie at that particular time, that's interesting to me because I'm interested in Oliver Stone, and I think that that film is a little bit like Ken Russell. Sometimes these very baroque and extravagant imaginations go over the top. Fellini, for example, was able to hold everything in balance, then all of a sudden it went completely excessive, and it all fell apart, and his characteristic imagination seemed not to be in control anymore. So, whatever

Oliver Stone chooses to do, I would watch it and think about what he is thinking about now. His is a very long career with many phases in it. Again, as a lapsed Catholic I am totally opposed to people marching into art – which I think is what popular culture is – with a political or moral agenda. No one has any right to be preaching any code to any artist, that is my position. The moment you start getting people preaching, you start to get the beginning of censorship. I believe that art opens a window on the dark human soul – that's what it does. I could understand if a film like *Natural Born Killers* was being piped into the schools or something and people were being forced to watch it, but no one is being forced to watch any film. I just totally disagree with the idea that, 'Oh, we must clean things up and we'll have a better society, a utopian society. Then if we have all very positive images of life in art, there won't be any crime and there won't be any bad behaviour.' That is ridiculous! From the beginning of time people have been murdering each other. Did the Aztecs need any movies to model their ritual executions on. A thousand victims a week, their chests slashed open and their living hearts pulled out and the bodies thrown down the bloody steps of the pyramid. When you look at the atrocities of history, the grisly human imagination is all you ever need. So what I see in modern movies is that we are looking directly into the dream-life, the nightmare dream-life of mankind. It is realistic, it is not a distortion of reality.

I believe in artistic standards, I really do, and I think that in the greatest films as in the greatest novels there isn't excess. Take films like *The Godfather* for example – I think that it is an absolute work of genius. *The Godfather III* does not reach the level of parts one and two. The way the violence is done in those scenes, the executions and so on – at the time some people were put off and felt it was too much. I have seen those films so many times, again and again and again on television. I just know them frame by frame. I think they are some of the most accurate films made about Italians, first of all, but

50   the violent executions, they are done so well. Each execution scene has some particular signature. It is so carefully thought out in terms of how the human body actually does or would react in a particular scene – as in *Godfather II*, flashing back to the beginning of the whole story in Sicily, where the young Godfather is taken by his mother to see the mafia chieftain and she begs for her son's life and pulls a knife on the chieftain, and then she's blasted by this shotgun – Boom! – and they pull her body back by wires and show exactly what the effect is of a shotgun hitting the body. Each execution is done with enormous imagination and as if it were choreography. I am someone, first of all, perhaps I should mention, who had a summer job in college in the emergency room of a city hospital. I was the ward secretary of St Joseph's Hospital in Syracuse, New York, where I grew up. And the thing is, I sometimes think that possibly that experience has made me a tiny bit more workmanlike in talking about the way the human body can be mutilated and so on. When I went there for my job interview, my knees went weak at the mere sight of the silver instruments, but I forced myself over that summer to look at every single casualty and injury that came through the doors from the ambulance. And after a while I think I got the kind of joviality or jocularity that soldiers get on the battlefield and that all doctors get. If you knew the kind of joking that goes on inside the emergency rooms! People just sing out, 'Here's another one!' and so on. So I saw everything from bullet wounds to stab wounds to people very cut up or dead from car accidents.

Also I think the Italian attitude towards death and violence is very based in rural life. People who are horrified by violence are very middle-class, and they've been separated from the elemental life, the life out in nature, that farmers live. You know, a farmer is very used to disaster and to animals being injured and they're used to all the messy processes of birth an death. I think that I have a kind of robust, instinctive, rural realism about violence and suffering and death that most middle-class writers

and academics have utterly lost. They tend to be horrified by
the slightest thing and go, 'Oh, no! Oh, oh, oh, how awful!' I was
very aware of it when I got to my first job after graduate school at
Bennington College in Vermont. We talked about this actually.
When people from the city arrived to teach at Bennington, they
would go, 'Oh, that poor dog has hurt its leg!' And the farmers
would say, 'Oh, yeah. Get that dog out of here,' or something like
that. There's a kind of sentimentality about physical injuries and
death that people have gotten from the Victorian period onward,
from the sanitisation and over-protection of middle-class life. So,
I would say that as well.

Time to Face Responsibility

MARY WHITEHOUSE

It was the late Sir Hugh Greene, then Director General of the BBC, who described television as 'the most powerful medium ever to affect the thinking and behaviour of people'. And one is bound to ask – if this is true of television, how can anyone doubt it is not also true of film? Especially as film forms the foundation of so much of what we see on our television sets, not least after the 9 p.m. watershed.

This watershed has itself been established in order, so we are told, to protect the young from unsuitable material. Not, of course, that it does, because we now live in a society in which well over 50 per cent of children have TV sets in their own bedrooms and are adept at switching them on long after Mum has kissed them goodnight, switched off the light, and gone downstairs – probably to watch the very films she did not wish the children to see!

There is a long history of concern about the effect of film upon the young. Way back in 1950 the Home Office published a report on 'Children and the Cinema'. As I browsed through it again I came across the following, to my mind, very quotable quote – 'The harmful moral effects attributed to "bad" films are commonly centred on the exhibition and glorification of crime, violence and sexual licence, the latter none the less deplorable because it is often coated with a thin layer of conventional morality ... that many films do contain sequences that are brutal, anti-social or licentious is undeniable. Some of these sequences will pass over the heads of the youngest children and it may be that only a few films err seriously in these ways, but these few must, on the grounds of ordinary human experience, be accounted bad influences on the minds of those who see them. We have no doubts at all about such films. We think they are bad and we should like to see them banned altogether to children' – and that was best part of fifty years ago!

If that is true of the cinema how can anyone deny its truth when applied to television – not to mention video?

Concern grew as evidence of the use of violence in film multiplied as internationally respected psychologists and social scientists like Leonard Berkowitz, writing in *Scientific American* in 1964, concluded that 'film media violence is potentially dangerous . . . (it has) increased the chance that an angry person and possibly other people as well will attack someone else'.

The problem persisted and in 1975 Dr Michael Rothenburg appealed for 'an organised cry from the medical profession' against violence on television and its effects on children. Working as a child psychiatrist in Seattle's Children's Orthopaedic Hospital and Medical Centre he stated that '50 studies involving 10,000 children and adolescents from every conceivable background all showed that viewing violence produces increased aggressive behaviour in the young' and went on to call for 'immediate remedial action'.

How far did this get us? The truth is – nowhere at all. In 1994 the Independent Television Commission criticised Channel 4's *Brookside* for violence culminating in the use of a kitchen knife as a murder weapon during its omnibus edition – at 5.05 p.m. on a Saturday afternoon!

I find now that I have a very real problem and it's this – in order to illustrate one's argument one has, as it were, to multiply the crime! Take the film *Nightmare on Elm Street,* shown not only in the cinema but also – where else – on Channel 4 TV (17.10.94). Here follows an assessment of some of the violence it contains:

54   Girl attacked by satanic force in bedroom. Her body flung round room and hoisted to ceiling. Her chest slashed. Blood-soaked body flung onto bed, walls splashed with blood. Young girl pursued by maniac with knife-blade fingers in dream. Girl in bath with legs wide apart. Hand with knife-blade fingers appears out of water between her legs. Girl then pulled under water by satanic force. Youth attacked in prison cell by satanic force and hanged by bedsheet. Fountain of blood hitting ceiling in torrents. Girl throws petrol on man and then sets light to him.

And then, of course, there was the film *A Clockwork Orange*, without an assessment of which no study of violence would be complete. After watching the film sixteen-year-old Richard Palmer hit a tramp over the head with two lemonade bottles until they smashed, beat him with slabs of crazy paving and when the old man staggered away battered him with two bricks and beat him with a stick. Then he left him, cycled home, and went calmly into his own home.

During his trial the prosecuting counsel told the Court that if robbery had been the motive it was only for ½p, the change the tramp had in his pockets after someone in the fish shop queue had given him 15p to buy his supper. But, he added, 'the conclusion that the film had some terrible influence on what is happening is inescapable'. And the psychiatrist who examined the boy said 'the real explanation is truly macabre and frightening. It seems as though momentarily the devil had been planted in the boy's subconscious. In my submission, it is the irresistible conclusion that whatever was planted there followed the violence of *A Clockwork Orange* which perpetrates violence in its ugliest form. This is the only possible explanation for what this boy did.'

Palmer's defence counsel, Roger Gray, said there was no evidence whatsoever that the boy was suffering from any mental disease. He was not drunk, neither had he taken drugs – 'what possible explanation can there be for this savagery other than the film?' The lawyer spoke of yet another 'callous comparison'. He said that, in the book, the gang, following the attack on the old man, were quoted as saying 'then we went on our way'. Palmer, after his attack on the old man, told police 'when I got home I noticed I had some blood on my trousers, then I went to bed'.

Mr Gray continued, 'how many impressionable young men have these sadistic tendencies which film directors and TV producers turn into mindless sensationalism producing a dreadful canker among them? All responsible people desire to see this dreadful trend stamped out.'

But far from being 'stamped out' the film, well launched with Stephen Murphy's X Certificate (1971), became a cult with a language of its own. The film, with its masochistic setting, reiterates a theme which is fundamental to much now freely available pornography – woman is there to be raped, she deserves to be raped and raped she must be. 'Gang-bang' suggests a romp – give crime a jolly name and even depravity and multiple rape sounds fun. The mascaraed, clockwork orange 'droogs' with their archaic speech, mannerisms and clothes, engaged in tellingly formal acts of rape, robbery and murder, had become the 'heroes' upon whom, as Scotland Yard reported, a dozen gangs in Central London alone were modelling their life-styles. And in May 1976, Herbert S. Kerrigan, one of Scotland's leading advocates, spoke of the three murder trials in 1975 which to his knowledge had been 'triggered off by seeing *A Clockwork Orange*'.

All this did not – could not – happen in a vacuum. As Enid Wistrich, then chairman of the Greater London Council's Film Viewing Board pointed out in her book *I Don't Mind the Sex, It's the Violence* (1972), the public backlash against the so-called 'liberalisation' of film and television resulted in the GLC itself coming under pressure to ban both Kubrick's *A Clockwork Orange* and Ken Russell's *The Devils.* It is interesting, and significant,

56   that Alexander Walker of the *Evening Standard* (29.1.72) made a statement to the effect that the Committee's decision to see *A Clockwork Orange* meant it would 'have to consider the social and political implications of such films in the light of the chaos in Ulster, the Aldershot outrages and the violence in the picket lines'. He pointed out that the broadcasters were anxiously watching all these developments 'with their own medium of television in mind. If such films were to be shown in the cinema where would that leave them?'

Alastair Milne* has told how the governors of the BBC became so concerned about the increasingly violent and obscene films becoming available for television that a private session was arranged for them in the office of the British Board of Film Censors in Soho Square early in 1973. After, apparently, being handed a warm glass of gin, they were regaled with the burning at the stake in *The Devils*, the rape and mutilation scenes from *Straw Dogs* and the gang rape from *A Clockwork Orange*.

Apparently, Alastair Milne tells us, 'the Governors were stunned; indeed two lady Governors were speechless while the Chairman, Michael Swann, was moved to articulate their anxieties'. However, Mr Milne and his colleagues at the BBC comforted the Governors by telling them that the Corporation already had 'pretty tough guidelines' to help them handle such productions.

That's as may be, but what is certain is that the problem didn't even begin to go away and it was Sir Michael himself who argued that violence, and 'society's attitude towards it should be based on the assumption of adverse effect until that is disproven'.

It was around this time that I addressed the Royal College of Nursing and referred to the fact that the techniques of conditioning used in the film *A Clockwork Orange* were similar to those being used by the American Army to train assassins. I went on to say:

---

* Alastair Milne, Director General of the BBC, 1981–85, in *Memoirs of a British Broadcaster*.

When the movement which I represent was founded in 1963, we said quite simply that the constant presentation of violence on our television screens would significantly promote and help to create a violent society. We were ridiculed for our pains, called cranks and accused of being squeamish. We sensed then and believe strongly now, that the screening of violence, horror, shock and obscenity into the home, where the viewer sits comfortably, detached, in his easy chair, where he can switch off mentally or physically whenever he wishes, can have nothing but a destructive effect upon our sensitivities and our society. So do the real horrors of war, death, and poverty become no more than conversation pieces, fantasy worlds, increasingly accepted as no more than entertainment.

As an example of the conditioning power of television I referred to *Dr Who*. I said I 'detected a pronounced increase in what one might refer to as conspicuous violence: strangulation – by hand, by claw, by obscene vegetable matter – is the latest gimmick, sufficiently close up so that they get the point. And just for a little variety show the children how to make a Molotov Cocktail.'

The evidence for this corruptive power of the mass media, I argued, lay in the equation we now make between sadistic violence and entertainment – we are, I said, becoming desensitised as well as corrupted and that is good neither for the individual spirit nor the social climate.

I then went on to argue 'television violence has not only made man more violent and less sensitive, it has, paradoxically, also made him more passive. The effect of television has, I suppose, never been more clearly seen than in the coverage of the war in Vietnam. That is the other side of the coin.' We increasingly took it in our stride.

To say that there is no end to the problem of violence on film and television is to put it mildly. It not only does

58   not lessen, neither does its impact decrease nor its contents soften.

This has been highlighted by the controversy which has surrounded the release of certain 'Video Nasties' amongst them the notorious *Serial Killers* labelled, almost gleefully, 'Unbelievable True Horror', which includes graphic first-hand accounts from 'some of the most infamous sexual psychopaths'. The film includes interviews with 'Harvey the Hammer', who bludgeoned to death with a claw hammer, and also with Arthur Shawcross, 'The Monster of the Rivers' now serving ten consecutive life sentences. Apparently, despite warnings that the film 'contains footage which is not suitable for television and material and language which some may find offensive' – really! – it was never submitted to the BBFC because its makers said that it was 'educational'.

James Ferman, then director of the BBFC, admitted that film-makers use the 'educational' category as 'a loophole' and went on to say that he found the cover description of *Serial Killers* really alarming and that he had to admit that he had 'a good deal of sympathy' with Nigel Evans, Conservative MP for Ribble Valley, who called for the system to be reviewed – 'Films are coming in under the guise of education but they are going through sensational subjects to make a fast buck'. Indeed.

All that, of course, was twenty years ago. So where do we stand now? Readers will be aware of how, as I write in the summer of 1995, hardly a day goes by without the report of a callous murder, so often of a child. *The Times* (17.8.95) carried the headline 'Wife stabbed sailor after watching *Basic Instinct*', and tells how 'a depressed housewife took a knife and went out looking for a stranger to stab only hours after watching the film on video. The woman, aged forty-one, put her two young boys to bed, went to a Portsmouth night club and met a stranger – a sailor – who became her victim. She led him down an alley and stabbed him with a serrated kitchen knife which she had taken from her home.'

She told the Court that the film had suggested to her that 'it would be a good idea to stab a man'. *Basic Instinct* was described as an 'exotic thriller' in which a naked woman sits astride a naked man, reaches for an ice pick and lashes up and down on the man in a frenzy until his body is covered in blood. And that's by no means all. The whole film is incredibly violent, finishing with police looking at photographs of teenagers lying dead with their throats cut.

So who can be surprised at the effect of all this on the 'depressed housewife'. The Recorder at the Crown Court told her 'you were sadly suffering from a very severe depressive illness at the time. But for the illness you would be looking at a very long term of imprisonment.' As it was she was committed to hospital under the Mental Health Act.

When one is involved in a fight – in itself a violent word – to reduce and in certain cases to eliminate violence on film and television, it is necessary to document the content of such material, and pretty harsh, evil and repetitive a great deal of it is. Nothing original, nothing uplifting, nothing to inspire any generation to challenge and change.

It is, of course, necessary to know one's facts and between July and December 1994 members of National VALA watched and analysed sixty-four films all shown on terrestrial channels and transmitted, with one exception, on and after 9.00 p.m. I dealt with the matter of film and TV violence at some length in my book *Quite Contrary* (Pan Books, 1993) and I believe that what I said then is equally applicable today.

I quoted from Dr William Belson's report 'Television Violence and the Adolescent Boy' (1977):

Serious violence is increased by long term exposure to: plays or films in which close personal relationships are a major theme and which feature verbal or physical violence; programmes in which violence seems just thrown in for its own sake or is not necessary to the plot; programmes featuring

60   fictional violence of a realistic kind; programmes in which the violence is presented as being in a good cause; Westerns of the violent kind.

Dr Belson found, for example, 'that teenagers exposed to violent programming committed 49 per cent more violent and anti-social behaviour than those in matched low exposure'.

Violent video and computer images are desensitising young people, according to Sir Paul Condon, Commissioner of the Metropolitan Police. In the age of electronic equipment, he said, there was compelling evidence that lack of family stability and a mistaken view of violence acquired in video arcades and from unlimited access to television can be very destructive. Sir Paul said that some cities in the United States were now 'reaping a murderous harvest' as a result (*The Times*, 2.3.95); while latest crime statistics in Britain show that violent offences have increased by 17,300 to 311,500.

On February 27th 1995 the BBC's current affairs programme *Panorama* examined the question of screen violence and its effects on children and society as a whole. The film *Natural Born Killers* had just been released at the cinema after a three-month delay while the BBFC investigated claims that this film had been a factor in a number of murders in the United States. *Panorama* examined the case of Nathan Martinez, a seventeen-year-old boy charged with killing two members of his own family after watching *Natural Born Killers* ten times.

Oliver Stone, the film's director, said in the programme, 'film is a powerful medium, film is a drug, film is a potential hallucinogen – it goes into your eye, it goes into your brain, it stimulates and it's a dangerous thing – it can be a very subversive thing'. Professor Rowell Huesmann of the University of Michigan said that he was in no doubt that 'fictional screen violence raises the level of belief in the appropriateness of aggressive and violent behaviour, it raises people's beliefs that this is a mean world, a violent world and it just makes aggression more acceptable'.

In the same programme Dr Susan Bailey said that 'in the early Eighties I encountered over a five-year period, twenty youngsters who had murdered and a quarter of that group presented me with descriptions of how they had watched violent and pornographic films in the weeks leading up to their offence of murder – films where there were particular issues of violence against one person or another and where quite often the message in the film was that being bad and being violent brought with it rewards and power and this seemed to be an important issue for them'.

Speaking on the same programme, James Ferman of the BBFC said, 'I won't be here in the next century doing this job. I think there will be a problem, I think our children will be assaulted from all sides. They will all have television in their rooms by then, probably video, probably satellite dishes attached to those televisions so they will all be seeing everything. We must somehow give them the strength to resist.'

And that, it seems to me, raises, as they say, the 64,000 dollar question. But there is another question, very much related: how do we fill the film-makers with a sense of their own responsibility for the health and welfare not only of the whole of our society, but especially, for pity's sake, the welfare of the children who are the future?

The Poetry of Violence

POPPY Z. BRITE

Frank Booth is kissing prettyboy Jeffrey Beaumont with bloody lips as Frank's henchmen hold Jeffrey in a vice lock against the side of the car. Roy Orbison is singing about dreams. His angel voice and candy-coloured words take Frank back to something horrible in his past that he must return to again and again and again. 'Hold him tight,' says Frank, and drives a fist into Jeffrey's pretty mouth. Their bloods mingle there. Jeffrey is spun around by several pairs of hands and pushed facedown across the hood of the car. At this point a scene is rumoured to have been cut, and as the screen goes black, I always imagine that I can hear a zipper being undone.

(Blue Velvet, 1988)

Sonny Corleone is on his way to beat the hell out of his asshole brother-in-law for abusing his sister. Sonny's the number one son, the one the Don is grooming to be Godfather. His humpy black sedan screeches to a halt at the tollbooth; he pays his toll and tries to speed off, but the car in front of him has slewed sideways and stopped. The guy in the tollbooth ducks. It takes Sonny about two seconds to realise he's been set up. He is no more prepared for it than we, the audience, are. The rival family's bullets come from everywhere, machine-gun hail shivering glass, punching through metal, peppering Sonny's big body. He makes it across the seat and out of the car, roaring in

pain and rage, and the bullets stitch his flesh, the bullets jerk   63
him into a dance. It takes him an eternity to stumble over a
concrete abutment and fall face-up, dead. When he does, one
of the gunmen stands over him and rakes him up and down
once more before they all speed away.

(*The Godfather*, 1972)

A man enters a stark room, removes his clothes, ritually cleans
his body, and locks himself into an enormous complex machine
designed for the purpose of mutilating him slowly until he dies.
Steel needles slide into the veins on the backs of his hands.
A metal claw grabs at his genitals, pinches and twists. A drill
slowly penetrates his abdomen and churns his guts into a bloody
porridge. Throughout the process, the camera keeps cutting to
the man's face, and his expression is beyond pain *or* ecstasy: it
is simply transcendent. All this is filmed in glorious black and
white, which somehow makes it gorier.

(Nine Inch Nails video *Happiness In Slavery*, 1992)

A bicyclist has ridden into the path of an eighteen-wheeler. We
get a brief glimpse of broken white limbs under huge tyres,
just long enough to see that she was, in fact, wearing a cycling
helmet. Emergency workers are attempting, in this moment
long past emergency, to reassemble the contents of the body.
The camera closes in on a flat piece of metal scraping gobbets
of gore off the asphalt and tipping them into a plastic bag. The
gore looks wet, rich, savoury red and purple. Our narrator, 'Dr
Francis B. Gröss', effusively ponders the fragility of life.

(*Faces of Death*, 1979)

*   *   *

The poetry of violence is loathed by many and denied by
even more. Violence cannot encompass beauty, claim these
squeamish souls; by its very nature violence is crude, base, evil,

64   and nothing but. Those of us who savour it, even on paper or
film, are probably evil too: we've surrendered our very humanity
for a peek at someone's innards. These are the film critics who
aren't content to pan *Natural Born Killers*; they cannot rest until
they have proven the moral bankruptcy of those who liked it.

I enjoyed *Natural Born Killers* at face value, as a tale of
predatory love. The supposedly heavy-handed messages – media
glorification of murder; the murderer as cult darling and the
journalist as his whore – were secondary to me. What captivated
me was the personal, erotic joy Mickey and Mallory Knox found
in each other, and how violence became an extension and an
expression of that joy. I did not feel that the film condoned this
joy *or* condemned it. As much as in any film I've seen, and more
than most, the camera was simply an observing eye.

Furthermore, despite all the stereotypes, I believe that the
media *scrupulously avoids* glorification of murderers and violence. The American news show *Inside Edition* aired an interview
with Jeffrey Dahmer because they wanted good ratings and they
knew that an enormous portion of their viewing audience would
be interested in Dahmer's 'revelations', but their reporter felt
compelled to ask him moralistic, unrevealing questions rather
than the things everyone really wanted to know – such as,
perhaps, 'What did it taste like?'

The media capitalises on violence just as it capitalises on
whatever else it thinks it can sell, but capitalisation and
glorification are not necessarily the same thing. More often
than not, mass media assures its consumers that they are
normal and those who commit acts of violence are abnormal
or subnormal. Despite the amount of violence depicted, most
newscasts and current-events shows are designed to make the
viewer feel like a well-protected sheep who will come to harm
only if he strays from the herd.

Films make no such promises. Like any other type of fiction,
they offer admittance to a world where the rules of reality do
not always apply. I believe that many viewers are upset by films

like *Natural Born Killers* not because they encourage violence, 65 but because they offer no reassurance against it. The bad guys aren't punished at the end; we aren't even sure who the 'bad guys' are.

Rather than the black and white of the traditional horror or crime story, these films explore the grey areas, the unclaimed zones. In *Blue Velvet,* Frank Booth is almost a parody of evil, but he is also a complex, deeply charismatic, mysterious and tragic character. His partner in crime, Ben, is perhaps even more intriguing: he wears gaudy makeup, lives with a gaggle of fat ladies in cocktail dresses, lip-syncs a mean version of Roy Orbison's 'In Dreams', and has the unique ability to pacify Frank. By contrast, the 'good guys' – Jeffrey Beaumont and his girl-next-door sidekick Sandy – are dunderheaded caricatures given to observations like 'It's a strange world'. When this gem of a line is spoken, Jeffrey and Sandy have yet to learn how strange a world it is. One gets the feeling that Frank and Ben already know.

The judgement of the squeamish masses will never stop some of us from finding a poetry in violence, an awful intimate beauty. This is one of the things I have attempted to express over the course of three novels and many short stories. But no matter how I strive and sweat to describe this beauty, I can never capture it as perfectly as film, which can just *show* it in all its undeniable splendour. I am grateful for this reality; it keeps me on my toes, and it keeps me watching movies.

Not all violence is poetic, of course. Series films like *Faces of Death* and its more recent (and less faked) cousin *Traces of Death,* billed as 'shockumentaries', claim to present footage of genuine, live-action death for audience delectation. Try watching every instalment of *Faces* or *Traces* in a single weekend. You'll end up reeling brainlessly, not from horror as the film-makers would have it, but from sheer repetitive boredom. Ten minutes of racing crashes backed by an awful speed metal soundtrack. A murky thrashing blob that *might* be a crocodile biting a man's

66 leg off. Occasionally, a gem of dark irony: the tormented bear or lion turning on the ecotourist, the bull goring the matador, the stupid deaths of stupid people. And maybe twice or three times in every series, the glistening moment you will remember forever, for whatever reason: the sound of a flat piece of metal on asphalt, scraping spilled life into a plastic bag.

At the beginning of each *Traces of Death* instalment, we are offered the creators' definition of a shockumentary: 'An unflinching view of life's horrors which takes the viewer to the outer limits of his brief and fragile reality!' For me, at least, *Traces of Death 1–4* failed to fulfil this promise. But, to be fair, I've spent much of my life attempting to explore the outer limits of my own brief and fragile reality. And the definition does a good job of explaining why I started watching such films. At first I was testing myself: can I handle this, will it haunt me, will it change me? As a young child I'd been fascinated with guts, gore, and the inner workings of the body. As an adolescent I became squeamish about them, for they had begun to symbolise a confrontation with death I dreaded but had never been forced to face.

At 18, I had an inexplicable crying jag after seeing an odd, ambisexual, hyper-religious movie called *The Fourth Man*. I was especially upset by a scene in which an unlikeable and otherwise unmemorable character is killed by a metal rod run through his eye in a car accident. Even today, I cannot encounter something gruesome involving the eye without recalling the torn membranes and yolky fluids spilling down that actor's cheek.

In my late teens and early twenties, during a time of intense depression and drug use that turned out to be one of the most creative periods of my life, I rediscovered my childhood fascination with gore. I rented *Faces of Death 1–3* and spent a day watching them by myself. Though there was certainly an element of reeling boredom, some of the images from those films still haunt me: they were among the first true images of death I had ever seen. Our culture hides death,

forcing those who are curious about its faces actively to seek
them out.

But I wasn't satisfied to see what gore looked like; I wanted to see *beyond* what it looked like to any truths it might hold. I felt compelled to imagine how injuries had felt in the infliction, to search for the visible imprints of death and pain. I wanted to release myself from the thrall of violence, and to enthral others with it if I could. I wanted to find the poetry in it.

This is not an original urge, or even a particularly unusual one. Commenting on the gory subject-matter of his own paintings, Francis Bacon wrote, 'It's nothing to do with mortality but it's to do with the great beauty of the colour of meat.' When a viewer reacts to Bacon's work with revulsion, is he revolted by the gore, or by the evident joy Bacon took in portraying it?

When I speak of those squeamish souls who cannot abide the thought of violence encompassing beauty, I know whereof I speak. An anecdote from my recent career will illustrate this.

In 1991, I signed a contract to write three novels for Delacorte Books. The first two, *Lost Souls* and *Drawing Blood*, have since been published. *Exquisite Corpse* was to be the third.

Exquisite Corpse is a necrophilic, cannibalistic, serial killer love story that explores the seamy politics of victimhood and disease. The first chapter and several others throughout the book are narrated by Andrew Compton, an English murderer who has escaped after five years in prison to pursue what he calls the art of killing boys. The story is punctuated by rants from pirate radio talk show host Lush Rimbaud, who is dying of AIDS and intends to disrupt the status quo as much as possible before doing so.

In early 1995, I turned in the finished manuscript of *Exquisite Corpse* and was soon informed that Delacorte would be unable to publish the novel due to its 'extreme' content. I never received an explanation from anyone at Delacorte, but in the words of my literary agent, the VP 'had to change her underwear after reading it'.

Soon afterwards, I received news that Penguin, my UK publisher, was declining to publish *Exquisite Corpse* as well. Unlike Delacorte, they had the decency to offer me an explanation. 'I was very sorry not to feel able to offer to publish it,' wrote my editor, 'both because I have so enjoyed the success we have had with your first three books and because I admired the book's ambition and what I felt was a considerable development in your writing. But I did have very considerable reservations about the subject; which is not to say that fiction shouldn't handle shocking and dangerous subjects, rather that I felt very uncomfortable with the mixture of a [journalistic] approach to the characters and a tendency to see them as admirable, almost vampire-like figures. There would be bound to be some negative response to the book, and I am afraid I couldn't feel that I could wholeheartedly defend it, given my own reservations.'

My agent and I watched the manuscript bounce from publisher to publisher on two continents, receiving the same frustrating comments everywhere it went: *it's your best writing ever, but it's too nihilistic, too extreme, a bloodbath without justification.* I wasn't interested in arguing these points, but I did believe any reader who was willing to crawl inside the head of a serial killer and experience the twisted world there would find the novel a fascinating (if not a comforting) read. There is nothing to be learned by dismissing the serial killer as an unfathomable monster or portraying him as a series of cause-and-effect clichés. He is human; he comes from any number of diverse backgrounds; he is the predator of our times.

Eventually the book was purchased by Simon and Schuster in the US and Orion in the UK. But by then I'd come to feel that I had written something almost divine in its loathsomeness. After going through the usual fear that I'd simply written a bad book and no one was telling me, I began to feel that *Exquisite Corpse* was the most powerful thing I'd ever written. Its power seemed to lie not in its violence, but in its seductive presentation of that violence and the characters' erotic responses to it.

Though I have received no definite offers as of this writing, my film agent tells me that *Exquisite Corpse* has caused far more of a stir in Hollywood than either of my two previous, nicer, ostensibly more filmable novels. Perhaps this is due to the success of dark, nihilistic serial killer movies such as *The Silence of the Lambs*, *Seven* and *Copycat*. But where did their popularity come from?

It may be simplistic to say these films are successful because of a public desire to understand a phenomenon that is becoming more and more prevalent in society, that of the human predator. But I believe it is also undeniably true. The vampire, who used to be the ultimate symbol of sexual predation, has become a romantic figure in the 1980s and '90s. There are many reasons for this, but one of the foremost is that a fictional Count Dracula's power to terrify is greatly diminished when a real-life Ted Bundy is prowling the highways. We need to know our monsters, particularly if they are human. Films that offer a candid look inside the mind of a serial killer can give us this knowledge.

It has been claimed that such knowledge can be misused by those already disposed to violence, that violent films and publicity given to serial killers can provide a blueprint for nascent criminals. This idea is explored in *Copycat*, where a young serial killer commits murders after the styles of Albert DeSalvo, the Hillside Strangler(s), David Berkowitz, Peter Kürten, Ted Bundy, Jeffrey Dahmer, and others. Though he apparently considers his murders as 'tributes', both to the original killers and to the female serial killer expert with whom he becomes obsessed, it is obvious that he would have been an unstable character even without these 'inspirations'. However, he is not presented as a sympathetic character, and so this film has not encountered great controversy.

Let's look back at one of the examples I used in the beginning. When *The Godfather* came out, its extreme violence was much remarked upon, but its true controversy lay in the fact that

70 it presented career criminals and murderers as sympathetic characters. Seen for the first time, the slaughter of Sonny Corleone is emotionally harrowing whether or not the viewer censures Sonny's criminality. Other controversial films – *Blue Velvet, A Clockwork Orange, Natural Born Killers* – feature great moral ambiguity as well as carefully choreographed, exquisitely depicted violence. The recurrence of these two factors in tandem spans decades of film and centuries of art and literature. We can see a similar ambiguity in less plotted excursions like the shockumentaries and the Nine Inch Nails video. These people (or characters) exist only so we can watch them die, and they must die spectacularly. As with the controversial films mentioned above, there is no tidy moral lesson at the end. We are allowed to draw our own conclusions.

This is the ultimate value of seeking the poetry of violence. It forces the viewer to arrive at his own conclusions about death, pain, and the visceral soup inside us. It forces him to understand his own feelings about these highly personal matters, rather than reinforcing what society says he *should* feel (fear, disgust). When I really started looking, I found that the things I had imagined I would see in violent films were often much more fearsome than the things I actually saw. So I wrote about the things I had imagined I would see, and often the scenes that disturbed readers the most were the scenes I had found most beautiful while writing them.

Those who say there is no poetry in violence aren't looking hard enough, or are refusing to look at all. But no matter. Even if the poetry never finds them, the violence eventually will.

The American Vice

WILL SELF

What happens if you put a man's head in a vice of a sufficient size that each of the metal plates fully clasps his temples, and then slowly tighten it, and tighten it, and tighten it?

Well, in this case, the man – who is overweight and wearing a patterned, short-sleeved shirt that rides up over his belly – begins to kick out, to flail his arms, to scream and plead for mercy. The men who are tightening the vice scream abuse at him, grab at his limbs, carry on tightening. This is all taking place in a behind-the-scenes, warehouse-cum-storage space. The overhead strip lighting, the piles of discarded boxes, the odd tools and other impedimenta, all serve to emphasise the very workaday nature of the evil being witnessed.

There's that – and there's also the way that our POV is being manipulated, moved about. One instant we're up in the metal strut rafters, the man whose skull is being cracked spread beneath us; the next we're eyeballing him, watching his eye bulge; hardly daring to listen, lest the synaesthetic crack widens to embrace us, engulf us, as the human shell is broached and the shards of bone and brain pierce us, the piss-jets of blood drench us.

Not, you understand, that we're altogether without motivation ourselves in this vice-viewing; without any kind of input. The sensation of observing this torture, this sadism, is not as you might imagine, like a reconditioning session, through which

72   we are compelled to sit, Alex-like, deprived of our droogs, our eyelids pinioned open. No, we went into this thing, this episode, with a mixture of keenness and frenzy that is worse than nauseating. The way in which it segued with the rest of our experience heretofore – the other sights we have seen – had the complicit, retrospectively assembled air of a dream; a dream in which we find we have committed some awful crime – such as cracking a man's skull in a vice – for reasons we can no longer explain, even if we knew them to begin with.

At this precise point the *we* became an *I*, and *I* stopped watching Martin Scorsese's *Casino*. I became utterly childlike, to the extent of holding both my hands over my eyes and peering between parted fingers, as if my flesh were some psychic screen, able to filter out the enacted pain. I squinted at the screen, hummed, talked to my companion who was similarly afflicted. To be frank – I cannot remember whether the man's skull was popped like a ripe melon dropped on a pavement, or not; I was considering whether a dramatic work in which catharsis is effected by a series of acts, the representation of which *cannot actually be viewed*, could be said, in any meaningful sense, to be cathartic?

There has, of course, always been screen violence. Arguably film has always – in some primary way – been about violence. The violence of the modern: the shock of the new. The apocrypha of the medium include many instances of neophyte audiences being shown films of oncoming trains, and fleeing the theatre in terror. But there is a difference between the kind of straightforward catharsis imparted by witnessing events you are relieved to have avoided, in which case the *stylisation* of that threat is sufficient to effect it; and the catharsis that modern depictions of violence on screen seem to be attempting.

That catharsis lies behind much contemporary, filmic depiction of violence cannot be doubted. And not just violence *qua* cracking men's heads in vices. There is violence in the insertion of a catheter, or the slicing of a scalpel, that is depicted in a hospital soap. There is violence in the hanks of mebraneous stria, and dollops of bio-goo, dished out by horror and science fiction movies (genres that are, interestingly, tending towards convergence). And, of course, there is violence in the choreographed, clash-of-extras that helps to misrepresent our history to us in the form of epic movies, war movies, and epic war movies.

(To digress: it's interesting to note that while, in contemporary historical epics such as *Braveheart*, the depiction of the political realities of the place and time (in this case twelfth-century Scotland) is hopelessly bowdlerised, the depiction of warfare has now achieved an impressive level of seeming-verisimilitude. A reversal of what was the case in the films of the past, e.g. Olivier's *Richard III*.)

The form of catharsis induced by any particular depiction is as diverse as the depiction itself. We moderns itch everywhere, so every itch must be scratched. We fear everything, so every phobia must be given its own name. So polymorphous has this form of catharsis become, that it now seems that the very dialectic of film violence itself is being propelled forward by depictions of violence that are themselves a kind of meta-depiction: examples that give an opportunity for a critical evaluation of the state of screen violence.

The scene from Scorsese's *Casino* described above doesn't have quite this meta-critical status. Although it's worth noting that it's an impressive addition to some memorably violent scenes he has directed. Scenes that have themselves provoked, goaded, and formed the scaffolding of the debate. Salient have been the long, backward-staggering, punches-to-the-face sequence in *Mean Streets*; the fingers shot off by spring-loaded Magnum sequence in *Taxi Driver*; and, of course, the psycho-leg-breaking sequence in *Goodfellas*.

But Scorsese's screen violence, while often gifting the viewer, through the manner in which it is filmed, with this same, awful mixture of keenness and frenzy, a curiousness about the

74 intoxication of violence, at the same time takes place within the context of films that themselves adhere to older narrative conventions. They represent the world with, if not realism, at any rate not surrealism or stylisation. Scorsese also does not equivocate *that much* about the division in moral responsibility between the auteur, the viewer, and the character.

As Scorsese also sets most – although not all – of his films in milieus that are explicitly criminal, amoral, and otherwise beyond the ethical moral pale, there is a suggestion that we are not to judge our response to this violence as we might to that meted out against the innocent, the straight, the solid citizen. Around Scorsese's depictions of intra-gangster violence hangs the heavy scent of dog eating dog.

The same cannot be said for the way that Quentin Tarantino has dealt with violence in his films. From the first scene of *Reservoir Dogs* we know that we are dealing with a film that has factored into its thematic scape a number of different genres; and in the third scene we are given the pay-off from this ironic miscegenation: the aftermath of the shooting of a character during a failed heist, that is depicted in a self-consciously hyper-real fashion; depicted in such a way as to raise insistently in our minds the question of the degree to which what we are viewing is naturalistic or not.

Could a man live that long having been shot in that way? Would he articulate his pain in this fashion? Would he bleed this much? And would the blood be this red, this obviously treacly, oily? These questions didn't simply come off the screen alongside the clever, parodic 'Sound of the Seventies' soundtrack, they made their way into post-viewing conversation, into the newspapers, into the culture.

Reservoir Dogs achieves its meta-critical status by mashing together genres; this gives an instant synergy of irony as the gangster comments upon the gangster commenting upon the gangster genre; and the knowing audience titters along. Tarantino's film is thus arch, self-referential, not altogether to be taken *seriously*. Not, that is, until you consider in hard terms the questions concerning naturalism that 'that shooting' raises.

Say, for instance, that you wanted to find out just how plausible the scene was. Would you be prepared actually to call up a vascular surgeon accustomed to dealing with massive haemorrhaging from gunshot wounds, and ask him whether it tallied with anything in his experience? It would be the only way to find out – and yet the very idea is revolting. By hyper-realising the effects of the shooting, Tarantino has paradoxically produced the same effect as the under-realised, pre-Peckinpah depictions of gunshot woundings: stylisation. But in this case it is a stylisation that engenders a peculiar, moral queasiness: a stylisation of overkill.

This film has thus leap-frogged over our ability to suspend disbelief through the articulation of the convention of naturalism, by raising the stakes to a level where we cannot afford *not* to believe in the reality of what is depicted – because the alternatives could only be worse.

In a different scene in the same film, Tarantino shows us another, related way in which the contemporary depiction of violence on screen introduces issues of moral displacement in a novel way. Holed up in a warehouse building by a reservoir, the gangsters begin to torture a policeman they have taken hostage.

The scene is neatly blocked out. Our POV revolves around the pinioned head of the policeman. Stephen Wright, an American comedian with a peculiarly lubricious and insistent voice, provides the soundtrack in the form of the sugary tones of an imaginary disc jockey. But then something deeply sinister begins to intrude. We lose sight of whose, exact POV we are inhabiting. The sadist who is doing the torturing? The policeman? The incapacitated accomplice? It is this vacillation in POV that forces the sinister card of complicity upon the viewer. For in such a situation the auteur is either abdicating – or more likely *foisting* – the moral responsibility for what is being depicted on screen from himself to the viewer.

This particular viewer, as is his wont, at this point in the film decided to leave the theatre. I felt certain that I could watch the torture sequence through to its conclusion, but not that I would do so without vomiting.

This 'vacillation' is not only analogous, but profoundly related to the de-centring, the displacement, of the overarching, 'moral' narrative voice from the contemporary novel. The nineteenth-century novel relied upon – and was indeed created around – the notion of an impersonal, narrative voice, that was both able *deus ex machina*-like to set the plot up and running, then leave it be; and also to intervene in the lives – and even thoughts – of the characters, when called upon to do so. Such a narrative voice was compounded in part of the author-as-narrator, in part of the narrator-as-author. Sometimes the use of the first person as the narrative voice would further erode distinctions, or set up incongruities, between the three different levels of existence implied by these personae.

The onset of Modernism was heralded by a breakdown in the conventions that both separated these personae, and allowed for their admixture. Conrad's *Heart of Darkness* stands as a pivotal text in this sense: as a story told within a story told within a story, the instabilities of the disjunctions between protagonist, narrator and author become fully explicit. (Although it's worth noting that such inherent instabilities have always been toyed with by novelists, e.g. Lermontov's *A Hero of Our Times*.)

I believe that whereas the novel can fully cope with this loss of the convention of narrative locus, such a flux becomes far more morally and artistically problematic within the filmic realm. Of course, from the off there is no direct equivalent in film to the narrator of a novel. There can be two narrators, a voiceover and a POV. They can dispute with one another, or even abandon each other. Film allows as fully for the convention of the unreliable narrator as the novel. But where I think film spirals away and becomes something wholly other, is in its ability not to simply ⌐77 decouple the POV (which is the primary narrative locus) from the POV of any given character, or even from the POV of any 'notional' character, but from the POV of any notional auteur – or author.

The idea that *someone* is making the film is traditionally implicit in the mono-reality of a unified camera perspective: the camera is an I. Of course this was played with very early on in the medium's history, but in – for example – those sequences of *Citizen Kane* which are meant to be 'real' newsreel, there remains the sense that there is another, more primary camera, that is filming the newsreel. In other words while the disjunction between narrator and auteur may have been distorted, it has not been abandoned.

However, in these contemporary films that are providing stepping stones across a raging river of debate about representation and reality, the disjunction *has* been abandoned. In *Henry, Portrait of a Serial Killer*, the ultimate, amoral plangency comes when the eponymous serial killers, having videoed their own raping and killing of a family, then view the video they have made. This allows the auteur to intercut between: his POV; their POV when videoing; their 'real' POV when doing the killings; and their POV when watching the video they've made.

Such a mixture of both POVs and different filmic media – video picture quality and film picture quality, together with combinations thereof – means that the viewer's sense of what the ultimate reality portrayed by the film *is*, is lost. In such circumstances the viewer begins to feel not only that she is a real witness, but that in some sense she is complicit, responsible. The repeated depiction of the making of film within the film, leads the viewer in some, subliminal, way to imagine that it is in fact *she* who has made the film – and by extension become culpable for the violent acts depicted.

(It's worth mentioning at this point that thirty seconds were cut from *Henry* before it was granted a certificate by the British

78   Board of Film Censors, and that predictably those thirty seconds
come from the sequence that mashes together video and film
footage. A friend of mine – Farrah Anwar – who is an expert
on issues of film violence and censorship, offered me both the
cut and uncut versions of the film to view. Needless to say I
declined, and the views above are essentially derived from his
observations.)

A more radical enactment of this breakdown of narrative
POVs can be witnessed in Oliver Stone's *Natural Born Killers*.
Here there is the film itself, the film the director-within-the-film
wishes to make, the film the protagonists wish to make, and a
number of film-of-the-film-within-the-film asides that the auteur
feels it is incumbent on him to make. By explicitly tackling
the 'issue' of the media depiction of serial killers, within the
context of a fictionalised account of such serial killers, Oliver
Stone (and Quentin Tarantino his scriptwriter) obviously feel
they are provoking a debate within the viewer, at the time of
viewing.

In fact nothing of the sort takes place. In part this is
simply because the writing, the ideas, the characterisations
(or rather caricatures) are too banal. But also it's because
the effect of all this mixed media, rather than producing a
provocative, ontological confusion, rather induces the kind of
slightly nauseous queasiness that one associates with too much
channel-surfing.

What catharsis is there to be gained in watching acts of
violence that are depicted in such a way as to make you
suspect that you may be implicated, culpable? And how
could this particular catharsis have become so important to
the contemporary film viewer? This question provides us with
part of the answer, I believe, to the question I posed about
catharsis in relation to Scorsese's head-cracking scene at the
outset. The catharsis effected by scenes we cannot witness is the
emotional release of knowing that by *not watching* we cannot be
implicated.

(An interesting half-twist on this idea is the opening scene of
Mike Leigh's film *Naked*, in which a seeming-rape, that might
be a rape, is perpetrated by the film's protagonist. The issue
of whether or not the sex was consensual for some time stood
proxy for – if not actually supplanted – the debate about the
nature of consensual sex itself: the raping point had become
a talking point, and vice versa!)

By contrast the catharsis effected by those filmic depictions
of violence that attempt to place us in the driving seat, give us
the POV, is both manifold and disturbing.

A couple of years ago I was in San Francisco and went back
to someone's apartment at the end of an evening's drinking. A
tape of miscellaneous footage was fed into the video machine,
and we sat around chatting and looking idly at the screen. Most
of the material was at the disturbing end of the off-beat: stop-go
animations of Ken and Barbie dolls with outrageously gifted
genitalia, and the like. Each clip segued with the next, so that
I was at least thirty seconds or so into this particular clip before
I realised what it was I was watching.

It was a clip that had – I subsequently learned – gained
considerable notoriety amongst collectors of the macabre. A
Californian bureaucrat accused of fiscal misdemeanour had
put a long-barrelled Colt revolver into his mouth during a
press conference which he himself had called, and then blew
his brains out. The whole episode was – of course – caught by
one of the live action TV cameras at the press conference.

The juxtaposition between the beginning of the clip, when the
camera's POV is behaving in just the way you would expect it to
in order to render a dull press conference, and the suicide itself
is extreme. The POV begins to waver, the sense of the emotional
disintegration of the person operating the camera is palpable.
He or she pans in to catch the suicide's face as he seems about to
pull the trigger; then pulls away to try and avoid it; then zooms
in once again. Finally, the camera operator cannot resist the
denouement: the actual gunshot has so shocked him/her that

the POV jerks right away, but then it recovers itself, finds the face of the now dead politician (not a pretty sight), and zooms in on it, for a final, lingering, tight-focus shot.

Now, what is most notable about this sequence is that it is a kind of *inadvertent* snuff film. As such I believe that it is the pure form of the experience that *Natural Born Killers* et al. are trying to reproduce. We moderns now feel ourselves all to be passive victims of such snuff contexts, mediated by the media. This tracks back all the way to Vietnam, the so-called 'first television war'. It was at that point that McLuhan's Global Village gained its own global vandals, thugs, rapists and murderers, and the newly installed security cameras began to garner film of them.

Another surveillance-mediated, inadvertent snuff film was gifted to the British Public three years ago. Video cameras in a Liverpool shopping centre caught images of two ten-year-old boys who were leading three-year-old Jamie Bulger away to his death. The murder of a child by children was the most horrific thing, but somehow there was a further enhancement of that horror, a magnification provided by the camera's lens. The surveillance camera – representing as it does the idea of the ultimate *deus ex machina*, the court of last, all-seeing appeal – had let us all down, traduced and manipulated us. It is events such as these, and countless others like them, that the unwitnessable catharsis is designed to deliver us from.

Many responsible, contemporary film-makers attempt to grapple with the moral issues blasted to the surface of our culture by the twin depth charges of modern media and modern death-dealing; but I believe all too often they fail and become part of the problem, rather than the solution.

The medium itself may also be partly to blame. While fully interactive filmic experience lies some way in the future (held off as yet by technical constraint), there is no doubt that it will come eventually. Some years ago I was commissioned by Philips Interactive to do a consultancy on the possible narrative entertainment applications of CD-I. After giving the matter some thought I concluded that the contemporary viewer's ability to suspend disbelief in full motion video (or naturalistic film) is by and large predicated upon the acceptance of mono-linear narrative structure. There was, I felt, only one motivation that could circumvent this fact and make it possible for the viewer to accept 'control' of that narrative as part of the entertainment experience.

And the motivation? You guessed it: the opportunity to commit either immoral acts, or acts of violence; or more to the point: both.

In Front of the Children

NICCI GERRARD

Sometimes, at night, when I leave my children in their beds, and they lie there after their stories and quarrels, after their teeth have been cleaned, after I've sung half-remembered lullabies to them in my tuneless voice and hugged them and put their squashed and balding teddies under the crook of their arm and turned out the lights – sometimes, then, they shut their eyes against the orange street lamp just outside their window and play a game. It's called, simply, 'films' or sometimes 'videos'. They give each other titles (*The Wizard of Oz, The Wrong Trousers, Dumbo* . . .) and they run the films through in their head, their closed lids the private screens on which are projected oft-watched and well-remembered scenes. They switch films every so often ('one, two, three, *Basil the Great Mouse Detective* when Basil goes up in the balloon . . .'; 'one, two, three, the few of my favourite things song in *The Sound of Music* . . .'), and later they discuss them with each other like regular filmgoers.

Sometimes, later in the evening, one of them will appear downstairs, a pyjamaed stocky ghost lurking on the fringes of our adult evening (scenes from *ER* or from Bosnia are hastily turned off the TV), and say that they are scared. Scared of monsters, scared of wars, scared of you going away, scared of thunder, scared of a rustle outside their bedroom door, scared of they don't know what, just scared. And if we say, but there's nothing to worry about, you're safe, there's nothing there, then they reply that they know that: *it's inside their heads and they can't make it go away.* It's as if the images that flicker against their eyelids night after night are locked into their skulls when they sleep, and go on burning there.

When I covered the Rosemary West trial for *The Observer* I was for the eight weeks of its duration and for several subsequent weeks assailed by violent and distressing images. By day I would push them away; at night they would surface in my dreams – small fragments of horror. Sometimes I would wake with a gasp out of a nightmare, and only gradually realise myself back into my actual world where four children were breathing with the calm rise and fall of deep sleep upstairs, and beside me my husband snored quietly and the big black cat lay on my feet and the whole house seemed to purr with dormant life. It was as if something I had witnessed (not even participated in, mind, merely watched and reported) had poisoned my mind. Rosemary West used to stare at journalists from the dock; if you caught her dull, heavy gaze she would never look away, but fix on you unwaveringly. We used to say to each other – nervously joking – that she was giving us the evil eye. After the judge sentenced her ('life' it's called, though really it's a waiting for death) and she had disappeared from the view of the horrified public, I often recalled that sooty, brutish gaze: the curse of the *mal'occhio*.

It's not just real violence which unreels itself in the imagination, fast-forward, fast-backwards and pause. I have sat in a cinema and watched *Seven* with peeled-back sight and a whimpering heart, peering aghast at the claustrophobic corners of the screen – and for days after have been unable to relinquish the image of a woman fucked to death by a knife, or of a forest of Christmas tree air-fresheners hung above a rotting, still living body. I have endured *Cape Fear* by turning away from the screen entirely, bottom up and head down in the crevice of the furry seat, fingers in ears and moaning a dotty

84   little hum to extinguish even the dialogue and certainly the skin-jumping soundtrack – but still been haunted by Robert De Niro obscenely sweet-talking one of his victims, a soft mirthless smile on his big face; I've watched *Manhunter* through fingers and groans, *Dirty Weekend* through a haze of nausea. I always have to leave the room when Dumbo's mother leaves him and he folds his vast ears over his weeping grey face, or when Bambi sees his mother killed. I like *Bringing Up Baby* and *The Front Page* and Jane Austen adaptations. Maybe at heart I'm a subtitle girl. I get very scared by images of violence. I get very worried by images of violence towards women. I get weepy and terrified by images of violence towards children.

Many people – more of them all the time – believe that there is a direct relationship between the culture we consume and the people we become. See violence, be violent. See pornography, do it ('pornography is the theory and rape is the practice' went a famous slogan of the sloganising Seventies). See misogyny, become more misogynist. In this comforting world of cause and effect, Jamie Bulger died because his child-murderers had (maybe) watched a video nasty; Rosemary and Frederick West watched and made violent pornography with their hand-held camcorder and then watched and made it in real life. Conversely, I suppose (though this is not often spelt out): see happiness and be happier, see goodness and be good, see innocence and become more innocent. President Reagan liked to tell us that his favourite sweets were jelly babies and his favourite film *The Sound of Music.*

Men are more violent than women. Fantasised violence has often been directed by men against women, and so has been a central issue in any discussion about feminism, oppression and male sexuality – and never more so than in the millennially scarified Nineties when apocalypse and utopia seem to beckon from the future, and when feminism has been turned into a battleground between the puritans and the libertarians (with most of us cowering in the no-man's land in between, not too sure which way to go).

It's in America, of course, where the fiercest battle is fought out. On the one side are those who would legislate against fantasy. These are the utopians, who believe that we are socially engineered, tameable creatures, and that if you (well, actually, *they*) change the dominant culture with all its electronic messages of patriarchal oppression then, hey presto!, you produce a kinder and a better world. You can fix it. Another word for this is censorship. And yet another is acute anxiety about the modern world and all its slipshod cruelties. At the head of these perturbed puritans march Catherine MacKinnon – slim and trim and pedantic, with a prose that clicks like a card index and a legal mind that snaps shut like one of those satisfying bags full of face-powder and tissues that my granny used to carry – and Andrea Dworkin – fat and despairing, with a sloppy noisy style, and a paranoia about men and heterosexuality which chops off any subtlety like a chainsaw (Dworkin's own works about violence and pornography have been banned in Canada for their violent and pornographic content).

And on the other side is the glam gang, led by the operatic, linguistically gymnastic, ironic and iconic Camille Paglia (at least, I think she's the leader, but she could just be the trumpeter). She loves Madonna and Robert Mapplethorpe and prostitutes and athletic gay men and pornography. She loves images of violence, believing they reveal a deep and pagan impulse within all of us. She loves deep pagan impulses. She loves artifice. She hates tenderness, sentimentality, academic jargon, sense, compassion, new men and wimps. She hates Catherine MacKinnon and Andrea Dworkin, and they hate her right back.

For MacKinnon (and this is at the heart of the whole anti-violence, pro-censorship argument; this is what informs Mary Whitehouse et al.), the barrier between real life and fantasy, real violence and its images on the screen, is not just

86 osmotic: *it does not exist.* She argues, with exquisite pedantry that
wraps unsuspecting readers like a fly in its thinly sticky threads,
that if you watch rape on the screen the effect it has upon you
is the same as watching it on the street without intervening:
your passivity renders you complicit; guilty. MacKinnon does
not use metaphors; she uses the verb to be. Pornography *is*
violence. Watching *is* accepting, thinking *is* doing (doesn't the
Bible say that if you lust after someone in your heart you have
committed adultery?). Her literal position is wonderfully caught
by a literary scuffle that broke out following the publication of
her radically puritan book, *Only Words.* A reviewer (male), trying
to demonstrate the absurdity of her argument, imagined in print
that he was raping MacKinnon: was that the same, he asked at the
end of his exercise, as really doing it? You could almost hear the
jeering, triumphant 'Huh?' hanging at the end of the piece. But
apparently it was – MacKinnon felt that she'd been raped, and
her fiancé Jeffrey Masson wanted to beat up the reviewer, not
for his execrable taste but for his actual assault.

For people like MacKinnon and Dworkin (and they have
crowds of followers, many of whom are politicians, judges,
academics), the world must be a terrifying place. It must be
exactly the unremitting inferno that was depicted in *Seven.* Every
step they take, where I see a *picture* of a woman being harassed,
they see a woman being harassed. They are sexually assaulted
on every street corner by swear words and winks. Every film they
visit, they risk watching a woman being raped or beaten up. Every
movie is like a snuff movie to their attenuated sensibilities.

For people like Camille Paglia, such women have made
themselves into pathetic, whinging victims, terrified of sex,
crying rape when a man joyfully pinches their offended
buttocks, quivering in the corners of a world that's full
of exuberant violence. These cool, macha libertarians love
freedom, and they love fantasy, and they believe that the
feminist movement has been decoyed down a dull and narrow
blind alley of victimhood, where women huddle and weep.

Paglia isn't just against censorship, she's pro-pornography. She believes that violent fantasies liberate. She adores hard-core pornography because it's anarchic, subversive and shocking.

So there you have it: in the blue corner, the gloves-on outraged; in the red, the punch-drunk outrageous. The trouble is that for most of us our feelings about violent and misogynistic images are so much more troubled, more ambivalent and less entrenched than these absolutists would have it ('Bo-o-ring' shouts Paglia; 'let me explain' says MacKinnon). I have always been opposed to censorship and I do not think that I need to be nannied by well-meaning feminists who want to decide for me which of my fantasies is legitimate and which may corrupt me; which violent film makes me behave violently. I'm against any law which legislates against our private, consensual lives. So far, I'm with Paglia and her gang, though I sidle rather prudishly in the slipstream of their swaggery strut.

And I'm appalled that I live in a society which seems to think that by banning a video nasty it can perhaps prevent a murder or a rape (don't forget that the man who murdered John Lennon seems to have been motivated by *Catcher in the Rye* – so should we ban that too, or the Bible for all the copycat crimes that follow in its bloodthirsty vengefulness, or *Crime and Punishment*?). When we start intervening, where do we stop? How far do adults need to be protected against the nasty world in which they live? Go down this road, and we'll end up like Howard Hughes, sucking boiled sweets in a tent while his fingernails grew and his mind decayed.

Yet I part company with people who say, with the flat certainty that slams the door on discussion and doubt, that films have no effect whatsoever on life – that there's no exchange between life and art at all. When I saw *Seven*, I half-wished that I had not. In its rococo realism, it came too close to my reality, and I felt, yes, altered by it (don't ask me how; I don't think I became desensitised as the MacDworkinites would have it, nor do I think I was illuminated). I felt visually attacked. I didn't really mind

88   that there were only three women in the film, each of whom was turned into a deadly sin and horribly disposed of, I'm grown-up enough to deal with that; and I didn't really mind that, surprise surprise, it was two men – creased buddies with guns and tired faces – who were going to solve the mystery and save the world. But I did really mind that the camera dwelt so lovingly on the aftermath of lingering death. I minded the obese marbled body slumped into a puddle of spaghetti, the bucket of vomit, the scabby living corpse putrefying, the female body genitally mutilated. For days after the film, I felt the slight sourness of panic in my stomach. I minded all the tender devotion to detail because I believe it in a way that I don't believe in the bloody bits of flesh that exploded around the car in *Pulp Fiction.*

Quentin Tarantino has said that violence is just another colour in his palette. His films are so referential, parodic and playful that this can be true: everything is artifice, composition. But a movie like *Seven* is deeply moral – the way that it is set in the mythological city that is hell immediately signals to us that here is a work about the human condition. Violence is not just another colour now, not a cartoon Pow-Zap! It's an image bred in the bone for the way we live as we approach the end of the millennium; it feeds off the lurching fears we have about our society. And as such it crosses the boundary between fantasy and fact.

Or at least, it does so for the moment. We've always had violence in our culture, in the sublimest art as well as in the tackiest. The crucifix is an icon of agony and torture; Dante takes us through the circles of hell; Shakespeare gives us massacres, extreme torture, even cannibalism; Jacobean tragedies strew bodies about the stage. Film seems more visceral as a form than written or performed texts. Pro-censorship critics argue vociferously that we are constantly pushing back the barriers of what is acceptable. Every year, a film comes along that makes permissible what would a year before have been unthinkable. We see naked bodies, dead bodies, blood that looks just like blood and guts which look exactly like guts, and we're overloaded, desensitised, damaged.

A few years ago I went to an exhibition about forgery at the British Museum which had gathered together examples of some of the most famous con tricks through history. What was extraordinary, riveting, was that these tricks that hoaxed whole populations of sceptics *no longer looked convincing at all.* The Vermeer copy that had fooled the greatest Vermeer expert in the world was now a kitsch fake, unmistakably unreal. The forgers had unwittingly copied something in the fashion of their own time, and as time rolled by the genuine and fraudulent articles had separated out and the hoaxes looked ridiculously unbelievable.

The same conundrum is true of art. People used to faint at Jacobean tragedies; now they sometimes laugh at the melodrama of them, their unreality to a modern audience. Dante's works were literal for many of his contemporary readers; now we read them for their anguish and beauty. At the first showings of films the audience would scream and panic if a train hurtled towards them on the screen; one actor even refused to work in the new medium because he feared he would be flattened. As it is made, art can press up so close against its subject that it seems nearly impossible to tell the flesh from its reflection. Time pulls the two away from each other. Olivier's blacked-up, eye-rolling Othello, acclaimed as a masterpiece, now seems overacted. I felt jittery and squeamish when I saw *Pulp Fiction*, but I bet that even two years on, it would seem so obviously artificial and playful that I'd hardly be able to recall my original emotions. And I also bet that if I see *Seven* in five or ten years' time, it will no longer feel too close for comfort. It will have withdrawn into the mysterious world of art, which removes itself from us even as it touches us. That won't be because something even more shocking and 'real' will have pushed back the frontiers of violence, but because what is 'real' will have taken on a different form, will have a different fashion.

90   'I don't see why they feel the need to be so violent':
the bewildered or aggrieved refrain of so many filmgoers.
But they do feel the *need*. Who can dictate what sets the
creative juices flowing? Today, in the hectic uncertainties of
a millennium ending, many artists express themselves through
violence. That's their voice, their context; that's the woeful and
jagged darkness where they feel at home. You can't exile them
to gentleness or optimism. Some of the most powerful cultural
works of the last decade have been couched in the language of
disturbance and pain. Protest and hope are often to be found
in the bleakest places.

A few months ago we showed the video of *Indiana Jones and
the Last Crusade* to my children and their slightly older cousin.
Snakes writhed in pits, spiders and scorpions crawled up the
back of the hero, skeletons shot out of hidden crevices with
empty eye-sockets staring, all the children squealed in terror
and delight and plunged heads into cushions. After it was over
and the microwaved popcorn had been eaten, they ran around
the house, fighting with each other, throwing shoes at the adults
and cushions at the cat, screaming euphorically. 'Can't you',
asked my mother-in-law as five children bolted past her, eyes
a-gleam, 'show them a nice film like *Lassie* next time?' But if
I show them *Lassie* they'll want to buy a dog and they'll still
throw cushions at the cat.

Yet when I go to look at them as they lie sleeping, cast by
slumber into a resemblance to each other that they never possess
when awake, arms flung above their heads, mouths slightly open,
a puff of breath fluttering on their upper lip, and I see by their
rapid eye movement that they must be dreaming – then I confess
that I want them to dream about peaceful comforting things.
Not cartoon wars and car chases and shiny robots with shiny
guns, but horses in fields and dogs in baskets and blue skies and
all the saccharine and childish things that only unimaginative
adults ever think belong to the fierce and dark imagination of
a child.

Suffer the Little Children

ALEXANDER WALKER

When children are mentioned today, they are frequently represented as being at risk from adults. But my argument is that, in the context of film and video censorship at least, it is adults who need protection from children. Since violent imagery, regarded by the law as potentially subversive and a mimetic invitation to children, became available for screening in the privacy of people's homes, it's been pursued with unprecedented tenacity and retribution. Those who police society – not all in blue uniforms – have always wanted access to places and powers that society usually thinks it better for them not to possess. The sanctity of one's home used to be the traditional defence for doing what one wished, so long as it didn't harm others. Not any longer. Children have placed the key to the door in the possession of the law. And the laws of film and video censorship have permitted the police to cross the threshold. Once inside, however, it's not children whom they seek to 'protect'; it is adults whom they constrain. It is adults on whose freedom they trespass.

Representing children to be the objects of its care and protection is simply the most respectable way that the law has yet found to sanitise a kind of censorship that would be thought oppressive, odious and downright ridiculous if its advocates came straight out with the admission that the real targets of their attention were adults.

Other countries no doubt make use of similar back-door

92   means of social control. But Britain does so – as it does much else – with that especial relish for moral condescension, legal hypocrisy and puritan zeal that forms the alloy of the Anglo-Saxon character. A country that customarily tops the list of nations which physically abuse their children lags behind none in its profession of moral care for them. In Britain, the family is fetishised as the ideal conduit for love and living, despite the fact that only a tiny minority of British households have families living in them. The country's divorce rates suggest that the impacted tensions of family life are implosions simply waiting to happen. More and more, censorship encroaches on family life without apparent benefit to its stability, but, as I hope to illustrate, with very practical consequences for the freedoms of the vast majority who don't have children of their own to raise.

The dominant themes of social control down the ages have been deterrence, retribution and repression. All three motives have lately been enshrined in film censorship laws inspired by violent events, or pseudo-events, intended to restrict the free dissemination of the visual image. All three have had their progress on to the statute books eased by the occurrence, and sometimes the deliberate creation, of moral panics. Invariably, these centre on children. Not always children as blameless innocents subjected to corruption by adults. Sometimes children as demonised threats to other children. Sadly and crucially, the sense of outrage that recently facilitated a sizeable and unwarranted extension of censorship powers was provoked not by adults, but by the violence done by children themselves.

The James Bulger case rightly shocked the nation, indeed the world. James, a Merseyside child just a month short of his third birthday, was enticed away from his mother in a crowded shopping mall in Bootle, a town in the north-east of England, one February afternoon in 1993, dragged by his abductors, two boys aged ten, to a lonely stretch of railway line and there tortured, mutilated and stoned to death. That in itself was abominable . . . shocking. But there was another factor which added a vivid dimension to the horror of the crime. Video pictures of the two lads leading the trusting child to his doom were soon retrieved from a security camera in the shopping mall. The blurred images showing a tiny tot hand in hand with two bigger boys, useless for specific identification purposes, actually made the pictures infinitely more potent. Lacking specific identity, their content was instantly generalised. It ceased to be an Identikit clue and became an iconic image. It was, in the words chosen by the Press Association journalist Mark Thomas for the title of his otherwise scrupulously dispassionate study of the affair, 'every mother's nightmare'.

The irony that followed was as clear-cut as the original image of the crime being committed had been fuzzy. Addressing the court after he had sentenced the two ten-year-olds to be detained for an indefinite period, Mr Justice Morland said, 'How it came about that two normal boys of average intelligence committed this terrible crime is very hard to comprehend. It is not for me to pass judgement on their upbringing, but I suspect that exposure to violent video films may in part be an explanation.' Thus the very medium that carried evidence of the crime was stigmatised as the possible cause of it. It didn't matter that the police, on checking the video hiring and viewing patterns of the defendants' families, never found a shred of corroborative evidence for the judge's speculative attribution, or perhaps his wishful thinking. What *was* found was circumstantial, yet sufficient to fall like a spark in the powder barrel of public morality. It was a violent Hollywood film called *Child's Play 3*, third in a horror series in which 'Chucky', a toddler-sized mannikin possessed by the soul of a killer, terrorises other children before the child hero of the film destroys him. The resemblance between it and the Bulger crime was only faintly coincidental, but it provided a powerful spring for the media's anti-video reflex.

Broadsheets as well as tabloid newspapers weighed in. An editorial in *The Times* of January 22, 1994, scorning the more

94   moderate and accurate term 'concern', spoke of wide public 'alarm'. 'The role which one particularly notorious film – *Child's Play 3* – played in the Bulger trial brought urgency in what had been an academic debate about the effects of screened brutality.' Where not simplistic, this was erroneous: the film, as mentioned, played no part in the Bulger trial. While half-admitting this in its next breath, the newspaper was nevertheless not going to be shaken off the scent that it had laid down itself. 'There was never any definite proof of it . . . But even if *Child's Play 3* was guilty only by association with that case, the episode left a deep sense of disquiet.' The sole person responsible for such 'association' had been the judge in the case. The 'deep sense of disquiet' was surely caused by the crime itself, not by a film that played no part in it, whose content bore only a slight resemblance to it and which neither child convicted of the crime had ever laid eyes on. Having grossly exaggerated and simplified events – the prescription for every moral crusade in history – *The Times*'s conclusion pointed the direction that the march should take: 'What kind of urban culture allowed such material to circulate freely in the homes of young children?' it asked. *The Independent*'s leader of March 20, 1994, repeated the same point even more peremptorily: 'We must protect young minds.' Aligning themselves with the angels, both influential newspapers left no doubt that they had sighted the devil. And he was making for 'young minds'. He was circulating 'freely' in videos. He was installed beside the VCR 'in the homes of young children'.

    All this came on the heels – the cloven heels, one is tempted to say – of a panic about satanic child abusers supposedly active in various covens dotted around the Scottish Hebrides. A completely false alarm, as it turned out. But it resulted in the children of half-a-dozen of the suspect families being forcibly sundered from their parents and taken into municipal care.

    The effect of the media barrage following the Bulger murder did create a kind of panic. Parents feared their children were somehow at risk from other demon children and from something even worse because more numerous, insidious and seductive – namely, films and videos. The 'children at risk' mood thus created has been basic to the promotion of every moral panic in recent decades – and for a very good reason. It makes it timely for the rule-makers and the rule-enforcers, the legislators and the police, to fall into step and march to the orchestrated beat of the media drums on a crusade whose objectives would be much vaguer, far more repugnant and (one hopes) more obstinately resisted if the salvation of adults was declared to be the holy mission. Moral panics have this in common with miracles: neither needs confirmation, only belief. Belief was reinforced by other events in 1994. During spring and summer, the moral panic over violent films and videos was amplified by Members of Parliament. Some acted out of genuine if misguided concern. Others – the usual suspects – saw a surefire way of commending themselves to their constituents, rather than their consciences. Those under threat, the film and video companies, would have done well to combine forces at this point. But anyone who knows the film trade also knows that it is in the business of, well, business – not civil liberties. Some eighty years ago, it set up censors of its own. The aim was to protect its wares, not the freedoms of those who bought them. Fearing censorship by state and/or local authorities, the film trade created the British Board of Film Censorship (now Classification), a privately appointed, self-perpetuating body, publicly accountable to no one. That broadly remains the case today – as far as film censorship is concerned.

But since 1985, the BBFC has also been the authority designated by the Home Office to oversee the Video Recordings Act 1984, which made videos subject to the criminal law. The BBFC thus represents British compromise at its worst – in other words, at its most hypocritical. At one and the same time, it is required to serve 'state' and 'trade' – to enforce the laws of the one and facilitate the commerce of the other, to protect

96   the public from exploitation by the trade and the trade from oppression by the state. What it does not do is protect the public from the incursions of the state. Established as a private body, it has been turned into an instrument of social control.

This transformation may not have been sought by it. But it nonetheless aligns its policies to conform to, indeed to *anticipate*, the diktats of the state.

In the immediate aftermath of the Bulger case, Twentieth Century-Fox submitted a film entitled *The Good Son* to the BBFC, paid its censorship fee – £1,030 was then the average rate charged film companies, non-returnable should the film fail to pass its examination. The distributors sat back and waited for a certificate . . . and waited . . . and waited. In the political atmosphere prevailing, the 'independent' BBFC dragged its feet. It kept *The Good Son* sitting so long on its shelf before tardily certificating it that the company judged the film's commercial prospects had been injured, and released it straight to video. What had caused the tactful (or cowardly) procrastination? *The Good Son* was scripted by the English writer Ian McEwan. Its child star, Macaulay Culkin, was the popular young daredevil of the recent *Home Alone* comedy, who had hurled vast objects down on the heads of the comic break-in men violating his household. But in *The Good Son*, he had been transformed into a more fundamental devil, a 'bad seed' child suspected of murdering other children. This was the sole resemblance to the Bulger case. But with a pack of hot-tempered MPs, eager to protect 'young minds', the BBFC did not rush to judgement on rating the film and thus allowing it to be shown. And nor, to their shame, did the film trade rush to the defence of one of their own. Twentieth Century-Fox got no backing – none at all – when it tried to enlist the support of fellow distributors to screw the censor's courage to the sticking place. What increased their reluctance to join in someone else's fight was their collective apprehension about Parliament's intentions. Here their anxiety was well based.

Over 100 MPs had already signed a motion supporting an amendment to the Criminal Justice and Public Order Bill. This catch-all rag-bag of repressive revisions, intended to plug gaps in the laws governing vagrants, squatters, trespassers, etc., was then proceeding slowly and controversially through Parliament as part of the Tory party's belated attempt in the face of rising crime statistics to redeem its 'law and order' election pledges. Most sections of the Bill were resisted by the Opposition. One was signally supported. Concocted by a backbencher, David Alton of the Liberal Democrats, its target was violent films and videos.

Alton's amendment went further than violence, however. It would have banned the sale or rental of *all* '18' certificate films by herding them into a new, even more oppressive pen where they would be branded with the stigma 'Not Suitable for Home Viewing'. The publicised aim was to prevent children of negligent parents from setting eyes on them. 'Under our proposal, people who want to watch the more horrific films can do so at the cinema,' Alton said, in a spasm of generosity. He was backed by the National Society for the Prevention of Cruelty to Children (NSPCC), which warned of more sinister uses for 'violent videos'. Adults might actively employ them 'to injure and harm children'. If Parliament had passed this bizarre amendment, neither liberal, nor democratic, nor rational, nor even enforceable, it would have removed many a film with an '18' certificate from sale or rental, whether or not it contained any violence of the 'horrific' kind, simply because it might be seen by under-age children. Once again, children were made the defensible excuse for further curtailing the availability of material lawfully intended for adults, simply because other adults of the David Alton persuasion found it offensive.

This whole agenda had an eerie and familiar ring. Like a blueprint being traced line for line, the Alton campaign matched the one almost exactly ten years earlier which had brought into being the Video Recordings Act 1984, the statute that ended the free circulation of films on video by requiring their separate

98   certification under the criminal law and not simply, as was still
the case with cinema films, by private agreement with the trade.
Then, just as now, another backbencher, Graham Bright MP,
had sponsored a private members' bill. Then, just as now, it
had been debated in Parliament and outside in an atmosphere
of moral panic. Then the hysteria had been provoked by the
unfettered circulation of so-called 'video nasties' with titles
like *Driller Killer*, *I Spit on Your Grave* and *The Evil Dead*. A
loose coalition of powerful moral-interest groups including
Scotland Yard, the NSPCC, Christian Unity and a group called
CARE (formerly the nationwide Festival of Light, a notoriously
reactionary body) backed the Bright bill. And again, the cry of
children-at-risk supplied the motive for a repressive measure
affecting every adult in the country.

In such campaigns of virtue, there is nearly always one moment
when prejudice and animosity are abetted by what appears to be
respectable evidence. Invariably, this is supplied by academia,
or what now passes for it. In 1983, it was the impressively titled
'Video Violence and Children Report', issued on November
23, by the equally authoritative-sounding Parliamentary Video
Group. The report made alarming claims: forty per cent of the
children in the country had seen one of the forty or fifty video
nasties presently circulating; and 57 per cent had seen films
intended only for the eyes of those aged eighteen and over. The
inference was clear: there was a direct link between watching
violent videos and the emotional and behavioural problems of
the young.

Rather more relevant, and demonstrable, was the link between
such a tatty document and the campaign for extending social
control over adults. Material for the report had been collected by
a reputable institution, Oxford Polytechnic; but it later emerged
that polytechnic staff had not collated it, had not seen the report
in advance, had not had a chance to check on the claims of
seeing 'video nasties' made by children in the questionnaires.
Dr Brian Brown, of Oxford Polytechnic, who had collected the

raw material for the report in good faith, later claimed that it had been assembled in haste by others unconnected with his department in order to catch the first Parliamentary reading of the Graham Bright bill, scheduled for November 23, 1983. He alleged that the conclusions were written before the research material was adequately assessed. The report, he claimed, was substantially the work of a consultant on violence for the police. Dr Brown later wrote, 'Nothing in the answers to the research questionnaires we had seen could lead to the conclusion that children watch videos in friends' homes' – here he quoted from the report – '"without the knowledge or permission of their parents," and that "young children are shown horrific films by older children" and that young boys regard watching video nasties as a macho sign of growing up'.

The public presentation of the report (supplemented by a 'Part Two' published shortly afterwards) reinforced these suspicions. It was 'sold' to the clamorous media as a) an official churches' report (an ex-Archbishop of Canterbury was present at the press conference at St Bride's church: that was its sole ecclesiastical imprimatur); b) as bearing Parliamentary authority (two peers had chaired an ad hoc unofficial group meeting, three or four MPs had attended meetings in the House of Lords); and c) as the findings of an academic working party (it was a pressure-group publication of no academic standing whatever). In the panic of the times, with the then Prime Minister, Margaret Thatcher, letting it be known that she took a sympathetic interest in the Bright bill, none of these flaws carried weight with the government, and were largely ignored by the media lest they spoil the story. Children were at risk, weren't they? Therefore 'protect' them. And if the shackles were actually clamped round the sort of adults who watched violent videos, what was wrong with that?

The Video Recordings Act supplemented the powers, income and staff of the BBFC – whose roster of examiners swelled from a half-dozen in 1983 to over fifty a year or so later in order to

100   vet a backlog of five to six thousand video films. Few, if any,
of them could be classified as 'nasties'. The face of freedom
had been given a new and uglier expression by the pressure
groups' distaste for what they had not hitherto been able to
bring under state control.

In 1995, a similar objective was attained by identical means.
A few weeks before the Alton amendment was due to be
debated, a piece of pseudo-evidence to support it came out of
the academic backwoods. This one was compiled by Professor
Elizabeth Newsom, head of the child development department
at Nottingham University, and carried the endorsements of
twenty-five doctors and academics. Called 'Video Violence and
the Protection of Children' – an almost word-for-word echo of
the tainted 1983 document – it forged the familiar link between
screen violence and child delinquency. Support for such a link –
one that was not proven, still isn't, and likely never will be – again
came from the very sections of the media that should have given
it the coolest examination. *The Independent*'s editorial concluded
that 'the report lends weight to suggestions that brutal attacks,
of the kind inflicted on James Bulger last year, can be traced
to the viewing of violent videos by young children'. Of course,
it lent no such weight at all to what was anyway the speculative
obiter dictum of an imaginative judge; and it soon emerged that
the 'report' itself was simply 'the prof's own work'. No one had
commissioned it, at least no independent (with a lower-case 'i')
authority had done so. Professor Newsom, genuinely worried
in her own mind by screen violence, had put her thoughts
down on paper, then circulated them, rather in the manner
of a 'round robin', to academic colleagues. These were experts
in their fields. But their fields were not those of violent films
and videos. One was an authority on the Byzantine papacy!
According to Dr Guy Cumberbatch, senior lecturer in applied
psychology at Aston University, there was 'not a name [in the
report] who has done research into the effects of the media, or
is from the media industry. What do they know about film?'

But what did one need to know in order to ban films? Very little, it appeared. The Newsom 'report' received more prominence in news and opinion columns than the views of its academic detractors, who denounced it as 'naive and depressing'. How welcome something is if it makes life simpler by confirming what many wish to hear! The government, for one, welcomed it. Alarmed at the support for the Alton amendment, it feared the worst. The worst, in this case, being not violent videos, but a violent Opposition augmented by some of its own supporters. With a Commons majority almost down to single figures, a coalition of cross-party MPs in the 'No' lobby would inflict a humiliating defeat on the Criminal Justice and Public Order Bill: not an issue of confidence, maybe, but one that would strengthen Labour's charges that John Major had lost control of his own party. Very quickly, the Alton amendment was taken into Downing Street, a foundling child too embarrassing to be left on the doorstep, given a wash and presentable clothing, and emerged in official dress as yet another of the hypocritical constraints on adult freedoms.

In the form in which it passed into law, it required the BBFC to take special account of any film, or any elements in films, that could 'cause harm ... to potential viewers'. The last phrase explicitly included young children. Lord Ferrers, a Home Office minister, said: 'If [the BBFC] concludes that the work will set a bad example to very young children, it need not ban the video altogether, but can place it in an age-restricted category. But [the BBFC] must bear in mind the effect it might have on children who may be potential viewers.' This is the heart of the matter. The context in which the child views such a video is immaterial. A child wandering into a family living room, or present in a friend's house, and who then views material considered 'harmful' in a video not classified for its age group could create, prima facie, a serious breach of the law by the responsible persons – presumably the householders, parents or other adults present. The government

102   resisted attempts to alter the amendment to mean 'any harm that may be caused to *a significant number* [italics mine] of potential viewers', including children: a revision that would at least have brought the reactionary measure into line with the Director of Public Prosecutions' policy under the Obscene Publications Act. Whereas the Video Recordings Act had simply meant that any unlicensed video exchanged by way of trade was unlawful, the effect of the rejigged Alton amendment to the Criminal Justice and Public Order Act meant that the BBFC had a statutory duty to consider whether or not a video might be harmful to *any child* [italics mine] regardless of the context in which it was viewed.

Any sensible person would immediately see that this requirement was unenforceable. But sensible people are not the ones currently policing adults' freedom to view. No amount of video law can solve the problem of unsupervised children. But the new laws do directly affect the freedom of unsupervised adults by making certain videos unavailable to them, or cutting them lest their content might be harmful to a child who might see them, or putting the onus of legal responsibility for not letting children see them on adults. On civil liberty grounds alone, if not on grounds of its doubtful enforceability, the new measure deserves to be struck down. It is right that responsibility for what children view is first and foremost a parental one; the law can devise no fail-safe system as effective as a parent who says 'no'. But it is wrong that the rest of the adult community, with no responsibility for children, should be denied the exercise of its freedom to view material in the privacy of its home and in a state unaffected by considerations of what an immature child may see in it.

Even when a parent says 'yes' to a video that's been legally certificated for children to view, human nature may make nonsense of such safeguards. The belief that 'unsuitable' videos may harm immature children – a belief now punitively enforced by the Alton amendment – has to be measured against recorded instances of it. There exists no reliable evidence, so far. On the other hand, evidence was recently – and tragically – provided of a video that had been categorised by the BBFC as eminently suitable for children turning out to be a suspected cause of one child's suicide. Or so it appeared at the inquest held in Newcastle-under-Lyme by the North Staffordshire coroner on 10 April, 1996.

It's painful to touch on any child's death, but especially on a child of fourteen who killed himself, in November 1995, in what appears to have been an attempt to 'become' the Lion King in the Disney cartoon film of the same name. The child, Imtiaz Ahmed, was found hanging from a tree near his Stoke-on-Trent home. A note in his handwriting said: 'I am going to die because I want to be a Lion King. Mum and Dad please put the Lion King film in my grave with me.' Police enquiries turned up the child's diary, which recorded his fantasies about the film, in which Simba, a heroic lion cub, grows to become a jungle king after the death of his father. Recording an open verdict, without suspicious or sinister circumstances, the coroner speculated: 'The question that [perplexes] me is what was [the boy's] state of mind. Was his wish actually to bring about a metamorphosis, a physical change or rebirth, so that he was still Imtiaz Ahmed and the Lion King? I have no doubt from the evidence that Imtiaz was obsessed by *The Lion King* and I think he fantasised secretly about it. I ask myself, was Imtiaz a naive, curious cub? Did he properly address his fourteen-year-old mind to the enormity of his actions or was it an inward voice or a macabre compulsion or was it an acting out of fantasy? I do not pretend to know . . .' And nor should anyone else pretend to know. But one may imagine the national hue and cry that would certainly have ensued had such a child's death been associated with a violent video classified for viewing by adults only. The pathetic irony is clear: in this single case, the video associated with the child's suicide was one that had been properly classified for children. In this instance, the silence of the media was deafening. No letters, columns or

104   editorials followed the publication of the coroner's remarks;
no demands were made for the withdrawal of *The Lion King*
video from public sale; and no one drew the lesson from this
tragedy that 'protecting' the young and vulnerable by imposing
ever more rigid restrictions on the adult and mature may have
little or no bearing on the influences at work on the under-age
and impressionable. We are left with calculable penalties and
the loss of adult freedoms, but without any additional assurance
that what we have been forced to surrender by bigoted and
ignorant legislators offers realistic compensation.

The most stringent film and video censorship laws in Europe
have been given a boost by the most irrational means and for the
most questionable motives. What next? I fear that controls will
more and more shift from the end product to the process. Having
policed the points of sale, or manner of viewing, they will next
restrict the means of dissemination. The government recently
banned the sale of decoders capable of downloading satellite
TV material regarded as corrupting to adults and minors. Very
shortly, technology will make it feasible for most homes to have
video films sent into the living-room down the telephone lines.
Such a unitary source is far easier to police than tens of thousands
of video stores. It removes 'ownership' of the image from the
renter's hands, retains (or withholds) it at the discretion of
the central supplier, and delivers to the consumer only what is
considered 'safe'. The regulatory powers are currently fretting
over the new technologies of the Internet and the uncensored
imagery still possible for the homeowner to download via his or
her modem by simply dialling a number. To enforce a ban on
the Internet, thus crippling the newest and most 'independent'
system of communication yet devised, might be thought totally
unacceptable. Wait till the children-at-risk lobbies get going.
They have had plenty of practice on what adults used to call
their freedom to view.

Pictures and Secrets

PTOLEMY TOMPKINS

'Be not afraid of the universe.'
            Eskimo shaman, quoting the supreme self,
                        or soul of the universe.

'Everything means something I guess.'
            Character in *The Texas Chainsaw Massacre*.

As dull a place as it was to grow up in, McLean, Virginia, had
terrific thunderstorms. Arriving in the deep summer afternoons
when the air was heavy and dead and everything felt as if it were
held in suspension, these storms bore down upon the landscape
with a vengeance. In my years at the Barn I knew ahead of time
when such a storm was coming, for doors and windows would set
to rattling and slamming urgently under the advancing winds.
Whenever I heard these warnings, I would drop what I was doing
and head out into the middle of the field that stretched behind
the Barn and watch the storm as it approached, marvelling as
the trees dipped violently beneath the cold, erratic blasts of air
and the leaves on their branches blew silver and rustled with a
sound like mounting applause.

So dark and strong and concentrated were these storms that
I could follow, foot by foot, the progress of the wall of falling
water as it made its way across the lawn towards me. Just ahead
of its arrival, I would retreat into the Barn and watch the steady

grey pandemonium of the storm's passing from inside. In ten or twenty minutes it would all be over, the storm would have moved on, and I would walk back out on to the sparkling lawn, the air now chill and charged and fresh, the grass covered with tattered leaves and fallen branches lying about like leftovers from a party thrown by some now departed group of titans. I loved the violence of these storms – the way they broke the spell of sameness that could lie so heavily over things in the summer months. Indeed, it often seemed as if the landscape actually awaited these storms with an eagerness that paralleled my own.

The understanding that destruction can be nourishing – that the world itself craves a certain kind of violence and cannot go for too long without it – was a lesson I learned in a number of ways as a child. First and foremost, however, it came from watching movies. My father and I spent countless nights at the cinema together, for he loved films even more than I did and had the true aficionado's unconditional open-mindedness about what he was willing to see. The films we saw together in those years were varied in the extreme, but most were united by the all-important quality of being, as my mother disapprovingly put it, 'over my head'. Sex, violence, profanity: for me these were not the inaccessible adult mysteries they tended to be for my friends, but items of easy and frequent acquaintance. By the age of about ten, I had already seen it all.

By far the most formative and beloved of the movies my father took me to were horror films, which in the early '70s were enjoying a lively and unprecedentedly bloody renaissance. In *The House That Screamed*, I watched as the unbalanced son of a girls' school headmistress murdered one student after another so that he could assemble the woman of his dreams out of their assorted parts. In *Mark of the Devil*, I marvelled as a woman's tongue was pulled from her mouth with giant iron pincers. In films like *Willard* and *Frogs*, I witnessed the unlikely but fascinating spectacle of rats, snakes and alligators deciding they had had enough of human domination and turning on people *en masse.*

After a few years of watching horror films with my father, I picked up the habit of decoding the world around me using the messages I thought I found at work in them. Like most children, I was a tireless and open-minded theorist, and these films provided an especially generous source of material from which to build up my own, custom-made explanations for why life was the thing it was. Of the many lessons that horror films taught me, one was primary. Again and again, these films drove home the message that ordinary existence – the one I woke up to and spent most of the day involved in – was something of a sham. Life, these films seemed to argue, was not the solid and reliable affair it pretended to be, but something much more tentative and fragile. Powerful forces lurked beneath the surface of day-to-day reality, and it was only a matter of time before those forces would make their way to the surface.

Effective as they were at convincing me of the existence of these hidden forces, most horror films didn't provide much of an explanation of them beyond that. The point was not to understand why things were going to go wrong – only that they inevitably would do so. One watched as a reassuringly ordinary scenario was first slowly and subtly, then loudly and graphically torn apart by some menacing presence or other – a giant animal perhaps, or a vampire or an axe-wielding maniac. Of course, there were always those who refused to believe, even when the evidence was staring them in the face. 'This can't be happening,' someone up on the screen would gasp. Down in the audience, I knew better.

By the end of the film, either the menace, whatever it happened to be, was put at least temporarily to rest, or else chaos and pandemonium won out once and for all. Generally, the endings of these films were something of a disappointment. The joy lay not in the climax but rather in watching things fall slowly and implacably apart. And the strange thing was that joy was indeed – for me, at least – the emotion most involved. Watching these films, I experienced a wonderful if paradoxical exhilaration as the safe and secure lives of the protagonists were turned upside down in order that this hidden dimension could at last emerge into the light.

Like that of an addict with a substance that at once fulfils and destroys him, my relationship with these films was double-edged. For although on one level I found some great and indefinable satisfaction in being told that the life so many people seemed satisfied and secure with was a mere stage of cardboard props and pulleys, on another level the concept was deeply unnerving.

'How about a film, Ptolly?' my father said one Friday night after dinner. 'Go check the paper and see what's playing.'

My father was on friendly terms with the owners of a group of theatres in Washington, and we could see any film showing at them for free. I looked over the list of free films showing that night, letting my instincts lead me to the most potentially unpleasant. On this particular night, the choice was easy.

'Here's one. It's at the Inner Circle, at midnight. *Night of the Living Dead*. What a great name.'

'Midnight. That's a bit late. It's not even nine yet.'

'Yeah, but if it's on that late it probably means it's good. Can we go?'

'All right. If you're still up for it at eleven, we'll go.'

Night of the Living Dead had only been out for a few years and was still considered shocking for its unprecedented violence, but neither my father nor I had heard anything about it. I had simply picked it out of the movie listings on the strength of its straightforward, no-nonsense title. It sounded like a film that would deliver.

And deliver it did. Jaded as I was, *Night of the Living Dead* managed to present me with something new – so new, in fact, that I left the theatre feeling I was not quite the same person I had been when I entered it. The street outside the theatre, the cars whizzing past through the late summer night, everything around me took on a frightening unreality, and on the drive home this sense of unreality did not decrease but seemed to grow. Things had unfolded on the screen that I had not previously thought possible, even in the pretend world of the movies, and as a result the world around me had become an entirely less trustworthy place than it had been a mere two hours earlier.

Upon reflection, I realised I had many reasons to gravitate to *Night of the Living Dead*. The forlorn farmhouse from which the main characters battle against the encroaching army of zombies looked a good deal like a number of houses I had lived in over the years. In addition, the desperate hammering of the film's hero as he nails planks of wood and bits of splintered furniture against the doors and windows was oddly reminiscent of the sloppy, rapid-fire style of carpentry my father tended to practise in his perpetual remodellings and improvements.

But these were just small and coincidental details. Above and beyond them, the movie both frightened and fascinated me because it stated, in unprecedentedly vivid terms, what I had long been told, and loved hearing, from the lesser horror films that had come before it: life was a place of deep uncertainty, ruled in secret by huge and dangerous forces. Like the lonely, pathetically vulnerable house in the film, lost in a night-time landscape where the dead staggered and lurched about in search of human flesh, the ordinary world was a fragile and precarious island set in a sea of mystery – a sea that at every moment threatened to overtake it.

All this I knew, or at least strongly suspected, already, but *Night of the Living Dead* gave my theories back to me in such a direct and vivid way that I was thoroughly unhinged by it. Having witnessed such an uncompromising confirmation of my darkest suspicions, I found it perverse and ridiculous that the ordinary, workaday world should dare to continue around me at all. Telling my schoolfriends about the picture did little

110   or nothing to help me make sense of it. No one else in my
class had parents permissive enough to allow them to go see
it themselves, so I was left to ponder the unspeakable events
I had witnessed without the benefit of peer opinions to check
against my own. The more I tried to give my fellow ten-year-olds
some idea of the uncanny and horrific truth I had uncovered
at the heart of this film, the more I realised that, like a mystic
returned from an encounter with the divine in the trackless
wastes of a distant desert, I had no hope of truly conveying
what I had witnessed.

'So the woman goes down to the basement to where the
daughter is, and the daughter is *eating her father*.'

'Whoa, that's cool. That's like when Godzilla grabbed that
guy and just his legs were sticking out of his mouth.'

But of course it wasn't like that at all. Godzilla was a plastic
Japanese dinosaur: a mere entertainment. What I had seen,
while 'only a movie' in the technical sense, was decidedly
something more as well. With this film, I began to realise, I
had stumbled upon something genuinely adult – something
which, as my mother put it, I was 'not ready for'. And as a
result I suddenly found myself living in a world where true
surprises were possible; a place where anything – absolutely
anything – could happen.

Sitting on the steps outside the kitchen one day shortly after
seeing the film, I overheard my mother and father talking
inside. 'Peter,' my mother said, 'I'm worried about Ptolemy.
He seems so preoccupied with that ghastly movie you took him
to last week. He's got circles under his eyes, and he's terribly
pale. He told me there's a scene in the film where a young girl
eats her father and stabs her mother to death with a gardening
trowel. What is on your mind that you can take a child to see
something like that?'

'Pretty grisly stuff,' my father remarked offhandedly. 'But I
didn't know anything about the film. He wanted to see it, and

I'll see anything as long as I don't know what's going to happen.
I like the surprise.'

'Well you certainly succeeded in surprising him! I think you
ought to stop going to these pictures altogether. He has enough
to cope with in his life at the moment without worrying that
some zombie is going to eat him.'

My father perked up at this last statement, as did I from my
spot on the steps outside.

'Are you suggesting I censor what the boy sees?'

'Oh for heaven's sake. Protecting him from films he's not old
enough to understand isn't censoring. It's being a parent.'

'Shield a child too much from the world,' my father returned,
'and you implant the idea that the world is a place that one
needs to be shielded from. One shouldn't keep secrets from
children about anything. That film may have been a little
much for Ptolly, but on another level it's never too early to
learn about what frightens you and to confront it. It's only
by examining what we fear most that we can learn to defuse
those fears and the negative energy they generate. When that
happens, that negativity can be transformed into love and
positive energy.'

'Positive energy! I hardly see where the positive energy is to
be found in a girl stabbing her mother with a gardening trowel.
But in any case I'd like you to talk to him.'

I had been monitoring this conversation closely, for I
understood that my future movie-going privileges were at
stake. It seemed to me that if I did not want those privileges
to be drastically curtailed, I had better set about giving the
impression that I was not as unnerved by *Night of the Living
Dead* as I actually was. In the days since I had seen the film,
I had indeed been sleeping less than usual. Those lurching,
shabbily dressed zombies appeared as soon as I closed my eyes
at night, and when I opened my eyes I saw them too, crowding
about in the large black windows of my bedroom, reaching out
to me with their pale, rubbery fingers.

That evening, my father came into my room as I was once again steeling myself for a night of fitful sleep.

'Ptolly,' he said, sitting down at the foot of the bed, 'you've got to stop letting this silly movie get under your skin. We'll have to stop going to the movies – or at least some of them – if they're going to have this kind of effect on you.'

'But I like seeing movies with you, and horror movies are the best kind.'

'So do I, but if they're going to upset you like this . . . Listen,' he said, leaning forward and talking seriously, addressing his remarks to the floor in front of him. 'I'm going to let you in on a little secret. This kind of stuff only has energy to frighten you if you let it. The thing you, the thing most people, don't realise is that they have the power to control the things that frighten them. You have the power to control your own imagination, and all the images that move through it, only no one's told you so. Now, what scared you most about that film?'

'I don't know. The little girl in the basement, I guess.'

'Fine. Now let's do a little experiment. Try to imagine the girl. Picture her with your mind's eye. Can you see her?'

'Sure.'

'Good. Now take her out of the context of the film. Take her out of the basement, and put her somewhere else.'

'Like where?'

'Anywhere!'

'On a bicycle?'

'Perfect. Imagine her on a bicycle. Can you see her?'

'Yeah.'

'What's she doing?'

'She's going down a hill.'

'Good. Now, make her reverse direction. Make her go backwards up the hill. *You're* the boss. Just as you can decide what situation you want to see the girl in, so you have the power to control what kind of effect the images in the film have over you. It's all just pictures, pictures, pictures. They're frightening because you allow them to be frightening. All the images that move through your head every day are under your control if you want them to be. You're the one creating them in the first place, and once you come to understand that and learn to act on it, they won't have any negative power over you any more.'

'I make the images in my head?'

'Of course.'

'But I didn't make the girl in the basement. I saw her.'

'You saw the image because someone else made it up in their head, then got actors and cameras so you could see it as they did. You know that a film always has a director, right? The one who tells people what to do and how to do it and decides where the camera is going to be.'

'Yeah.'

'Well, *you* are the director of the scenes and pictures that go through your head every day. You're even the director of the dreams you have at night – the director and the audience at the same time – only you don't know it.'

'Where do the pictures come from, though?'

'From you! That's the whole point. You're the boss.'

'I sure don't feel like I'm the boss.'

'Most people don't,' said my father enthusiastically. 'And if you can come to the realisation that you are, you'll be better off than ninety-nine per cent of the adults out there. That's really the great secret: knowing who's behind the scenes making it all happen – knowing who the man behind the curtain is.'

'There's a man behind the curtain? What curtain?'

'No, no. That's just a way of talking. What I mean is there's a whole world out there that you don't know about.'

'I know. That's why I'm scared.'

'But it isn't the kind of world you think it is. You think it's a wasteland full of ghouls and little girls with blood on their chins and all that sort of shit we see in these movies you like so much. But it isn't that kind of place at all, really. You shouldn't

114 be frightened of it, because it's the place where you really belong.
You, me, all of us go through our lives thinking we're this tiny
little person, trapped inside our own heads, and that the world
out there is some big alien nightmare. And because we think
it's that way, that's the way it appears to us. But it's all a big
illusion. It's not real.'

'So what's real?'

My father turned from the floor and stared at me, tapping
his head with his finger as he did so.

'This,' he said triumphantly. 'This is what's real. The you who
mistakenly thinks it's a frightened little nothing trapped inside
your brain. It's what's real, only it isn't really so little at all, and
it isn't trapped inside your brain, either.'

'I don't get it. If I'm not in my brain, where am I?'

'You're everywhere! You're out there in the dark beyond the
window, and up in the sky, and in the past and in the future. The
real you isn't limited by time or space or the body, because the
real you is everything. That asinine school we send you to tells
you there's some grim-faced God up in the sky looking down
at us making sure we all behave correctly. But there isn't any
such God out there at all. In fact, it's really just the reverse of
that, because deep down each of us, you and me, if we look
hard enough, discovers that we are God ourselves. We actually
are the ones who have made the world and who control it. The
world is really us, only we don't want to admit it because we
don't want the responsibility of all that power.'

'So I shouldn't be frightened about that movie because
I'm God?'

'You aren't *literally* God, but you are the creator of your own
reality, which is almost the same as being God.'

My father straightened up now and patted my foot through
the blanket.

'Listen, I've got to get back out to dinner because we have
guests. But I don't want you lying awake thinking about this film
any more. Think about some of the things I've told you instead,

and remember,' he said, smiling and tapping his temple with his index finger, 'who's really in charge.'

However well intentioned, my father's insights weren't much use in helping me to fall asleep that night, or on those to come. The trick of picturing the zombies that crowded my imagination dressed in party hats or eating green ice cream worked for a moment or two, but the process took constant effort, and as soon as I relaxed they went back to what they had been doing before, staggering and gaping, their tattered arms reaching out towards me with the same old grim hunger. Out beyond the dim lights and shaky walls of my ten-year-old self-consciousness, the world continued to appear a dark and deeply alien landscape, dead set on doing what it, not I, wished it to do.

Having failed to command the zombies of my imagination through force of will, I developed other anxiety-avoiding strategies – the simplest and most effective of which was simply to avoid going to bed for as long as possible. This was easiest when there were guests over. At around ten o'clock my mother would tell me it might be a good idea if I got off to bed, but my father would always intercede on my behalf, telling her I shouldn't be discouraged from listening to the adults if I wanted to do so. There usually wasn't much to interest me in these conversations, but I stayed at the table anyhow, chin in hands and eyes half closed, letting the adult voices wash over me in a comforting and largely meaningless babble.

It was during this intensive period of dinner-party attendance that I first started to notice a pattern of sorts to my father's talk, as he sat, booming away, at the head of the table. What I noticed was that he always seemed to be talking about secrets of one sort or another, and about how knowing those secrets could set one free. Sometimes, as had been the case in my bedroom that night, the 'great secret' would be that you and God weren't really different, but on some mysterious inner level one and the same. But at other times it would be about something else – that

116   love was the engine that drove the universe, or that everything possessed consciousness, or that all things good and bad that happened to one came from actions committed in a past life.

In addition to the various 'great' secrets, there was any number of lesser ones that came up on occasion as well. Who built Stonehenge? Who wrote the plays attributed, by the dull-witted academicians, to Shakespeare? Who ran the banks in America? What were the ancient Egyptians really up to? Gradually it became clear to me that if there was in fact any real 'great secret' to life, it had to do not with any single, specific secret, but with the nature of secrecy itself. Life was essentially a carnival of misleading appearances – a papier mâché landscape set about with hints and inconsistencies, which when examined closely enough pointed the way to a realm beyond. The mass of humanity, it seemed, chose for some reason to ignore these little openings and inconsistencies with which the world was strewn, but my father, to make up for this negligence, had apparently cornered the market on all of them himself.

'That whole period has to be seen in reference to such-and-such a secret society, or it makes no sense at all,' he would remark, or, 'If you want to know anything about his *true* motivations, you have to realise that so-and-so was in reality a third-degree mason,' or, 'Of course, once you see what was *really* going on with this or that ancient civilisation, it turns all of conventional history upside down.' With all of these innumerable hidden intrigues, secret histories and shadowy, occult goings-on, the basic argument was the same. Nothing was ever what it seemed on the surface, but if one knew this and stared at that surface long enough with this in mind, openings in the small and all-too-normal world would appear: openings that would then turn into roads leading into a vast dimension where all kinds of things that had previously been mere impossibilities were made gloriously manifest.

Of course, I was already more than well aware that the world possessed a secret life. The message had been instilled in me by every horror film I had ever seen, and *Night of the Living Dead* had driven it home once and for all. The problem lay in the nature of this secret world. Was it a place of cacophony and terror, as the movies I saw insisted, or was it rather, as my father so vociferously maintained, a place of happiness and love and communion? The paradoxical joy that horror movies gave me – the fact that I somehow couldn't help loving them even when they destroyed my nights and haunted my days – suggested that my father was perhaps correct in his optimism about the secret world and its true intentions. Perhaps all those zombies were really only allies in disguise, waiting to do my bidding once I discovered, as he so confidently put it, who was really in charge. Yet the possibility that this wasn't so – the nagging anxiety that that great unknown dimension did not hold only good intentions – continued to trouble my sleeping and my waking hours. How did my father *know* it was all so good out there in the dark?

According to the documents of countless religious traditions, from Native American prophecies to the Revelation that closes the New Testament, the real intentions of the universe are well hidden for a reason, and are not to be revealed until the Final Day, when all our troubled suspicions and carefully guarded hopes will be fulfilled or dashed once and for all. In the meantime, the general wisdom goes, we must be content with our ignorance – improvising visions of the secret world from our imaginations if it pleases us to do so, and remembering not to be either too troubled or too consoled by the results. After all, they're only pictures.

Why I Love Violence

JOHN WATERS

I'm hardly what you'd call a mellow person. When audiences
see my movies, they always seem appalled that I find such
humour in the violence I lovingly depict. 'How could you
think of such awful things?' liberal critics always ask. 'How
else could I possibly amuse myself?' I always wonder. I tremble
to think how boring my life would be without the throbbing
excitement of violence always surrounding me. It makes the
newspapers worth the quarter, perks up local news shows, helps
the economy, and can even make a mundane walk to the store
exciting, if you're lucky enough to see a mugging or a car
accident.

It's not that I want to harm anyone – I've never initiated
physical violence in my life – but thinking about violence
seems to relax me and give me comfort. Even when violence
is directed at me personally, I've managed to keep a cheery
attitude. Recently mugged in New York and given a serious
concussion, I managed to stagger to a rather snobby friend's
apartment. As she opened the door and saw me covered in
blood, I'm told I blurted out, 'I've just killed five people and
I've come to involve you.' Life is nothing without a good sense
of humour.

Even as a toddler, violence intrigued me, and I've always
identified with that Diane Arbus photo of a child holding a

toy hand grenade and grimacing in mock terror. My parents claim they suspected something was wrong with me from the beginning, and my childhood obsession with car accidents seemed to confirm their worst fears. While other kids were out playing cowboys and Indians, I was lost in fantasies of crunching metal and people screaming for help. I would sweet-talk unsuspecting relatives into buying me toy cars – any kind, as long as they were new and shiny. As soon as I was alone, I would rush out to my favourite place, a tree stump surrounded by mud, located in an obscure section of the woods near our house. Here was my own little fantasy world – a child's version of an auto collision centre. I would take two cars and pretend they were driving on a secluded country road until one would swerve and crash into the other. I would become quite excited and start smashing the car with a hammer, all the while shouting, 'Oh, my God, there's been a terrible accident!' I would linger over the destruction for a while until finally I would take my little toy tow truck (the only one that was never damaged) and tow the wrecks into my play junkyard, which was filled with smashed cars from other days' games.

My parents, not knowing what to make of my creative play, threw up their hands in despair and agreed to take me to a REAL junkyard filled with REAL LIVE AUTO WRECKS! It was quite embarrassing for my mother. We'd pull up to a local junkyard and some oil-covered grease monkey would approach us. My mother, trying to be very proper, would try to explain: 'Uh ... my son ... uh ... would like to look around at some of the wrecked cars.' The junkyard man would look at her like some kind of a leper and glance down into the face of a child fanatic. As my heart pounded a mile a minute, I would clutch my little toy tow truck and give him a crooked smile. He would shrug, laugh in our faces, and walk away, shaking his head.

My mother, not wanting to interfere with my fantasies, was decent enough to let me explore the junkyard alone. I was in total awe. My favourite sight was cars that had overturned.

You could always tell by the dented roof. I also loved broken windshields and the thoughts of the people who might have gone through them. Once I saw bloodstains on the seats and this I still treasure as my happiest childhood memory.

Another childhood obsession related to violence in my mind was amusement parks. I've always loved scary rides and, to this day, I'll drive hundreds of miles to go on a roller-coaster if I've read that someone has recently been killed while riding it. If I could pick my own death, it would be on a roller-coaster that jumps the tracks and careens into a packed crowd at a cotton candy stand at a state fair.

I used to beg my father to take me on the most hair-raising rides possible. For a while he would give in, but he always hated the rides and would turn green from nausea. If he wasn't available, I would force my younger brother to go on rides that would terrify him to the point that the attendant would have to stop the ride and let him off. Once, as a child, I either saw or had as a fantasy – I can't remember which any more – a seat fly off a ride and land on the roof of a nearby building. Ever since, it has been one of my favourite rides, and I still go on it every chance I get. Another time, on the Wild Mouse, a high-speed minicoaster, my car started up the first hill, but the chain pulling the car broke and we slid back down to the bottom. Other riders fled in panic, but I stayed put as the attendant just rehooked the chain under the car and I started up the hill again. I remember it being quite a thrill. I also used to watch the ride called the Roundup for hours, because nothing holds you except centrifugal force, and I always wanted to see, if someone got sick, whether the vomit would fly back in his face.

When amusement parks ceased to provide violent fantasies, I went even further and thought up my own ride, which I would draw over and over in my school classes instead of paying attention to the boring teachers. It was called the Crush, and was based on the Ferris wheel. Instead of cars, you were strapped to a giant wheel. The wheel was about ten feet off the ground and it would go around and you'd be terrified when you'd be at the top upside down. After the wheel turned for a while, it would start getting lower to the ground until you were at last crushed to death on the final spin. My drawings always had terrified riders on one half of the wheel and bloody pulps on the other half. Luckily, my teachers and classmates never saw my little sketches.

Another childhood obsession was hurricanes. I loved them and always prayed one would hit our community. Once, one did – Hurricane Hazel – and I will always remember it fondly. The high winds uprooted trees on our lawn, and I sat for hours and looked lovingly at the damage. But the best sight was right up the street where a giant tree had fallen into a neighbour's house; you could see right into their bedroom from the street, and I would sometimes take my lunch up to the corner so I could look at the damage while I ate. I remember being heartbroken when the workers came to finally make repairs.

Fires also fascinated me as a kid, and this was one fixation my father seemed to understand. Whenever we'd hear the siren that alerted the local volunteer firemen, we'd drop what we were doing, race to the car, and speed for the firehouse just in time to follow the fire trucks to the local blaze. 'It's a good one,' my father would whisper if the flames were raging out of control. I always felt closest to my father when we stood together and watched a neighbour's house burn to the ground.

Another thing my parents could never understand was my hatred for sports. Knowing I loved violence, they incorrectly figured that sports would be a healthier outlet for my interests than my little games of destruction. But violence in sports always seemed so pointless, because everyone was prepared, so what fun could it possibly be?

My father always dragged me to football games, and I would be disappointed to see that the players actually wore special costumes designed to protect them from injury. I noticed ambulances waiting on the side of the field, so what was the big danger? Bored to tears, I fantasised the stadium bleachers collapsing, all the while thinking of the famous photo of the Indianapolis 500 tragedy that I had secretly clipped and hidden under my bed. Gazing intently at one section of screaming fans, I would imagine them falling to their deaths so my father and I could experience some real excitement.

Baseball games were even worse. Grown men chasing balls for no apparent reason held little interest for me. I only hoped that a fly ball would conk some spectator on the head and knock him unconscious for being stupid enough to sit there in the first place. Unfortunately, this happened rarely, so I had to content myself with eating junk food and praying the game would end so I could rush home and concentrate on some imagined disasters.

In grade school I was forced to participate in sports, but was always the last chosen when teams were picked. This was a relief rather than a trauma, because at least my fellow teammates accepted my attitude and didn't expect the slightest effort on my part. I would always be relieved to be assigned to the position of right field because no balls ever came there unless a powerful left-handed hitter was at bat.

Happily making up weird little stories to myself, I would always be startled if the dreaded ball ended up anywhere near me and would make no attempt to catch it. Or pick it up. Or do anything with it: my teammates would be screaming 'Waters! Waters!' as the opposing team's players raced around the bases; but I never paid much attention, figuring it was *their* problem.

If ever I was unlucky enough to be called to bat, I would just stand there, refusing to swing and hoping the pitcher would strike me out quickly and quietly. The few times I was 'walked' to a base, I panicked at actually having to be involved in the stupidity of the game and tried to make conversation with the disinterested, wildly competitive first baseman.

'Did you see Dagmar on TV last night?' I'd ask, trying to be friendly.

'No!' he'd growl, furious that I was paying absolutely no attention to the game.

'She was real good,' I'd continue, forgetting that you were supposed to keep one foot firmly planted on the base.

Suddenly everyone started yelling as if there was a national emergency and someone threw the ball to the first baseman and he lunged at me with it and the umpire screamed, 'Out!'

'Thanks,' I mumbled in all honesty as he scowled in my face, unable to comprehend my eagerness to get out of the hot sun and sit back comfortably on the bench.

To this day I'm a confirmed sports bigot and even the mention of sports riles me up uncontrollably. 'How about those Birds?' some ignorant cabdriver will ask, referring to the Baltimore Orioles and trying to be friendly. 'I hate sports,' I state flatly, ending the conversation with a dud. Just because I'm a man, why does he assume that I want to talk about sports? It's as ridiculous as if I got in the cab, slapped the driver on the back, and screamed: 'How about Fassbinder's latest movie? Wasn't it a knockout?'

Whenever I hear a friend casually mention an interest in a sporting event, I immediately reconsider our friendship. After all, I argue, sports are responsible for lowering college academic standards and ruining holidays by dominating every family get-together with a loud and obnoxious TV 'big game'. All sports are contemptible. Basketball: freakish giants with midget IQs 'dunking' balls in macrame baskets that are the exact height of the players. Football: fat hogs knocking each other down and huddling to tell secrets that no one in his right mind would care to repeat. Boxing: ugly, notoriously underprivileged men beating each other up without the thrill of breaking the law. And skiing: eager-beaver masochists in polyester outfits anxious to break a leg in the name of fitness.

Unfortunately, as an adult in Baltimore, I used to live near

124 Memorial Stadium – 'the Atrocity Centre' – and my memories are anything but pleasant. Nightly, thousands of drunken fans would cause traffic jams, take up parking places, and become human eyesores, decked out in obvious fashion violations. If your hometown team is ever unfortunate enough to be included in the World Series, cross-country idiots will pour into your city, filling up hotel rooms that otherwise might have been rented by interesting people. They hog bar conversations and insist 'the game' blare from every TV set. If your team ever wins, a dangerous celebration takes place where crazed enthusiasts hoist one another on their shoulders and stagger around drunkenly, waving flags, starting dangerous bonfires, and pissing on your lawn. If they should lose, the entire city becomes morose and seemingly normal sales clerks become hostile if you don't seem properly devastated by the outcome of the game.

God, I'd like to bomb that stadium! I silently curse it every time I drive past. But once, and only once, did something wonderful happen there. An entire scout troup was eaten by a berserk escalator on 'Scout Day'. The escalator was packed with baseball-crazed scouts (some of whom probably even carried baseball cards) when the escalator suddenly speeded up to five times its normal rate and began grinding up the little sports fans. Maybe next time their parents will send them to the movies, where they belong.

Despite sports I had a happy childhood. Naturally I loved horror movies or any kind of movie that had good villains. *The Wizard of Oz* is still my all-time favourite movie and, even as a child, I rooted for the Wicked Witch. To hell with Dorothy. The Witch had pretty green skin, a beautiful castle and all those wonderful winged monkeys. Dorothy just had a dull home in Kansas, dreary farmer aunt and uncle, and an ugly little dog that bothered the neighbours. I even tried dressing up like the Witch to terrify my neighbourhood friends, but succeeded only in raising a few eyebrows.

Another favourite villain was the Wicked Stepmother in Walt Disney's *Cinderella*. I used to gaze for hours at her picture in the soundtrack album storybook and play her entrance line over and over until the record wore out and started to skip. 'Cinderella!' I'd hear again, knowing every inflection of her wonderful voice. I'd repeat this line over and over, shivering in appreciation and glowing in childhood happiness.

Cyril Ritchard's portrayal of Captain Hook in *Peter Pan* also obsessed me for years. I went through entire years of my childhood convinced I *was* Captain Hook. Every day I'd awake in the suburbs, block it out, and pretend I was on a pirate ship. From my vast collection of childhood props, I'd choose an especially nasty-looking hook made from a bent coat-hanger, scrunch up my arm and insert the hook in my coat sleeve. Trying to imitate Captain Hook's long hair, I'd swipe my father's neckties and tape them to the crown of my head. Finally dressed, I would nod a silent approval in the mirror and stalk out of the house, feeling quite evil.

Once, our fat maid Clara discovered me deep in fantasy, dressed in complete Captain Hook drag. Talking to myself and cackling away, I was in seventh heaven. She stopped in her tracks, tried to comprehend, and burst out laughing. Instead of being embarrassed, I sneered at her in my best Captain Hook fashion. She quit soon afterwards.

As villain-worship took up more and more of my time as a child, I decided to design 'horror houses' in the family garage and charged a nickel admission. Kids would enter the pitch dark through fake spider webs and risk breaking their necks on little traps I had set all through a maze. After selling a ticket, I'd sneak back into the horror house and wait at the exit. As annoyed customers groped their way to the door, I'd leap out and spray them with a fire extinguisher that made a horrible noise and shot forth an icy thick smoke. Pretty soon parents began forbidding their children to enter and my little business was forced to close.

I also started giving puppet shows and became good enough to be hired by parents for their children's birthday parties. I earned as much as twenty dollars a show and sometimes had three or four a week. The show consisted of *Cinderella* and a more violent version of *Punch and Judy* that ended with both Punch and Judy being eaten by my favourite dragon puppet. After this abrupt ending I would come out from behind the stage and let the dragon puppet bite the children's hands for 'good luck'. Sometimes I'd chase the few terrified children who had refused until they finally gave up and let the dragon have his way.

At about the same time, I discovered William Castle movies, and they quickly became a fetish. Especially the ones that included gimmicks such as plastic skeletons flying out into the audience ('Emergo') and electric buzzers going off under the seats ('Percepto'). I tried to jazz up my puppet shows by using some of those very same gimmicks and spent hours trying to rig up the apparatus, but unfortunately the kids were never too impressed. When I started using fake blood, the parents began to get alarmed and word spread throughout the ice-cream-and-cake circuit that the shows were getting 'too sick', so I gracefully retired while I was still ahead.

Today, I am lucky enough to have friends like Pat Moran and her husband, Chuck, who allow me to take their daughter to any horror event I choose. I really identify with little Greer. She is only six, but she loves violent films and hates kids' movies. She even wanted to walk out of *Superman* halfway through, saying in disbelief, 'You mean we're going to sit through the *whole* thing?'

One day Greer and I were walking down the street on our way to the local downtown theatre when a neighbourhood busybody stopped us and said, in her worst cutesy voice, 'And where are you going, honey?' Greer wearily said, 'To the movies.' And the woman, thinking this was oh-so-precious, said, 'To see what?' Without blinking an eye, the little horror buff blurted out,

'*The Bloody Pit of Horror*,' and the woman almost collapsed as we trotted off down the street.

I had a children's birthday party for Greer and her friends, and I showed an early film monstrosity I made called *Multiple Maniacs*. All the little kids had ice cream and party hats and laughed and cheered at the movie like it was Punch and Judy. Later, when I mentioned to my mother how nice the kids' party had turned out, she snorted, 'I'm glad none of *my* kids were there.' In disbelief I reminded her, 'But, Mother, one of *your* kids made the movie and *gave* the party.'

I couldn't wait to be a teenager so I could get pimples. I craved braces for my teeth, but the uncooperative dentist insisted to my parents that I didn't need them. Undaunted, I unbent paper clips and wrapped them around my teeth and felt much better.

I loved rock 'n' roll and was always insanely jealous of the teenagers who could attend rock 'n' roll riots. I wanted an Elvis Presley haircut more than anything, but my parents insisted on taking me to a horrible barber shop filled with *Field and Stream* magazines where no one understood the 'drape' look I so feverishly desired. Ignoring my elaborate instructions, the barber would give me a crew cut and I'd rush home and try to turn it into a flattop with the aid of Butch Stick hair wax, but somehow it never seemed to work.

When I entered junior high, I received the thrill of my life. Actual girl juvenile delinquents were in my class, and, to my astonishment, they got into cat-fights. I immediately lost interest in the school's curriculum and concentrated completely on every move of these cheap girls. I had never seen anything like it. Dressed in black, straight skirts, white 'angel blouses', and pointy-toed 'fruit boots', they hung in packs, combing their Debra Paget bangs and discolouring their lips with pimple medicine. They never did their homework and were proud of it. They were only 'wasting time' until they could legally quit school, run away, and become full-time 'skags'.

128   My favourite 'skagette' was Debbie Sue, a fifteen-year-old seventh grader who loved to terrorise substitute teachers by grabbing their pocketbooks and throwing them out the window. This girl really hated school and even the other mean girls were scared of her. I always tried to sit near her, and although we never spoke, I think she knew I was her fan. She wore the whitest lipstick, the tightest skirt, and had the biggest fake-leather pocketbook, monogrammed 'D.S.' in huge gold letters. She used this bag as her deadly weapon.

On the day of the school election, Debbie Sue was in a sour mood. She waited outside the student government association office, and when the goody-goody girl candidate emerged victorious, Debbie Sue sprang into action. Screaming like a banshee, she lunged at the new class president, slapped her across the face, stabbed her with her rattail comb, and hit her over the head with her pocketbook. Soon after, Debbie Sue was expelled, but on her last day of school she winked at me and handed me a Lucky Strike cigarette before throwing her books in the trash can. I watched in total admiration as she sulked her way across the schoolyard for the last time. I think Debbie Sue was my first real heroine.

Another girl who fascinated me was Vikki. She didn't fight, but God, this girl was trash personified. I remembered her fondly from the seventh grade, so when the teacher called her name on the first day of the school year, I was thrilled to learn she would be in my class: I could watch her all the more closely. Craning my head, eager to see Vikki's version of the 'back to school' look, I was disappointed to learn that she was absent. Later that day I found out why.

After school I hitchhiked to the state fair to go to the freak shows. The Fat Lady was my favourite, and every day I would pay my quarter and enter the tent to gawk at her seven hundred pounds poured into a polka dot housedress. Precariously balanced on a specially built chair, she'd look up from the peach she invariably ate and scowl in my face, never once giving me a nod of recognition. Refusing to leave until I had gotten my money's worth, I'd stare right back, memorising every detail of the tent, her old pocketbook, the cigarette butts she threw to the ground, and the soggy coffee cups that littered her makeshift table.

Finally moving on to my second-favourite attraction, the Octopus Man, I was momentarily distracted by the sight of my truant classmate, Vikki, as she brazenly flirted with some lecherous midway workers. I was overwhelmingly impressed when I realised she had hooked the very first day of school, and shocked by her outfit – skintight short-shorts that exposed her scabby, mosquito-bitten legs and a see-through blouse over a stiff white pointy-cupped bra. Her hair was a peroxided rat's nest. I began following her, all the while imagining how appalled her parents must be and praying that she would come back to school to horrify the teachers. I later learned that she eloped with the Ferris wheel man, which *really* impressed me, since running off with the carnival is, beyond a doubt, the trashiest thing you can do with your life. I'm really sorry we didn't get to become friends.

Since all my favourite girls quit school or were expelled, I started imagining fantasy ones. Instead of doing my homework, I'd draw monstrous teenage brats, give them fictitious names, and jot down autobiographical horror stories on the backs of the drawings. I'd amuse myself by sorting through my collection and recalling the grisly stories of their lives in much the same way that normal kids linger over batting averages on the backs of baseball cards.

There was Big Leslie, fifteen and pregnant, charging boys quarters to feel her bra straps. Placed in the 'special ed' section for slow learners, she eventually burned down the school.

And Bobbi and Betty, twins – one evil, the other good. I'd draw the same face but apply completely different hair and makeup and imagine the hell of their home life. Bobbi would try to study, but Betty would punch her and force her, at knifepoint, to fill in all the wrong answers on her homework.

As long as I was alone, I had a million friends.

Luckily enough, I also had a career in mind. The nuns at Catholic Sunday school initially interested me in forbidden films, and I thank God for pointing me towards my vocation so early in life. Each week at our religious brainwashing sessions, Sister Mary Something-or-other would begin the lessons with the rosary. 'Hail Mary,' we'd chant over and over until she felt we were sufficiently blanked out and dizzy. We'd then sit in rapt attention as she read us the list of comdemned movies. 'You will definitely go to hell if you see these movies,' she'd state infallibly, and for once I paid attention. It was always such a thrill to see her flinch over some of the titles. '*And God Created Woman* . . . *The Naked Night* . . . *Mom and Dad* . . . *Love Is My Profession* . . . *The Bed.*' She'd spit out each title as if she were being forced to utter the vilest obscenity.

But *Baby Doll* was the worst. If you saw *Baby Doll* it was worse than killing the pope. The nun even used visual aids to convince us to stay away from this film. 'See this picture?' she'd challenge us, holding up a photo of a huge crowd outside the theatre playing *The Ten Commandments.* 'Now, look at this,' she'd sneer as she held up another photo of a theatre playing *Baby Doll*, with not one person waiting in line. 'See?' she'd beam triumphantly, and we all got the message. I immediately sneaked downtown to see *Baby Doll* and made a point, from then on, to see every condemned film I could.

I started getting *Variety* in my early teens and was thrilled to see ads for movies even the nuns hadn't warned us about. Violent ones, like *Poor White Trash, The Mole People, I Spit on Your Grave.* It was a whole new world opening up, and I devoted all my time to the exploration of cinematic garbage. I'd sneak to a hill near our home where I could see the distant drive-in screen and watch all the 'adults only' gore and horror films through binoculars. I'd pore over the local entertainment pages, clipping and collecting the most violent movie ads. I'd pretend I owned a movie theatre and book the most notorious films, redesigning their ad campaigns in a much more sensational manner and imagining the outrage it would cause in the religious community. At last I had a goal in life – I wanted to make the trashiest motion pictures in cinema history.

from *Shock Value*,
Thunder's Mouth Press, 1995

Journal of the Plague Years

KIM NEWMAN

Though not without precedent in 1930s anti-horror film agitations that led to the introduction of the H certificate (and a wartime ban on such films) or the 1950s drive to rid these shores of American horror comics, the 'video nasty' kerfuffle of the early 1980s was a unique collision of an unexpected technological revolution, moral panic, legal action and press hysteria. The period, which some now might regard as a golden age, also offered brief and unprecedented access to material which was hitherto almost legendary in its unavailability.

When I first read about H.G. Lewis's work or *Last House on the Left*, I assumed I'd never see these films. Paging through Walt Lee's three-volume *Reference Guide to the Fantastic Film* in the 1970s, I wondered at titles which might as well be lost for all the opportunity I had of seeing them. Growing up in the West Country in the 1970s, my cinematic diet was confined to what played TV or came to the local cinema. *The Hideous Sun Demon* was never going to be on television, *A Bucket of Blood* would not get a 16 mm rerun in Bridgwater and *Two Thousand Maniacs!* would never get into Britain and past the British Board of Film Censors. I thought I might live to visit the moon but never considered that I might physically own a film, much less an obscurity on the level of *Devil Girl from Mars*.

Less than a decade later, films which had seemed impossible artefacts imaginable only from stills in American magazines were freely available from high street shops in every town and city in the country. Returning to Bridgwater in 1984, I saw a tape of *Blood Orgy of the She Devils* available for rental. It might not be a direct correlation, but at the same time the Palace Cinema – where I had seen films from *Cheyenne Autumn* through *Dracula AD 1972*, *The Wild Angels*, *Let's Scare Jessica to Death*, *Dog Day Afternoon*, *Doomwatch* and *Barry Lyndon* to *Southern Comfort* – had closed down.

A young horror fan of the post-Video Recordings Act era might now feel similarly deprived, though the inaccessibility of, say, the full cut of *Zombie Flesh Eaters* must be all the more frustrating to kids whose older brothers and sisters provide testimony of a time, literally within living memory, when such amazing obscurities could be easily hired without breaking the law. Those titles officially tagged as video nasties were but the smallest sampling of a flood of bizarre material that has been swept away by the Video Recordings Act and never re-released. Among the thousands of horror titles once available and now gone from the shelves of bankrupt video shops were a great many that were too tame or pathetic to be thought worth prosecuting and which are now gone forever, removed from those completists (such as I was) who wanted to see any horror film, no matter how bad, banal or dull: *Night Fright (The E.T. Nastie)*, *Fiend With the Electronic Brain (Blood of Ghastly Horror)*, *Death Bed: The Bed That Eats*, *Boarding House*, *Poor Albert and Little Annie (I Dismember Mama)*, *The Black Room*. I don't want to see any of these (or dozens of others) ever again and I guess no one will ever bother to acquire re-release rights to them, but I regret their disappearance.

Most studies have concentrated exclusively on the censorship issue. The focus has been not on the films themselves but on the tabloid campaigns against them, police actions against video dealers and distributors, studies on the effects of such videos on impressionable minds, ludicrous attempts to 'blame' specific films for specific crimes and the imposition of an apparatus

134   of still-confusing censorship by the Video Recordings Act. This is a remarkable and absorbing story, intensely frustrating for those of us who feel that no matter how many arguments we might win, the cloud of misinformation on the issue is so thick (alleging, for instance, that *Child's Play 3* is some sort of pinnacle of horror) that it can never be dispelled.

Here, I'd like to address the question of what exactly is, or was, a video nasty. Sub-genres thrive and perish in cinema with the swiftness and adaptability of the mutant cockroaches of Jeannot Szwarc's *Bug*. Usually, film critics and fans get the job of labelling and categorising specimens. We note for instance the recent mutation of *film noir* and softcore porn, inspired by the big screen success of *Fatal Attraction* or *Basic Instinct*, in a run of direct-to-video items which includes *Animal Instincts* and *Night Rhythms*. Labelled 'erotic thrillers' by the trade, these top-shelf titles have prompted the sub-generic coinage 'suspense and suspenders'. Considering Dennis Etchison's credit as 'genre consultant' on *Night Life (Grave Misdemeanours)*, actually a contractual synonym for rewrite man, it is tempting to imagine the distinguished author looking at a rough cut of the film and helpfully informing its makers 'yep, that's a teenage zombie comedy'.

The video nasty, however, was named by the trade and the popular press (adapting publishing jargon used in the 1970s to describe the early novels of James Herbert and Guy N. Smith). It was defined not by critics and fans who might be expected to argue the issue of whether *The Bird with the Crystal Plumage* is a post-Hitchcock thriller or a post-Bava horror but by the Director of Public Prosecutions, who drew up the initial nasties list. Issued in the early 1980s, this consisted of titles against which obscenity prosecutions had been attempted. The mutable document was often plagued by trivial errors in titling (consistently referring to '*Frankenstein* (Andy Warhol version)' rather than *Flesh for Frankenstein*), and so no-frills that it failed to make a distinction between Tobe Hooper's nasty *Death Trap* and Sidney Lumet's respectable *Deathtrap*. Various titles came and went from the list according to the vagaries of prosecutions, recuttings and distribution. All told, about seventy titles were tagged, at one time or another, as video nasties.

Though the strict definition of a video nasty requires that it have made an appearance on the DPP list, usage of the term has persisted well beyond the demise of the list (rendered obsolete by the Video Recordings Act of 1984). Recently, it has cropped up repeatedly in the debate surrounding David Alton's attempt to revive the ten-year-old controversy for a new parliamentary generation. Alton's definition of a video nasty seems to be any horror film, or indeed any film involving a depiction of violence. Although Alton's draconian pro-censorship amendment did not become part of the Criminal Justice Act, the fact that the overwhelming majority of MPs supported it suggests that either our politicians have no real experience of our media or that a significant faction in the country will not be content until (as with comics in the 1950s) the horror genre is entirely eradicated. This will, of course, be no great loss to anyone but the few perverts who might enjoy the umpteenth TV reshowing of *Dracula, Prince of Darkness*. Next, I would imagine these witch-hunters will apply themselves to the thriving genre of teenage horror fiction.

A fact no one was much interested in raising in the 1980s was that the DPP list arbitrarily excluded a great many titles which would seem comparable with the films they did single out. The list was dependent on random complaints from the public (which is how someone somewhere got *I Miss You, Hugs and Kisses* on the list), given to a guilt-by-association tendency to include anything with the word 'cannibal' in the title, and compiled by people who could hardly be expected to show any great depth of knowledge about cinema in general or horror in particular. Thus, Hooper's *Death Trap* and *The Funhouse* made the list, but not his more notorious (and effective) *The Texas Chainsaw Massacre*.

Any horror fan, had the DPP consulted him or her, could

136   have pointed out that such unlisted items as *Mark of the Devil,* *Zombi Holocaust* or *The Hills Have Eyes* were far more likely to conform to the public perception of a nasty than such milder, listed efforts as *Frozen Scream, Madhouse* and *Unhinged.* It seems especially odd, given the equivalence of many horror films, that *The Burning, The Gestapo's Last Orgy, Terror Eyes* and *Inferno* made the list but *Friday the 13th, Deported Women of the SS Special Section, Prom Night* and *Suspiria* didn't. A few high profile items, including *The Exorcist* and *Straw Dogs* (still unavailable on video in Britain), never made the list but were quietly refused certificates when video came under the remit of the BBFC. An odd effect of this was that *Straw Dogs* was available at knock-down prices in Woolworth's (of all family image places) in the period leading up to the enforcement of the VRA, presumably because the retailer needed to get shot of the cassettes before the cut-off date, thus disseminating them among a much wider audience than would otherwise have made the purchase.

To state the obvious, one thing all commentators agree on in defining the video nasty is that a film only qualifies for the mark of Cain once it is released on video. However, a sizeable number of the pictures listed by the DPP were made in the 1970s (and even, in the cases of *Blood Feast* and *Night of Bloody Apes,* the 1960s) before video was considered as an ancillary market for films. My initial experience of a great many of these pictures was theatrical: on double bills, in all-nighters, one-day-only reissues, semi-major releases, grindhouse escapees.

My earliest exposure to a film that later became an official nasty was at a Yeovil cinema in 1974, where *Flesh for Frankenstein* (shown flat in the provinces, sadly) was double-billed with *Blood for Dracula* (both films were slightly choppy through censor cuts). At fifteen, I went with my adventurous Dad, who was presumably persuaded to indulge my interest in horrors because of the involvement of Andy Warhol. Critical response to the films had been mixed, ranging from a thumbs-up on *Kaleidoscope* from David Pirie (whose *A Heritage of Horror* had helped develop

my nascent disagreement with accepted horror pundits like
Denis Gifford and William K. Everson) to an extraordinarily
humourless rant from Forry Ackerman in *Famous Monsters*. As
with *The Evil Dead*, the gore in these films struck me then (and
strikes me now) as essentially comic; my father and I both felt the
films to be amusing and effective parodies of the Hammer Films
style, bearing much the same relation to Terence Fisher's films
that Mel Brooks's *Young Frankenstein* does to James Whale.

Though I remember the films as containing more sex and
violence than most pictures of the time, they were also more
good-humoured and, I still believe, fundamentally inoffensive.
From about the same time, I recall being far more disturbed
by the grottier *Open Season* and *House of Mortal Sin* double-bill.
It now seems arbitrary that *Frankenstein* made the nasties grade
but *Dracula* did not. The latter film climaxes with Joe Dallesandro
coercing a fourteen-year-old virgin into having sex with him and
Dracula licking her hymenal blood from the floor, a scene I
found then and still find both amusing and squirmy but which,
described or shown to a moral campaigner, seems like a true
depth of depravity. I can only argue that context is all, and
that Paul Morrissey has set up a pretty, silly, disgusting film
where everybody is rather likeable and nobody seems to get
hurt during their ordeals.

I spent the late 1970s living in Brighton as a student and the
early 1980s in a bed-sit in East Molesey as an unemployed (indeed
unemployable) graduate. Both these situations afforded me far
easier access to a wider variety of cinemas than I had enjoyed
at home: not only were there regular cinemas within walking
distance, but I was an easy commute away from London, with
such venues as the National Film Theatre (where I saw *Last
House on the Left*), the old Scala Cinema in Charlotte Street
(which made available Ed Wood, John Waters, Tarkovsky and
Godzilla) and the Charing Cross classic which premiered double
bills (*The Bogey Man* and *The Beyond*) and programmed bizarre
all-nighters mixing Al Adamson with Don Siegel. At this period,

138 I knew people who had VCR machines – only just penetrating the market – and saw a few films in friends' houses, but still I saw most of my films in cinemas.

It may well be that the key event in establishing exactly what a 'nasty' would come to be was the release on a double-bill of Lucio Fulci's Italian *Zombie Flesh Eaters* (minus eyeball-skewering) and the American *The Toolbox Murders* (with nail-gunning trimmed) in 1980. These films represent radically different, if equally 'nasty', aesthetics. *Zombie*, though a cheap cash-in on *Dawn of the Dead* (it was called *Zombi 2* in Italy where *Dawn* was released as *Zombi*), seems quite lavish: it has widescreen photography of Caribbean locations, superior make-up effects, the odd distinguished player (Richard Johnson), an effective score. It is also badly paced and torn between the conventions of 1930s pulp and 1970s splatter. *The Toolbox Murders*, in which Cameron Mitchell uses various implements on various nubile girls, is cramped, ugly-looking (note how bad lighting makes nailgun victim Kelly Nichols, who appears glamorous in her porno movies, look goofy) and threadbare. Both films are mean-spirited and misogynist, but the sillier fantasy context of *Zombie* is easier to forgive than the TV-movie-with-guts look of *Toolbox*.

Between 1980 and 1983, while video ownership was booming, many of the films later tagged as nasties played theatrically, usually on double-bills. Fulci's follow-ups to *Zombie Flesh Eaters* (*The Beyond*, *City of the Living Dead* and *The House By the Cemetery*) and a rush of American psycho movies that flooded in the wake of the success of *Halloween* and *Friday the 13th* (*Terror Eyes*, *The Bogey Man*, *The Burning*) all played, in various BBFC-approved versions, in regular theatres. By 1983, I was working as a film critic, so I got to see a few of the nasties in the rarefied circumstances of a press show. My first significant piece was a review of *The Evil Dead* for the *Monthly Film Bulletin*, which gave me an early look at the film Mary Whitehouse would tag as 'the number one nasty'. I even remember a publicist telling me how much I wasn't going to enjoy *Unhinged*, a film it now seems incredible folly to have released theatrically. At this time, the issue of violence was being raised, but usually in relation to films that did not make the nasty list: Brian De Palma's *Dressed to Kill* and Barbara Peeters's *Humanoids from the Deep* were signalled out for feminist paint-throwing protest during the years of the Yorkshire Ripper.

With video came the availability of uncensored prints of many of these films – though a significant number of the nasties had been pre-censored by distributors (Vipco accidentally lost a key and violence-free expository scene of *Driller Killer* by botching a reel change) – which was perhaps the first alarm signal to the censorious that material the BBFC were snipping (that *Zombie* eye-gouging, finger-snipping from *The Burning*, a quarter of an hour of killing from Mario Bava's *Blood Bath*) was being made available. I didn't have regular use of a VCR until 1984, but I had started researching and writing my first book, *Nightmare Movies*, a year earlier and took advantage of friends' hospitality and patience to turn up for day- or weekend-long sessions with piles of tapes, mostly hitherto unavailable or unheard-of horror films. Throughout the mid-Eighties, I was writing about horror for various publications and knew enough like-minded types to make mass consumption of direct-to-video genre movies, often in marathon sessions, worthwhile. At that time, I saw most of the nasties (I doubt if I'd have seen *I Miss You, Hugs and Kisses* if it had not been on the list), but also an enormous number of horror (and other) films which never made anybody's list of anything. I can confirm that though the DPP listed most of the most violent pictures, little separated the average video nasty from the average video horror.

Looking back from a decade or more, the overwhelming memory I have of the nasties and their like is not of horror, disgust, titillation or excitement but of boredom. My friend Julian Petley has written eloquently in defence of Italian cannibal movies and Carol Clover mounts an interesting analysis of *I Spit*

140 *on Your Grave*, but neither the sub-genre nor the single notorious example prompts in me any feeling of nostalgia or an interest in repeating the dreary, unpleasant experience of watching the things. In retrospect, the great discovery of the nasty era was Abel Ferrara, whose *Driller Killer* I continue to rate quite highly even as it now seems to have been superseded by his more polished (*King of New York*) or focused (*Bad Lieutenant*) films. Yet, the nasty tag is not inappropriate for his films. It is just that he shows a thoughtful nihilism, tinged with a complex personality and a conflicted attachment to New York, that gives even his misfire films a real texture. One could not say the same for Andy Milligan, auteur of *The Ghastly Ones*, or even the venerable H.G. Lewis.

The Italian films included in the nasties list range from comparatively expensive Argento (*Inferno, Tenebrae*) through mid-range Mario Bava (*Blood Bath*) and Ruggero Deodato (*Cannibal Holocaust, The House at the Edge of the Park*) to Umberto Lenzi (*Cannibal Ferox*), Joe D'Amato (*The Anthrophagous Beast, Absurd*) and Fulci. In the first edition of *Nightmare Movies*, I singled out Argento and Bava and lumped the rest together; by the second, I had seen a lot more films and was able to find subtly different places on the pantheon (or tiers in the inferno) for them. These films are, in some ways, uncomfortable on video: many were shot in widescreen and inevitably issued either in pan&scan versions or the lazy option of pointing the telecine at the centre of the screen so dialogue scenes often feature noses intruding on the edges of empty space.

Combined with mostly indifferent dubbing and subtly unfamiliar narrative strategies, not to mention an almost total lack of humour (Bava and Argento marginally excepted), these squeezed and cropped films – they may have all the gore, but you only got half the image – seem alien artefacts. Most of the horror scenes in Italian films are staged slowly and with ritual care, as if they were already videos set on frame advance, and it is perhaps these meticulous, grand-standing displays of bodily abuse (the girl vomiting her intestines in *City of the Living Dead*, the girl hung up on skewers through her breasts in *Cannibal Ferox*) that so upset the anti-nasty campaigners. Without wishing to defend the attitude of cynical misanthropy endemic in the Italian exploitation industry, as distinct from the icy cynicism of its genre-transcending masters, it is hard to regard such cruelties as disturbing in the way the forty-five-minute rape filmed home-movie style in *I Spit on Your Grave* is disturbing. Ten years on, I find some of the Italian depravities almost endearing: I miss the comparatively lavish and oneiric fantasy epics Fulci turned out before entering his Utter Crap phase (*Cat in the Brain, Voices From Beyond, The Ghosts of Sodom*) and I even have fond memories, with the dullness edited out, of George Eastman's gibbering, liver-eating loon in D'Amato's ridiculous cannibal movies.

The American nasties were, well, nastier. They didn't often have the expensive special effects of their Italian cousins – an exception is *Dead and Buried*, which feels more like a Fulci movie than a Ferrara one – even when, as in *The Boogey Man*, they were trying for that supernatural excess. Most of them are grotty psycho movies shot on the extreme cheap, verging on the community play level. Something like *Don't Go into the Woods* or *Night of the Demon*, which feature dozens of deaths, are aimless and dull movies, disorienting because of their makers' ignorance of such basics as getting an audience involved with the characters and the story. These traipse travelogue-like from death to death, filming the interim police investigations or teenage gropings with all the skill and interest displayed in the non-sex scenes in porno movies. Unlike the Italian films, there aren't even impressive (much less convincing) effects: offal and gloop being manhandled by a maniac, to the accompaniment of inept actors screaming and droning synth scores, was rarely enough to relieve the overwhelming tedium of *Mardi Gras Massacre, Delirium* or *Forest of Fear*.

The degraded video image, as much a result of poor duping as

142 amateur cinematography, makes many of these films disturbing as chronicles of poverty. Occasionally a has-been like Aldo Ray or Cameron Mitchell might pop up among casts populated by friends and relations, but these mostly feature no-name nobodies wandering through regional nowheres. Of course, there were exceptions: *The Slayer* is just as formulaic, but happens to be well made; *The Witch Who Came from the Sea* is a hippy-trippy art movie which I found interesting but others have yawned through. The big controversies around *Snuff* and *I Spit on Your Grave*, especially with regard to the film-makers' intentions, are defused by actual viewings of the pathetic films, which render debate redundant since the film-makers are plainly incapable of carrying out any intentions they might have. *Grave*, which has raised heated debate pro and con, probably falls into the category of simple failure: intended as a balanced, feminist rape-revenge film, it is remembered for its forty-five minutes of humiliation rather than (the testicle-snipping bath scene aside) the ineptly staged revenge scenes. This may well be because it is easier to fake a gang rape than a convincing death-by-power boat propeller.

Somewhere along the way, a lot of films got lumped together and the video nasties remain discussed as if they were a homogeneous group. Quite apart from the fact that the old saw about horror films (and not all the nasties are even horror films) being alike is simply a fallacy (anyone with any depth of knowledge can distinguish between a Lenzi cannibal movie and a Deodato one, let alone between an Italian SS camp exploitationer and an American stalk and slash film), these films are separate entities in my memory and estimation because of the circumstances in which I saw them. Some nasties were London Film Festival choices (*Death Trap, Possession, The Evil Dead*) complete with programme, notes and director question and answer sessions; some were throwaway theatrical releases in long-gone cinemas (an abiding memory of my period of unemployment is cheap afternoon matinees doubling *My Bloody*

Valentine and *The Funhouse*); some were chance video rentals or borrowings, mostly watched in clumps with much other material while trying to catch up with the huge backlog of horror films that burst free during the video boom; and some were rep screenings at the sadly missed Scala cinema. I can attest that, cuts apart, *Zombie Flesh Eaters* is an entirely different experience when seen in a first-run multiplex in Leeds, in the Scala on an all-nighter, as an nth generation dupe or in a letterboxed widescreen sell-through video.

The individual films have become myths, memories, accepted classics, reviled turkeys, cult favourites, forgotten drek, academic footnotes, talking points, test cases. All of us, from the fan or critic who has systematically viewed the entire DPP list to the casual viewer who happens to have enjoyed *The Evil Dead* or disliked *Possession*, have a different experience of what a video nasty was. My own definition has long since diverged from the legalistic one of the DPP. The ecology of the business of horror has changed: the VRA 'cleaned up' rental video, which is now as withering as it was flourishing in 1983, and theatrical distribution is practically extinct, but cable and satellite, easy access to multi-standard VCRs, the proliferation of sell-through cassettes (you can buy *The Killer Nun* or *Tower of Evil*, should you wish) and more liberal TV programming policies (*Bad Taste* was screened on BBC2, *Howling VI* on Channel 4) mean that there is still an enormous amount of varied horror material available for the fan, the critic and the compulsive. To feel nostalgic for easy availability of *Headless Eyes* (a no-budget 1971 gore movie never tagged as a nasty but nevertheless swept away by the VRA) rather than *Mesa of Lost Woman* (a no-budget 1952 s-f horror now available to buy, which has even played network TV) is as useless as it is to wish for Margaret Thatcher rather than John Major. The times, and the horrors, have changed.

Muscle Wars

NIGEL ANDREWS

Something funny has happened to screen violence on the way to the end of the millennium. Thanks to a squirl or garble on the cosmic word-processor the words 'myth' and 'mirth' have became interchangeable. Great prototypes of movie heroism or antiheroism that used to command our respect, however wry, now command – indeed insist on – a gleeful, lyrical, blood-fed hilarity. The Strong Man, the Hero, the Gangster, the Outlaw: all go into the cultist-comical reprocessing machinery. As Hawks and Bogart shade into Tarantino and Travolta, Bonnie and Clyde into Mickey and Mallory (of *Natural Born Killers*), modern violence demands ever more intemperance and more absurdist, frame-breaking adventurism.

As we scan the land for reasons and origins, theories of possible suspects are legion. But one major formative identity parade surely includes the Austrian Oak and the Italian Stallion, possibly joined by the Muscles from Brussels and other supporting stars in the bicep firmament. Or reading from left to right, Arnold Schwarzenegger, Sylvester Stallone and Jean-Claude Van Damme.

Sometime in the late 1970s movies first began to be overrun by these mutant flora and fauna in human (more or less) shape and screen mayhem entered the oddest, most muscle-mad age in its history. After twenty years the two prime specimens, Sly and Arnie, are still being fed and watered by monster salaries

(Stallone $20m, Schwarzenegger close behind) and put out each summer in those vast exercise-grounds called action movies.

Over this time almost every part of the world, including the newly Arnoldised Republic of China (top box office attraction of 1995, *True Lies*), has succumbed to a vision of heroism in which no shirt button is safe from swelling chest measurements and no troublemaking country can resist one-man invasion by the super-warrior of the moment.

Stallone did democracy proud against Vietnam in *Rambo* and the Afghanistan-occupying Russians in *Rambo III*. Schwarzenegger has fought Russians (*Red Heat*), Colombians (*Commando*), Muslims (*True Lies*) and Martians (*Total Recall*), as well as whole armies of that worst scoundrel of all, the unpatriotic or psychotic American (*Raw Deal, The Running Man, Terminator 2*, the upcoming *Eraser*).

It is an old movie fantasy that one man can pulverise dozens or hundreds. Errol Flynn did it in Burma. Gary Cooper did it in the foreign legion. Charles Bronson did it with gun, moustache and inscrutable scowl all over urban America. But it has been a relatively new fantasy that sheer brawn, with the minutest admixture of brain, is an appetising, ticket-selling way to show it happening: and even, increasingly, an amiably comical one. For what began as a side order of po-mo risibility in these films and their descendants is now threatening to become the main course.

With Stallone and Schwarzenegger the action genre first ballooned into Brobdingnagianism. And far from trying to hide itself, the caricatural aspect of these movies has gone on to play its role in one of the great sensibility revolutions of late-century cinema. Violence As Variety Show. From Arnold and Sylvester it is but a short if bloody step to Quentin (Tarantino), Oliver (Stone), Robert (Rodriguez) and John (Woo).

Addressing the provenance of these hulks, a destiny theory of cinema would say that America was demoralised after Vietnam and needed a super-hero figure to reclaim national pride. A

146   series of symbolic warriors was born and reared, semi-naked intellectually as well as physically, from the broken teeth of past defeats.

A chaos theory of cinema, by contrast, would argue that it all happened accidentally and with a prophetic touch of comic improbability. Take one plug-ugly Italian-American actor frustrated by sneering and scowling in supporting roles (*Bananas, Death Race 2000*). Give him delusions of grandeur and a typewriter. And as surely as lower simians will reproduce Shakespeare this higher simian will bang out *Rocky*, the founding opus of modern machismo cinema.

By a follow-up accident, let an Austrian bodybuilder come to America and prove so blissfully improbable a movie presence that the god of perversity signs him up for the largest fees in history.

Cinema being the organ of dream-anarchy loved and formed by Vigo, Buñuel and Cocteau, any properly seditious movie buff will prefer the reasonless ontogeny to the earnest socio-political genesis. Yes, it is impossible to separate Arnie and Sly from Ron (Reagan) and George (Bush), or the cinema of late-century bicep-rattling from the politics of self-assertion in a West recovering from its first major military debacles in modern times. That West needed a Goliath, or several, to stage its wish-fulfilment re-matches with the Davids of South-East Asia or the Near and Middle Easts.

Yet the movies and their appeal have outlived such precise historical trigger points. Today they seem more compelling and resonant as a heralding of changing tastes and demands in filmgoing itself. The cinema of machismo has been a major precursor – *the* precursor – of the modern trend towards treating violence with a designedly 'desensitised' wit and irony, less as a real impact of pain on person than as a vivid, unbridled, at times outright joky colour in the kinetic palette of cinema as form.

Tarantino and Co. may be the new artists in residence, but long before them the muscle genre was coaxing outraged comments about the 'irresponsible' – that is, the surreal, humorous or imaginatively preposterous – use of screen mayhem. On one side of the battlefield frowning moralists observed the *Rambos* and *Commandos* and condemned the brute carnage whereby one ritualistically invincible humanoid coolly destroyed a series of ritualistically sacrificial homunculi. On the other side, fans of the subgenre exulted in this freely licensed dreamworld in which might was right or, more exactly and mystically, right was might.

For wasn't the volume-filling, muscle-expanding essence that had been poured into these heroes, with every filmgoer refusing to say 'When', our own belief in their righteousness: our crazed desire for an invincible, short-cutting justice more extreme and more exact than any that terrestrial action movies had given us before?

At the same time we loved the absurdist nativities which had brought these men into being. Before *Pulp Fiction* there was pump fiction – or fact. These hero-stars were built by themselves, for themselves, from themselves. They were self-born Frankenstein's monsters whose hissing natal laboratories, though called 'gyms', contained much the same high-wrought mixture of steamy vapour, mad pseudoscience and sudden grunts of triumph.

This athletic genesis allowed them to establish another, paradoxical and thereby potentially absurdist, mystique. The more naked they were – and stripping off has been a vital ceremony in hulk movies – the less vulnerable they seemed. For their bodies were designer products, sexless, formidable, pre-accessorised. And the next step after proving that you have preternatural pectorals and adamantine abdominals is to go onward and upward in the synthesising process. To don the battle-dress, the off-the-shoulder rocket launchers, the round-the-waist grenade belts, the down-the-calf hunting knives, the ten-pound army boots.

Thus was born the hero as one-man bio-mechanical army. And

148   the identification of man with machine became more explicit
with the years, as if some millennial Heath Robinson was
heading up Hollywood's futurism division. Taking its cue from
the darkside cyber-scenario of Schwarzenegger's *The Terminator*,
the *Robocop* series turned its injured cop hero into a full-grown
metal automaton. And the hero-as-android concept spread to
movies like *Universal Soldier* (Lundgren and Van Damme as
robot troubleshooters created by the US military) and *Total
Recall* (Arnie duelling with his own high-science doppelganger).
Even in the comical *Twins* the Schwarzenegger hulk is a kind
of noble cyber-savage, produced by a rogue bout of South Seas
genetic engineering.

From their inception the Stallone/Schwarzenegger films
prepared us for fantastical take-off, for cosmic comedy, from the
artfully deceptive starting point of an in-your-face Body Realism.
In the process they became part of a much larger coeval fantasy
genre that has dominated entertainment cinema for much the
same twentysomething years. The comic-book movie.

The muscle heroes were born from the same impulse that
has brought kinetic draughtsmanship to cinema in *Superman*,
Flash Gordon, the *Batman* series et al. If such films are about
violence they are about an aesthetic, calligraphic violence as
well as a physical, fisticuffing kind. Emulating cartoon tropes
and traditions, the comic book genre set out to dash plausibility
– visual, narrative, psychological – on the rocks of folkloric
wish-fulfilment.

Stallone and Schwarzenegger may seem more monolithic and
less flighty than Batman and his *bande dessiné* brothers. But there
is a caricatural dementia about both parties. Exaggerated size,
strength and steadfastness are no less surreal than hyberbolised
speed, agility and quick-change expertise. (And if we needed
one form of surrealism to call out to another we had the caped
crusader's batsuit, lovingly moulded into a he-man musculature
and surely a salutation to Cinema Stallonegger and its rococo
body worship.)

The dramaturgy in this broad-church action cinema is as distinctive as the image-making or character-drawing. Both the muscle films and their larger brotherhood of comic book movies use dialogue like speech balloons: with a fondness for laconic one-liners, catchy exhortations ('Hasta la vista!', 'Cowabunga!', 'Holy Batmobile!'), semi-crazed combat jargon and, in emergency, hilariously precipitate plot-babble. (For racy speech-balloon story exposition, nothing beats Michael Biehn's gabbled aria during a car chase in *The Terminator*, in which he explains the Schwarzenegger cyborg and his entire scientific make-up. 'All right, listen. The Terminator's an infiltration unit, part man, part machine. Underneath it's a hyper-alloy combat chassis, microprocessor-controlled, fully armoured, very tough, but outside it's living human tissue . . .')

As for violence, the muscle epics like the comic book genre have courted a high-style cartoony excess. Fantastical weapon arsenals have been favoured ever since *Conan the Barbarian* (surreal-ancient) and *The Terminator* (surreal-futurist). Vast rococo explosions, as improbable and casually motivated as in a comic strip, are created to climax individual scenes or entire movies. And shamelessly implausible numbers of villains are put away, as giggles vie with gasps among an audience aware that licence is being taken not just with the numerology of rough justice but with the whole concept of violence as a safety valve for audience aggression.

For perhaps, these movies suggest, catharsis *can* come through translating pain into paroxysmal serio-comic pleasures, into a world of fantasy derring-do where crunching Judgement Days come and go leaving scarcely a graze on the filmgoer's actual, deeper nervous system. (How many viewers have actually looked to these films for violent inspiration? In twenty years it is hard to recall a single well-publicised incident of copycat violence related to a Stallone or Schwarzenegger movie.)

This dallying with playful extremes has taken action cinema towards a new pop avant-garde and, on the way, crystallised a

150   truth about movies that we sensed but never quite, until this
last quarter century, or even this last decade, saw laid out as
a lucid, lucent proposition.

It's a medium whose perpetual-motion character and impulses
encourage diametric opposites to meet. The more violent an
action thriller, the closer it comes to the hyperkinetic brink-
manship of farce. (Directors like Tarantino and Rodriguez are
still upping the ante on this proposition.) The more farcical a
comedy, the closer it approaches to free-form violence. (Movies
like *The Mask* and *The Naked Gun* are today's live-action answer
to Tom and Jerry, with punchball humans replacing punchball
cartoon animals.)

In the same way that opposite styles in modern action
cinema collide or collude, multiple responses to the same
movie can be experienced by today's increasingly nimble,
postmodernism-reared film audiences. The whole concept
of 'camp' in cinema has evolved and broadened as if to
accommodate and recognise this new age. Camp invites us to see
and savour the contradictions between a film's aspirations and
its reality: between its solemn-or-hieratic style and softbrained
content, or between signalled meaning and the rich teeming
of inadvertent significances.

Camp allows a filmgoer to stand outside a film and see
it wryly from multiple angles. More and more this percep-
tual sophistication offers itself up as modern cinema's own
deconstruction programme. In the process it will make life
even more problematic for today's would-be censors, who will
find themselves aiming at a perpetual moving target.

The new action movies and thrillers not only rejoice in a
plurality of perspective, they are *about* that plurality of perspective. They offer audiences adventure thrills while inviting them
simultaneously to laugh at exaggerated characters, outlandish
decor and pulpy dialogue.

The muscle epic's place in this landscape has been especially
teasing and piquant. It is caricatural and postmodern while

appearing for much of the time to be solemnly, plebeianly serious. Stallone's famous 'Do we get to win this time?' in *Rambo*, spoken to the officer (Richard Crenna) trying to recruit him for an MIA-rescuing mission in Vietnam, is at once a forlorn banality and a hilarious irony, satirising every flag-waving action film that ever treated history as a simple-outcome geopolitical board game.

Likewise, Schwarzenegger plays a weatherbeaten army veteran in *Predator* who when asked if he 'remembers Vietnam' replies sombrely, 'Trying to forgeddit.' In a film that more than most resembles a comic book in its blend of Z-movie plotting and archly iconic camerawork, the haunted thinks-bubble portentousness of that utterance has 'camp' written all through it. (It is taken further to the edge of absurdism, of course, by being delivered in an accent closer to Vienna than Vietnam.)

The muscle movies delight in their own hall-of-mirrors narcissism. The semi-concealed agenda of self-derision co-exists with an unconcealed, irresistibly campy agenda of self-worship. The films are about macho chest-thumping on a grand scale, presented in a style of sculptural attitudinising glazed with kitsch.

It is possible, of course, for audiences to watch these films with no ironic perspective at all. And indeed nine-figure box-office revenues cannot all come from a coterie of sophisticates giggling into their copies of *Modern Review*. But even the bloodcurdling exhortations of filmgoers who side with Action Arnie or Bullet-spraying Sly during slaughter sequences – and anyone who has been in an American cinema has heard and winced at them – bespeak an awareness that this is excess as style. And that the wake-up call to reality will come as soon as the filmgoer is back out on the street.

There may soon be a larger wake-up call than this: one that rouses us altogether from the oneiric delights of these *übermensch* operas, as the millennium approaches. There are signs today that muscle fatigue is setting in in movies and that with the comparative failure of recent Stallone/Schwarzenegger films –

152 and of Van Damme, Seagal and Co. to topple the terrible twins at the box office – audiences are looking for new power-brokers in action cinema: for heroes who do not depend on special shirt fittings or guttural one-liners, let alone a familiarity with every known submachine-gun. Conquering heroes may soon have to come in another guise altogether.

Such as the anorak. In the mid-Nineties we are seeing the suspicious rise of the nerdic protagonist, from Tom *Forrest Gump* Hanks (natural wisdom) to Jim *The Mask* Carrey (natural quick-change adaptability) to Sandra *The Net* Bullock (natural computer wizardry).

Maybe film-makers are at last twigging to something the entire world twigged to the day before yesterday, but didn't want to spoil the party by telling Hollywood. Namely: that in the age of microchip intelligence, lateral thinking and off-kilter psychological agility are worth more than a hundred kilos of meat and muscle.

In the computer era, if you want to destroy your enemies you don't need a Hercules build and rocket-launcher. You need a laptop, a mouse and a pot of strong coffee. That way you can infiltrate agencies and governments, change records, communicate killer diseases (computer diseases) and generally take over the world.

'Do we get to win this time?' Maybe only if we offer Arnold and Sylvester honourable retirement and hand the Armageddon franchise to the ten-stone weaklings who used to have sand kicked in their faces. The age of the microsoftie has arrived.

Do we get to laugh this time? Only if we ensure that the great mischief-making trend of postmodern action cinema spreads not just to the antiheroic line – the Tarantino/Stone/Rodriguez outlaws – but to the Pentium do-gooders poring over their keyboards. Global justice is too serious a subject not to be able to laugh at it. Sly and Arnie taught us that, in the great religious mission of conquering everything in sight, it is a short but healthy step from the hieratic to the hilarious.

Explosions

DAVID THOMSON

We are not quite ourselves in the dark, waiting for the big bang. For consider: there is no way we would have wanted to be in the Federal Building in Oklahoma City on April 19, 1995 when that explosion occurred. Or even near enough to watch its amazing disruption. We understand how in split seconds human beings could be fragmented and obliterated in that blast. While the photographs of the wreckage may have a surreal beauty – shall we say a Dadaist shock? – with the structure's entrails hanging out and interrupted rooms naked for inspection, still we would sooner not be in the search party that has to discover pieces of meat and puzzle over their reassembly – so that real dads and mums can be persuaded that their three-year-old was once there but is no longer anywhere. It all happened so quickly, people say, struggling to find a reason for going on. But the searchers, many of them, after the seventh or eighth day of meticulousness in that stench, suffer breakdowns. They are never the same again, not quite their old Oklahoman selves.

We can imagine the force and the noise driving eyeballs out through the backs of skulls. We are all, in the age of TNT and *Terminators*, explosives experts. But then consider the situation twenty-five or so minutes into *Speed*. We have lived through the elevator alarm in the highrise (interesting word!). We are buddies of a sort with Keanu Reeves and Jeff Daniels – we are such dopes for comradeship. We have seen the demented Dennis

Hopper go out of the door in his pullover of explosives, and we have heard and seen the blast a moment later. We know no one could survive that, don't we. We are experienced enough to gauge the force.

Except that we are not idiots either, and we know that a big picture called *Speed* with Dennis Hopper in a starring part isn't *over* after half an hour. And we don't *want* it over: we want the bang for our buck, the bigger one yet to come. So that when we shift down to a sunny, tranquil morning in Santa Monica, and when we see Keanu Reeves out for his breakfast, chatting to a bus driver who has stopped for a coffee, we *know* something is going to happen. Something good for the show. And when the camera tracks and pans just a little to get a better view of that bus driving away, we know that bus is going to go. We're ready to push its button ourselves. And we get a hell of a kick – in the Dadaist sense – when the bus shivers and does its fireball thing and then still drifts down the street. There must be enough of a foot left hitting the metal. Wow! and Pow! and comic-book Crash! *Speed* is off again!

An explosion is the virtually instantaneous transformation or disintegration of matter accomplished with noise and, invariably, some eruption of flame, smoke and blast. It is notable that every dictionary insists on sound (for the word 'explode' has its origin and its first, now obsolete, meaning in the Latin 'explodere', which means to drive off the stage by clapping – applause comes from the same root). That theatrical basis is already suggestive, yet it leaves one wondering whether an explosion is possible in a silent film? At the end of *The Great Train Robbery*, when the cowboy fires his pistol at the camera, is that an explosion or just a kind of blooming?

Of course, not every gunshot is exactly a transformation or disintegration of matter – the definition just proposed. There are plenty of vigorous pops in life, from champagne corks to Oliver Hardy-like wrath, that deserve the word 'explosion'. But when we think of explosions in movies, we imagine the frame transformed. The fireball from that bus in *Speed* consumes not just the bus and the street; it occupies the frame. I make this point to remind us that any on-camera explosion resembles the innate capacity of film as a medium to transform its nature if not instantaneously then in a twenty-fourth of a second. Waiting for the big bang, we know deeper down than story operates that the medium can, as it were, blow us up or blow our calm away by cutting from some scene of ordinary bliss to . . . any kind of menacing horror. We are stuck there in the dark (and, ideally, trapped by surrounding audience), available to be cut to the quick – whether by Buñuel's razor, Norman Bates's knife . . . or the immediacy with which a match blown out becomes the blazing wide screen of desert in *Lawrence of Arabia*.

That cut is not, strictly, an explosion: indeed, the match goes out. But, imaginatively, the context of the film expands from a match-head to an infinity. Above all, we are reminded that the film and those in charge of it can do anything to us, blow us up or blow our minds, quicker than we can close our eyes. For in any cut, the shock of the new is delivered, and felt, before defensiveness can function. There is always something explosive, or invasive, something of an assault, in any unexpected cut – the looming appearance of Kane's lips saying 'Rosebud', the intrusion of Nevers in *Hiroshima Mon Amour*, or even the brief slippage of movie in the assembled stills of Chris Marker's *La Jetée*. The inherent violence and the concomitant healing of movie is demonstrated in the way every cut is also a suture, and every explosion a catalyst.

That ambivalence helps define the unique and uneasy status of the voyeur in the dark: he can behold the delightful – whether a sunny shore, the exhilaration of an automobile drive, or some woman undressing – without ever enjoying those actualities; he can watch the slaughter of the masses, as well as the destruction of material things, without feeling pain or loss. And because we submit ourselves to the constant threat of explosion – the unexpected, an outrage of editing – there is a mysterious and not entirely wholesome response in us, a feeling of the right to blow up, or assist in, the explosion of what we see. If that seems fanciful, or masochistic even, consider *Speed* again.

When Keanu Reeves chases after the shattered, burning bus, he can only get so close. As he stops, he hears a public telephone ringing (a kind of explosion in sound). He goes to answer it – he *has* to if the narrative of the rest of the film is going to operate. For there is Hopper on the phone to advise him that this bus was just a way of getting his and the city's attention.

There is another bus, on the highway: once it reaches 50 m.p.h., its bomb is primed; then once it falls below 50, the bomb will go off.

How could Hopper know that Reeves would be in the spot to hear that phone? Why does Reeves answer it at such a vexed moment unless, somehow, he knows it is for him? Hopper is presented in the movie as a madman, a warped seeker after vengeance. But let us not forget that he is also a brilliant high-concept screenwriter, for his plan and the movie's are effectively the same. He knew which public phone to call; he put Reeves there – this dark god is in the details!

We have fallen into camaraderie with Reeves and Daniels, but we are in league with Hopper, too. We love the trick of this bomb of his, its cute hook, and we will demand eventually that it go off. For it amounts to a kind of tumescence.

Explosions are beautiful and satisfying – if you're in the right location. When the bus ignites in Santa Monica, it's as if the Utrillo-like grid of an everyday street scene has suddenly had a Rothko or a Jackson Pollock dropped on it – or rather, as if those great abstract orgasmic expressions had burst through hitherto matter-of-fact canvases and then spread across them, like egg yolk soaking into bread. The subconscious feels food and sex – so it's happy.

There is one movie famous for the self-conscious formal splendour of its explosions – Michelangelo Antonioni's *Zabriskie Point*. Made in 1969, by a director who was stunned by the mystery and beauty of America, but who spoke very little English, *Zabriskie Point* is often mocked for its simplistic confrontation of idealism and materialism in America. One cannot put the movie's plot or theme into words without risking banality – thus, two students, Daria and Mark, fall in love and discover the hatefulness of the American system.

Mark is shot to death by L.A. cops. Daria has gone away to the desert home of her boss. This is a piece of palatial modernism embedded in a clifftop with a view of the desert near Phoenix, Arizona. The boss is a high-powered developer who wants to build in the desert and get Daria into bed. She is anguished because of the death of Mark. She observes the mindless chatter of corporate wives by the pool. She faces the glass and steel of the house and the pawing hands of her boss. It is all too much. She flees and drives her old car into the desert.

From that vantage, she both witnesses and seemingly invokes repeated explosions that destroy the house and its contents. There is no suggestion that she, or anyone else, has planted a bomb in the spirit of insurrection. Rather, it is her dream, or her desire, that that place and all it represents be blown to smithereens. Intriguingly, the first explosion – rippling across the CinemaScope frame – is silent, forcing us to *see* the sudden suffusion of fiery colour. There are then, by my count, eleven more versions of the explosion, all with sound. Two are exact repeats of the first shot. The next nine are angled close-ups of particular aspects of the house. Almost certainly, all the shots were taken at the same time.

These exterior shots are followed by interior, slow-motion studies of details of destruction (I think the objects have been filmed underwater to slow or drug their fragmentation). We see a rack of clothes, a TV set, a refrigerator and its contents, and a bookcase all bursting apart. We see such things as an uncooked chicken drifting across the frame, like a lunar module. We do not see bodies or limbs, even though the house was full of people.

One does not have to admire *Zabriskie Point* to feel a quite different kind of cinematic force in this sequence. For those who do like the film, it is the final proof that visually, spatially, cinematically, Antonioni has a comprehension of Americana that goes beyond the language, the politics of 1969, or 'common sense'. If *Zabriskie Point* were music, this coda would clarify everything. And at a sensual, plastic level, the reiterated explosions are liberating, cleansing and jubilant. For they understand the proximity of our exultation at beauty for its own sake and our glee at witnessing destruction.

That playfulness may be disconcerting as a principle. After all, it is not so far from the hideous alienation of pilots above the Vietnam jungle 'high' on the Rousseau flowers of napalm beneath them. But the notion also illustrates the value of explosions in comedy, and in animation. Is there any film form more violent than, say, Tom and Jerry cartoons, in which the cat is exploded, electrocuted, flattened, perforated and reduced to his own dust before, on a cut or a fade, he can be reconstituted so that the humour of destruction can begin again? That is a species of torture, as well as murder, yet it is deemed fit for children. Equally, there is something deeply rewarding in, say, Laurel and Hardy's *The Music Box* where a piano and a house, to say nothing of sanity and dignity, are taken apart before our eyes.

In the cool light of day and reason, we may disapprove of those urges, but in the dark there has always been an audience for spectacular car crashes, hubris succumbing to fire in *The Towering Inferno*, and the wholesale destruction of cities and scenery by Schwarzenegger, Bruce Willis and King Kong. In life, we agonise over a scratch on our car or a leak in the roof. Those nagging bourgeois longings for wholeness and tidiness inspire a demon of resentment that is itching to break out in riots of mayhem, the lovely innocent plenty of ruin.

I feel guilty writing that – as if ruin could be lovely or innocent in an age that has seen Dresden, Hiroshima, and, more recently,

Guildford and Oklahoma City. But then I recollect a marvel observed at the editing table – the serenity with which a cloud of flame may retract and the tumbling spill of wreckage flutter back, every bit falling in place, so that the terrible outburst returns to where it belongs, making the skin of a building as flawless again as hopes for calm. For that is what happens if you run the piece of film backwards. There is an astonishing, innovative beauty in seeing motion and time run backwards – and it is something that was only discovered with film. Of course, the majority of movies run forwards and employ explosions as displays of murder, terror, violence and menace. But in its deepest nature – and in the regular experience of editors – that reverse healing power is always present. And it is a secret sub-text of play.

In the practice of film-making, explosions have become a sport and a craft – nearly a cult. Sets are often crowded and merry when the intricate outbursts are being arranged. There is a special respect granted to those who measure and plant the charges and to the men who wired up the soldiers of Mapache in *The Wild Bunch* so that their tunics and their rascally beings would burst open with bullet wounds. Film-makers live with the daily grind of making the physical world act on cue: there may be a genius involved, but there are builders, plasterers and the clerics of continuity, too. And so crews love those moments when care relaxes and they can blast order to hell.

Never forget that extended first shot from *Touch of Evil* (as well as the night of re-takes before they got it right) is a prelude to explosion, the history of the brief life of a bomb. And though, later on in the movie, we hear that a shoe was found, with a foot in it, still that blast is witty, sardonic and lip-smacking because of Welles's virtuoso coverage. We want that bomb to go, too, and it is the final jab of irony that the blast comes just as Janet Leigh and Charlton Heston achieve their first kiss in America. Welles knew the dynamite in lips!

One of David Selznick's few unquestioned strokes of genius

160   was to begin the shooting of *Gone with the Wind* with the burning of Atlanta. More than a month before principal photography, he cleared his own back-lot (so that Tara etc. could be built there) by putting 1860s facades on all the old sets and then making a gorgeous bonfire of them. That Saturday night, 10 December, 1938, the Culver City fire service was besieged with alarms as the fire turned the night sky Technicolor. There was a party on the lot, and many visitors – one of them an English woman, Vivien Leigh, born as Scarlett on a night of flames.

I could go on, but that runs the risk of losing sight of movie explosions in which we have no doubt about danger, pain and violation. There is a difference between a bang that is dreaded, and one that comes out of the blue. In *The Small Back Room*, set in wartime England, David Farrar plays a demolition man. It is his task to pick apart wicked new German devices: he is miked, so that he can describe what he is doing in case the thing goes off. In the film's climax, he has to deal with a sort of thermos flask of doom stuck in the shifting pebbles of Chesil Bank. It could take away his face, but we share the risk as we watch. It's like doing surgery on yourself.

But then, in Fritz Lang's *The Ministry of Fear*, in a gloomy warren of intrigue and paranoia, Ray Milland and a young woman are charged with taking a suitcase to a particular flat in an apartment building. Milland believes its weight comes from books he is delivering. They are let into the empty flat, but there is no one there. As they look around, they realise that the flat is vacant. The cabinets and shelves are empty. Only the suitcase is full, or loaded. Milland opens it, and there is a rustling sound as if some creature is inside. He throws himself and the woman into the far corner of the room and there is a blast in which the pieces of furniture bounce around like balls.

They survive the bomb, but there is a way in which if bombs go off in movies they have to claim someone. As Robert Aldrich's *Kiss Me Deadly* works towards its climax, hardly anyone in the story deserves life. The hero, Mike Hammer, is as loathsome as the assorted villains. The 'bomb' in this film is a metal case, wrapped in leather, a box that contains a very bright light, a hissing noise that rises to a roar, and the promise of eternal fire and damnation. Viewers have argued as to whether it is a version of the Bomb – that very big one – or just a superb metaphor. But it is a force that threatens all existence. Despite warnings, the depraved villainess opens it and so, in modern prints, the fire consumes the Malibu beach house and, seemingly, all the world. Yet once I saw a version where a Bikini-like mushroom hung over the house while Hammer and his girl staggered into the ocean. I'm still not sure which ending I prefer.

But that close reminds me of one other movie explosion – too good a metaphor or warning to omit. We are watching a movie when the image jams in the projector. A second or so later, the picture begins to scorch, then the stain of meltdown ebbs across the frame. There are screams and smoke from behind us. The movie is on fire in the projection booth, and it is the old days when film stock was deadly nitrate. The fire has taken out the exits, and we are caught between the real and the mere image of explosion.

Gunfire

JASON JACOBS

The cinematic transition from the bloodless death to the crimson ballets of the slo-mo bullet-fest is generally dated, however casually, to the release of *The Wild Bunch* in 1969. Its opening and closing gun battles paid attention to the detail of bullet impacts in a sustained and stylistic manner rarely seen before. Death was no longer simply about Right shooting Wrong, Good triumphing over Bad: in *The Wild Bunch* it is spectacular, empty and nihilistic. Everyone loses. The pleasure is in witnessing the process of losing.

Gunfire battles *were* sometimes spectacular and excessive before this point; indeed, to a certain extent cinema and gunfire had *always* been intertwined. Guns and movies have been twin obsessions of American culture in the twentieth century, and both have mythic status. The movies represented glamour and excess, guns represented the Law and its democratic aspirations: as the Wild West proverb has it, 'God created men, but Samuel Colt made them equal.' Since the outlaw Barnes fired his Colt Peacemaker at the audience in *The Great Train Robbery* (1903), gunfire in films has continued apace, through the final shoot-outs of Howard Hawks's *Scarface* (1932), the gunfights of the Western, the casual gun-toting of *film noir*, right up to Peckinpah, De Palma, Tarantino and Woo.

Perhaps cinema and guns were made for each other. In both, the apparatus is mechanical, chemical, rhythmic. They share some terminology (the shot, the magazine), a point-and-shoot rationale, and a historical moment: in the late nineteenth century, the development of the fully automatic Maxim gun (mounted on a tripod) coincided with the first showing of the Lumières' films. If Hollywood cinema is fundamentally built around the drive of causal relations (this happened because that did) the gun also embodied a cause-effect apparatus (he bleeds because I shot him). It is precisely the rationality of this causal momentum which seems to disintegrate at the end of *The Wild Bunch* and in other modern gunfire sequences, such as those of *Bonnie and Clyde*, *The Godfather*, *The Getaway*, *Dillinger*, *Magnum Force*, *Taxi Driver*, *Assault on Precinct 13*, *The Long Riders*, *Blade Runner*, *Scarface*, *The Terminator*, *The Year of the Dragon*, *Full Metal Jacket*, *Lethal Weapon*, *Die Hard*, *State of Grace*, *Nikita*, and *Reservoir Dogs*. In various ways in each of these films (if sometimes very different ways) the shooting is no longer a means to an end but an end in itself.

Obviously there needs to be some qualification here. Modern gunfire should not be equated with everything Peckinpah did after *The Wild Bunch*, nor should one pretend that there have not been films since in which the gunfire remains subordinate to character and plot development. I'm talking about an influential stylistic *tendency* which emerged during the Sixties, which may indeed have been a culmination of earlier styles and forms (such as those of Spaghetti Westerns or the new forms of realism that European art cinema provided). But it is also clear that *The Wild Bunch* marks a departure from what came before, a change in the conventions of movie gunfire (just as the conventions of the car chase and the sex scene changed). The Sixties ushered in a greater realism in the depictions of death and injury. In part, a more liberal climate was a factor. But gunfire sequences also reflected and incorporated anxieties produced by the assassination of President Kennedy and the Vietnam War, events which provided a newly graphic and realist context.

164   The assassination of JFK brought a new immediacy to issues of bullet injury. The ballistic puzzle of JFK's death raised issues of range, calibre, entrance and exit wounds to the level of national importance: if the assassin was shooting from behind, why was Kennedy's head thrown back? The idea that bullets did not necessarily travel in a straight-line trajectory entered popular currency: a slug could travel in and out of the body, bend, expand, ricochet. According to weapon and type of bullet, bigger or smaller wounds could result. The Zapruder footage, screened on US national television in 1975, graphically showed the spectacular difference a frangible bullet could make compared to a regular one. One second Kennedy is shot in the neck but still together, the next his head is peeled open in a mist of brain and gore.

The Vietnam War had a different impact. The television reporting of firefights in the jungles of Indochina regularly noted the sense of confusion and frustration that US soldiers felt at the absence of a clearly identifiable target. Who is the enemy? What are we shooting at? Why? Such second-wave Vietnam movies as *Platoon* and *Full Metal Jacket* regularly stage this confusion in their gunfire sequences.

With these two events, the representation of gunfire was required to become both more visceral and out of control to be realistic. A wincing gunfighter nursing a flesh wound on his shoulder is no longer realism: life is messier than that. *The Wild Bunch*, its final holocaust especially, aimed to show you what it was *really* like to get shot.

However its realism operates not despite its heavy stylisation but largely because of it. Peckinpah used every cinematic technique in the book for its famous ending. Fast cutting between firing and bullet impact, snap zooms (sometimes into unfocused abstracts of red on white) cross-cutting between the slow-motion, bullet-ripped, blood-squirting leaps of Mexican soldiers – and Warren Oates as Lyle psychotically spinning the Browning machine-gun around and firing. Close-ups of blood

exploding from flesh, close-ups of roaring guns, close-ups of   165
faces screwed tight in agony, and all the time the symphony
of bullet report and men screaming. Peckinpah keeps the
screen ferociously busy with the dynamics of explosion (walls,
bodies, guns) with a cutting rate more rapid than MTV. It is
the founding bullet-fest, a heavily mediated *mise en scène* of
industrial barbarism. And yet it captured – more precisely
than anything before – the reality of gunfire as an excessive
and bloody confusion, in which it is increasingly unclear who
is shooting at whom and where the bullets are coming from.

This confusion is also achieved technically. Peckinpah uses a
vast variety of camera angles, and lenses with long focal lengths
to give a flattened perspective to the carnage, suggesting a
suffocating proximity between the combatants. Blood, bullets,
Mexicans and bandits appear to shoot and die almost on top of
each other. Like Kennedy's death, bullets come from nowhere
and without reason, and like the battlefields of Indochina, a
desperate and crowded confusion prevails. Hence it is the *active
mediation* of gunfire and bullet impact in this movie which
supplies the meaning of the sequence, even if that meaning
is painfully nihilistic.

However disturbing, the sequence is also exhilarating. Aside
from the ferocious stylistic fireworks, exactly where the pleasure
in the witnessing of such agony originates is difficult to identify
– but a few notions suggest themselves. The first is that the
sequence is an early example of the gradual transformation
of modern Hollywood cinema into a pure thrill machine,
offering sensation before story, the cause-effect narrative engine
becoming (at significant points, in various ways and to varying
degrees) subordinate to the spectacle. Seduction by spectacle,
providing sensuous and visceral pleasures, is now considered
characteristic of many contemporary Hollywood films (though
some critics regard it as an infantile characteristic).

In gunfire sequences, what constitutes the spectacle is not
simply the amount of gunfire released, but the visible impact on

166 the body. The special-effects bullet-impact squib has a dynamic of its own, an attraction as the spectacle of visible injury. Sometimes it seems that a pumping artery lies just beneath the material of the victim's clothing, and the bullet operates like a lance to a boil. Alternatively, there is a more messy and explosive form where the 'boil' itself detonates outwards in wild and runny rivulets of blood and stringy gobs of gore. The 'Odessa steps' ending of De Palma's *The Untouchables* offers some designer versions of these squibs: where each slo-mo detonation has a shiny liquid texture, as if Armani himself had sewn them, as accessories, into the fabric.

It is the cumulative effect of such spectacles – the sustained provision of visual and kinetic motion – which makes good gunfire sequences so enjoyable. John Woo's Hong Kong action movies are exemplary in this respect. Woo has said that he choreographs his gun battles with the precision of musical numbers: a Peckinpah on an inspired drug-bender, Woo uses every technique and every type of squib to deliver some of the most sustained and unlikely gunfire sequences on film. At the end of *Hard Boiled* the two cop heroes, Chow Yun-Fat and Tony Leung, are working their way through some hospital corridors, leaving a war-crime's worth of dead bad guys in their wake. Their squib-soaked progress is filmed and choreographed with a steadicam in one take: sometimes the sound and action groan into slow-motion (usually to extend a wounding frenzy), then groan back up to normal speed; the two even get into a lift and start cleaning out the *next* floor before we get a cut. Some dislike Woo's extended and bloody depiction of cops shooting bad guys, bad guys shooting cops, cops shooting cops, usually point blank with a gun in each hand, and few grenades to spare. As with those who hate Techno music, the fundamental misunderstanding is that it's all the same, just banal repetition: once you've seen one guy shot, why show the other twelve dozen? Those who like both Orbital and John Woo know that more *is* more, that repetition is part of a cumulative dynamic, that no part is ever the same as that preceding it: it is the constant and unbelievable accumulation of impact and firepower that makes a Woo film like *The Killer* akin to an all-night blood-and-bullets rave.

As my adoration of Woo might suggest, the pleasure of gunfire is also somewhat gender-specific, which leads to my second suggestion for the origin of such pleasures. Gunfire sequences offer particular pleasures for men, pleasures which often cannot be found elsewhere. Just as important as the shooting in this *Hard Boiled* sequence is the emotional relationship between the two cops; indeed, such relationships are often fundamentally bound up with the gunfire itself. In Woo's *A Better Tomorrow II* one character can only stop weeping and win Chow Yun-Fat's respect and love when he finally picks up a gun and starts shooting at something. Many men find the end of *The Wild Bunch* an exhilarating sequence, but it is also a tender one. Somehow the pain and agony of gunfire legitimates a kind of male intimacy usually outlawed in the Hollywood film, or else awkwardly displaced onto dramas of male camaraderie (as with much of Hawks). With Lyle and Tector (Ben Johnson) dead, their leader Pike Bishop (William Holden) finally succumbs to the amount of lead drilled into his bleeding body. Dutch (Ernest Borgnine) clambers over the carnage towards him, weeping: 'Pike! Pike!' – and then dies next to his friend. It is a tender moment because one feels that Dutch was about to express his love for his friend, to hold him tight and tell him, 'It's OK, we'll die together.' It's corny, but after all the four of them *have* been wearing their wounds like fluid brooches: they've earned the right to cry out, to scream, to weep, even if the price of that expression is terminal. Such intimacy and close physical contact between wounded men carries a powerful cultural message: it's OK to touch me *now* – I'm bleeding. I'm dying. Would Mr White (Harvey Keitel) tenderly comb Mr Orange's (Tim Roth) hair in *Reservoir Dogs* if Orange wasn't bleeding to death?

But this is only part of a broader pleasure, a pleasure which I think is less gender-specific and more universal than it might

168   at first seem (and this is my third suggestion for such pleasure's origins). It is connected with a modern fascination, centred on the body as a site of both perfection and decay. On the one hand we are told that our bodies are 'at risk' from disease, viruses, smoking, junk food and ageing; on the other, and in response, we are encouraged to 'take care of ourselves', to eat healthy food, to exercise, to give up smoking and aspire to the perfect body. If the responsibility for this is ours, so is the anxiety. A hitherto healthy body riddled by gunfire graphically reproduces this anxiety; what's more, it celebrates the abdication of responsibility for the body itself. So the pleasure gained from watching gunfire sequences is bound up with issues of control and its loss. This is strikingly illustrated in the standard shot routines of these sequences. Mastery and power (the cool handling of high-tech weapons) are directly contrasted with the loss of control over the body, the messy exit of blood and the involuntary convulsions. For example, in *Reservoir Dogs*, Mr White shoots two cops in their car. We are given a shot of White, cool, collected, powerful, firing a Smith and Wesson 645 in each hand; in the next shot we are given a chaos of injury, exploding glass and flesh, shrieking cops. This quick transition between mastery and vulnerability is certainly the characteristic trajectory of male orgasm, and there are further correspondences: a 'powerful weapon' is brandished, its contents released; there's an analogous cause-effect chain, in that the beating spurt of orgasm has its equivalent in the gushing of the bullet impact and consequent involuntary body movement. But one should be wary of the cliché which equates all specific cinema thrills to sexual pleasures: because control and its loss has a far more significant meaning in the real world.

This is best illustrated by those gunfire sequences in which the shooter is also the wounded. In *The Wild Bunch*, as noted above, a shot and bleeding Lyle screams as he spins around the machine-gun, spraying destruction indiscriminately. One gets the acute sense that the gun is controlling *him*, that he couldn't let go if he wanted to. The technology has overwhelmed its user. Similarly, at the end of *Taxi Driver*, Travis Bickle (Robert De Niro) is also shot and bleeding, but the logic of his on-board arsenal propels him to continue the killing until he runs out of ammo. Again, the gun becomes the agency of control to the extent that Iris's (Jodie Foster) cry, 'Don't shoot him!', becomes an impossible request: Travis evacuates the brains of the brothel keeper over the wall. In *Reservoir Dogs*, Mr Orange, lying in a lake of his own blood, empties his entire weapon into Mr Blonde, but continues pointing it even when it's empty, as if the gun itself was urging him to continue. Automatic gunfire creates automatic people.

But even this explanation doesn't give the entire picture. More than just the technology powers these characters. They have a heroic quality too. Tim Roth's blood-soaked Orange defiantly shooting and Warren Oates's Lyle swinging on the machine-gun have something iconic about them, something which recalls the paintings of the Crucifixion or of St Sebastian. The fifteenth-century painter Andrea Mantegna's powerful paintings of Sebastian depict him as shot through with arrows, bleeding, and looking heavenwards for redemption beyond the agony of the material world. But neither Orange nor Lyle has any such recourse. They can only turn to their guns and fire back.

And herein lies the profoundest desire and deepest pleasure in these gunfire sequences: in the will to fight back, to gain mastery over one's life even in circumstances so desperate and agonised. They give us a highly stylised spectacle in which are played out genuine dramas of mastery and loss. If these do reflect male pleasures and anxieties, this is because in a patriarchal world men have more to lose. The passivity and weakness associated with women are a direct reflection of the systematic way they have been denied access to that power. But there is nothing positive about passivity, no strength in lying back to wait for the next bullet.

170   Society continually offers us examples of how we cannot do
anything about our situation: famine, disease, war, interest rates,
inflation and job security. We seem to have less and less control
over what happens to us, however often we are told to take
responsibility for it. It is because most of us know what it's
like to be under fire (if only metaphorically), and what the
yearning to shoot back feels like, that it feels so damn good to
watch gunfire in these films. The desire to shoot back is positive,
and even subversive, at a time when our first instinct might be to
keep our heads down and not make trouble. Marx argued that
the fight against capitalism begins with 'the weapon of criticism
and the criticism of weapons'. That is, in critically and actively
fighting back, even as the odds and guns are ranged against
us. Pleasure in gunfire sequences simultaneously reflects our
recognition of our vulnerability and our desire to fight back. As
the screenwriter Charles Higson explained in his recent *Obsession*
(*S&S*, August), after his first youthful viewing of the end of *The
Wild Bunch*, 'I wanted to go out in a blaze of glory, I wanted a
Gatling gun, I wanted to be pierced by a hundred bullets.'

Sight and Sound, October 1995

Killing Time

PAULINE KAEL

Clint Eastwood isn't offensive; he isn't an actor, so one could hardly call him a bad actor. He'd have to *do* something before we could consider him bad at it. And acting isn't required of him in *Magnum Force*, which takes its name from the giant's phallus – the long-barrelled Magnum 44 – that Eastwood flourishes. Acting might even get in the way of what the movie is about – what a big man and a big gun can do. Eastwood's wooden impassivity makes it possible for the brutality in his pictures to be *ordinary*, a matter of routine. He may try to save a buddy from getting killed, but when the buddy gets hit no time is wasted on grief; Eastwood couldn't express grief any more than he could express tenderness. With a Clint Eastwood, the action film can – indeed, must – drop the pretence that human life has any value. At the same time, Eastwood's lack of reaction makes the whole show of killing seem so unreal that the viewer takes it on a different level from a movie in which the hero responds to suffering. In *Magnum Force*, killing is dissociated from pain; it's even dissociated from life. The killing is totally realistic – hideously, graphically so – yet since it's without emotion it has no impact on us. We feel nothing towards the victims; we have no empathy when they get it, and no memory of them afterwards. As soon as one person gets it, we're ready for the next. The scenes of carnage are big blowouts – parties for the audience to gasp at in surprise and pleasure.

172   At an action film now, it just doesn't make much difference whether it's a good guy or a bad guy who dies, or a radiant young girl or a double-dealing chippie. Although the plots still draw this distinction, the writers and the directors no longer create different emotional tones for the deaths of good and bad characters. The fundamental mechanism of melodrama has broken down, I think: the audience at action pictures reacts to the killing scenes simply as spectacle. A tall, cold cod like Eastwood removes the last pretensions to humane feelings from the action melodrama, making it an impersonal, almost abstract exercise in brutalisation. Eastwood isn't very different from many of the traditional inexpressive, stalwart heroes of Westerns and cops-and-robbers films – actors notoriously devoid of personality – but the change in action films can be seen in its purest form in him. He walks right through the mayhem without being affected by it – and we are not cued to be affected, either. The difference is a matter of degree, but it's possible that this difference of degree has changed the nature of the beast – or, to put it more accurately, the beast can now run wild. The audiences used to go mainly for the action but also to hate the ruthless villains, sympathise with the helpless victims, and cheer on the protector-of-the-weak heroes. It was the spaghetti Westerns (which made Clint Eastwood a star) that first eliminated the morality-play dimension and turned the Western into pure violent reverie. Apart from their aesthetic qualities (and they did have some), what made these Italian-produced Westerns popular was that they stripped the Western form of its cultural burden of morality. They discarded its civility along with its hypocrisy. In a sense, they liberated the form: what the Western hero stood for was left out, and what he embodied (strength and gun power) was retained. Abroad, that was probably what he had represented all along. In the figure of Clint Eastwood, the Western morality play and the myth of the Westerner were split. Now American movies treat even the American city the way the Italians treated the Old

West; our cops-and-robbers pictures are like urban spaghetti Westerns. With our ethical fabric torn to shreds in this last decade, American action films such as *Magnum Force* and *The Laughing Policeman* are becoming daydream-nightmares of indiscriminate mayhem and slaughter.

The John Wayne figure – the man who stood for the right (in both senses, I fear, and in both senses within the movies themselves) – has been replaced by a man who essentially stands for nothing but violence. Eastwood has to deliver death, because he has no other appeal. He can barely speak a line of dialogue without making an American audience smile in disbelief, but his big gun speaks for him. The concept of the good guy has collapsed simultaneously in our society and in our movies. Eastwood isn't really a good guy; you don't *like* him, the way you liked Wayne. You don't even enjoy him in the way you could enjoy a scoundrel. He's simply *there*, with his Magnum force. For a hero who can't express himself in words or by showing emotion, shooting first and asking questions later has got to be the ultimate salvation. In *Dirty Harry*, Eastwood said to the hippie psychotic, 'This is the most powerful handgun in the world, punk. It can blow your head off.' The strong, quiet man of the action film has been replaced by the emotionally indifferent man. He's the opposite of Bogart, who knew pain. Perhaps the top box-office star in the movie business, Eastwood is also the first truly stoned hero in the history of movies. There's an odd disparity between his deliberate, rather graceful physical movements and his practically timbreless voice. Only his hands seem fully alive. In Italian movies, the character he played was known as the Man with No Name, and he speaks in a small, dead, non-actor's voice that drops off to nowhere at the end of a line and that doesn't tell us a thing about him. While actors who are expressive may have far more appeal to educated people, Eastwood's inexpressiveness travels preposterously well. What he does is unmistakable in any culture. He's utterly unbelievable in his movies – inhumanly tranquil, controlled, and assured – and

174   yet he seems to represent something that isn't so unbelievable. He once said of his first Italian Western, *A Fistful of Dollars*, that it 'established the pattern', that it was 'the first film in which the protagonist initiated the action – he shot first'. Eastwood stands melodrama on its head: in his world nice guys finish last. This is no longer the romantic world in which the hero is, fortunately, the best shot; instead, the best shot is the hero. And that could be what the American audience for action films, grown derisive about the triumph of the good, was waiting for. Eastwood's gun power makes him the hero of a totally nihilistic dream world.

Hollywood's flirtation with the ideology of the law-and-order advocates reached its peak two years ago with the release of *Dirty Harry*, a Warner Brothers picture directed by Don Siegel and starring Eastwood as the saintly tough cop Harry Callahan. A right-wing fantasy about the San Francisco police force as a helpless group, emasculated by the liberals, the picture propagandised for para-legal police power and vigilante justice. The only way Harry could protect the city against the mad hippie killer who was terrorising women and children was by taking the law into his own hands; the laws on the books were the object of his contempt, because he knew what justice was and how to carry it out. The political climate of the country has changed, of course, and, besides, Hollywood is, in its own cheaply Machiavellian way, responsive to criticism. In *Magnum Force*, the sequel to *Dirty Harry*, and also from Warner Brothers, Clint Eastwood, again playing Harry Callahan, is just as contemptuous of the laws on the books, but he believes in enforcing them. John Milius, who had an uncredited paw in *Dirty Harry*, and who gets the screenwriting credit here, along with Michael Cimino, twists the criticism of the earlier film to his own purposes: he takes his plot gimmick from those of us who attacked *Dirty Harry* for its fascist medievalism. The villains now are a Nazi-style élite cadre of clean-cut, dedicated cops who have taken the law into their own hands and are cleaning out the scum of the city – assassinating the labour racketeers, the drug dealers, the gangsters and their groupies. They are explicit versions of what we accused Harry of being; they might be the earlier Harry's disciples, and the new Harry wipes them all out. 'I hate the goddam system,' he says, 'but I'll stick with it until something better comes along.' *Magnum Force* disarms political criticism and still delivers the thrills of brutality. Harry doesn't bring anyone to court; the audience understands that Harry *is* the court. The picture is so sure it can get away with its political switch that before it allows Harry to spout his new defender-of-the-system line it actually tweaks the audience (and the movie press) by implying that he is the assassin who's mowing down the gangsters. But the movie – and this is what is distinctively new about it – uses the same tone for the Storm Troopers' assassination orgies that is used for Harry's killing of the Storm Troopers. At no point are we asked to be appalled by homicide. We get the shocks without any fears for the characters' safety or any sadness or horror at their gory deaths. The characters aren't characters in any traditional sense; they're not meant to be cared about.

Studio-machine-made action pictures have the speedy, superficial adaptability of journalism. One can measure some of the past two years' changes in the society by comparing the two films. In *Dirty Harry*, the sniper villain (wearing a peace symbol on his belt) idly picked off an innocent girl in a bikini while she was swimming, and the pool filled with her blood. In *Magnum Force*, one of the young Storm Troopers machine-guns everyone at a gangland swimming-pool party, and you get the impression that the girls prove their corruption and earn their deaths by being bra-less. Generally speaking, the victims now are all guilty of something, even if only of taking drugs, so you're exonerated – you don't have to feel anything. You can walk out and pretend you didn't see what went on. If the élite cadre and their prim Führer (Hal Holbrook) represent what Harry the hero represented the first time around, and if it's

176 now right for Harry the hero to kill them, what of the writers who confect one position and then the next? Do they believe in anything? I think they do. Despite the superficial obeisance to the rule of law, the underlying content of *Magnum Force* – the build-up of excitement and pleasure in brutality – is the same as that of *Dirty Harry*, and the strong man is still the dispenser of justice, which comes out of his gun. Harry says it: 'Nothing's wrong with shooting as long as the right people get shot.' He's basically Paul Newman's Judge Roy Bean – another Milius concoction – all over again. Although Ted Post's direction of *Magnum Force* is mediocre, the picture isn't as numbing as *The Life and Times of Judge Roy Bean*, because it stays on its own coarse, formula-entertainment level, trying to turn on the audience to the garish killings and sustaining a certain amount of suspense about what's coming next. It sticks to its rationale. In *Magnum Force*, Dirty Harry is still the urban garbage man, cleaning up after us. His implicit justification is 'You in the audience don't have the guts to do what I do, so don't criticise me'. He says he does our dirty work for us, and so he invokes our guilt, and we in the audience don't raise the question 'Who asked you to?' If Milius were a real writer instead of a hero-idolater, he might begin to raise questions about whether Harry unconsciously manipulates himself into these situations because he likes to kill, and about whether he keeps his face stony so as not to reveal this. But *Magnum Force*, the new city Western, has no mind and no class; the moviemakers seem unaware that their hero lives and kills as affectlessly as a psychopathic personality.

'A man's got to know his limitations,' Harry keeps saying, and it's a comment not on himself but on his enemies' failure to recognise that he's the better man. Harry is tougher than the élite cadre, just as he was tougher than the mad hippie killer. The Nazis look like a troupe of juveniles in training for stardom in the old studio days, and are suspected by other cops of being homosexual, so Harry's weathered face and stud reputation (which is all hearsay as far as the audience goes) are like additional equipment for destroying them. But Eastwood is not a lover: women flock to him, but he makes no moves towards them. From what we see, they have to do all the work; he accepts one as dispassionately as he declines another. In one sequence, a woman bares her feelings and tells Harry of her desire for him while he just sits there, as unconcerned as ever; he's not going to get involved. Like the Western loner, he's almost surreally proper – lunatically so, considering what he does with his gun and fists. The only real sex scene in *Magnum Force* is a black pimp's murder of a black whore, which is staged for a turn-on erotic effect that I found genuinely shocking and disgusting. But the movie is full of what in a moral landscape would be sickening scenes of death: a huge metal girder smashes right into a man's face, and the audience is meant not to empathise and to hide from the sight but to say 'Wow!'

The right-wing ideology functioned in *Dirty Harry*; here the liberalised ideology is just window dressing. What makes Harry the sharpshooter a great cop is that he knows the guilty from the innocent, and in this action world there's only one thing to be done with the guilty – kill them. Alternatives to violence are automatically excluded. If we talk to Harry, if after he dispatches his thirty-fifth or eightieth criminal one of us says 'Harry, could you maybe ask the guy's name before you shoot, to make sure you've got the right man?' Harry's answer *has* to be 'All criminals are liars anyway,' as he pulls the trigger. Because that's what he wants to do: pull the trigger. What keeps the audience watching is one round of killings after another. *Magnum Force* is a far less skilful fantasy than *Dirty Harry*, and so is less involving, and it isn't likely to be as big a hit, yet my hunch is that the audience, after these last couple of years, rather likes its fantasies to be uninvolving.

It's the emotionlessness of so many violent movies that I'm becoming anxious about, not the rare violent movies (*Bonnie and Clyde*, *The Godfather*, *Mean Streets*) that make us care about

178 the characters and what happens to them. A violent movie that intensifies our experience of violence is very different from a movie in which acts of violence are perfunctory. I'm only guessing, and maybe this emotionlessness means little, but, if I can trust my instincts at all, there's something deeply wrong about anyone's taking for granted the dissociation that this carnage without emotion represents. Sitting in the theatre, you feel you're being drawn into a spreading nervous breakdown. It's as if pain and pleasure, belief and disbelief had got all smudged together, and the movies had become some schizzy form of put-on.

from *The New Yorker*, 1974

Alex Through the Looking Glass

TONY PARSONS

Only one character dies in *A Clockwork Orange*. Early on in Kubrick's lost masterpiece, Alex DeLarge, the teen with a taste for rape, murder and Beethoven, makes his last appearance in classic Droog chic – white shirt, braces and trousers, black bowler hat, right eye framed by a spider's web of heavily mascaraed false lashes – when he bungles a burglary and smashes in a middle-aged woman's skull with a sculpture shaped like a giant cock. And though the film is littered with battered and abused bodies (and another victim eventually expires quietly off camera), the woman who Alex kills in his valedictory appearance as a Droog is *A Clockwork Orange*'s only onscreen fatality.

By any cinematic standards this is a very modest death toll. For a work with the lurid reputation of *A Clockwork Orange*, one killing seems a remarkably low body count. Yet even now, it remains a supremely shocking film. There are countless films more violent than *A Clockwork Orange*. But there is not one that even comes *close* to matching the inflammatory power.

There's a chilling conviction about the sex and violence in *A Clockwork Orange*. Conceived by the novelist Anthony Burgess as a fable about man's choice between good and evil, when the film appeared in 1971 it was seen by some young hotheads – not to mention the majority of judges, policemen and tabloid editors – as a thesis on how good it feels to be bad. *A Clockwork Orange* was big box office and even bigger news, and was blamed for

180   inspiring a plague of teenage violence from every pulpit and soapbox in the land.

The hysteria eventually became too much for Stanley Kubrick, who told Warner Bros. that he no longer wanted *A Clockwork Orange* to be distributed in the UK, the country the American director has made his home.

In the deafening furore around the film, hardly anyone noticed that Kubrick never went on record to explain this decision. Did he pull *A Clockwork Orange* because he was sick of seeing his film carry the can for society's problems? Or because he thought that perhaps it really was responsible for inciting violence among some confused souls? Or because he was frightened to be seen as the man responsible for creating what one judge called 'that wicked film'? The honest answer is that we do not know, although sources close to Kubrick claim that he was profoundly disturbed by the reaction the film received in this country.

A Clockwork Orange disappeared into a black hole and has remained there ever since. But beyond the hysteria of the tabloid headlines, here was the greatest film ever made in Britain – a giddy cocktail of stark brutality, slapstick comedy and futuristic nightmare. It is a dazzling social prophecy (Alex is eventually brainwashed by a weak government attempting to stay in power by taking a tough stand on law and order). It is brilliant social satire (Alex and his Droogs sip milk spiked with hallucinogenics, sporting uniforms – the long girlie eyelashes, the gentleman's bowler hat – that are both celebrations and satire of every British youth cult from Teds to Punk). And, for all its horrors, *A Clockwork Orange* is frequently achingly funny (the leading man has Marty Feldman's eyes). Yet there is no denying that the film also has a touch of evil about it. What made *A Clockwork Orange* subversive was that it seems to rejoice in its dirty deeds. This is a film completely lacking in what screenwriting guru Robert McKee calls 'the centre of goodness'. There is no moral redemption at the heart of *A Clockwork Orange*. The fifteen-year-old hero has the choice between good and evil. Emphatically, he chooses evil.

When Alex and his Droogs rape a woman, the camera lingers on her face in leering close-up, as if it is the next in line. When a rival gang is beaten to bloody pulp, it is to the exhilarating strains of Rossini's *The Thieving Magpie* (classical music is all over the soundtrack, a classy counterpoint to all the GBH). And when Alex puts the boot into a man whose home he has invaded, it is while he is doing a tap dance and crooning Gene Kelly's 'Singin' in the Rain'.

And yet you can't help liking him. Alex (Malcolm McDowell in the performance of a lifetime) is one of cinema's most seductive heroes – articulate, witty, whispering his amoral philosophy in a breezy voice-over, calling the audience 'my brothers'. Alex rapes, murders and crushes testicles. And we want to be his friend.

A Clockwork Orange cruelly exposes the old liberal line about great cinema making us realise the horror of violence. *A Clockwork Orange* put forward a strong case for the symphonic beauty of violence, the glamour of evil. There are scenes where the violence is as choreographed as anything in *West Side Story*. But then Kubrick subverts the theatricality with a sudden close-up of a bottle being shoved in someone's face. Naturally, the boys in the back row of the late show lapped it up. *A Clockwork Orange* may have drawn the art house crowd in the rest of the world; in this country it attracted the lads, the mob, the masses.

The film had been running in London's West End for over a year when Kubrick pulled the plug. *A Clockwork Orange*'s steady ascent to mythic status in this country over the last twenty years often makes us overlook its initial commercial impact. In its day it was *huge*.

The director withdrew his film from distribution only in Britain. Here you can't buy it on video or see it at the cinema. But in the United States you can buy it on LaserDisc. In Paris it is still playing to packed houses. In fact in the rest of the world *A Clockwork Orange* is as fêted as *Citizen Kane* and as easily available as *Home Alone 2*. Only in Britain is it censored by the man who made it.

And so, of course, the dark legend continues to grow. *A Clockwork Orange* is the mainstream film that descended to the underground. In London – twenty-two years after it was released – there is at least one video rental store that displays a sign saying, 'No: We Do Not Have A Clockwork Orange.'

What is it with Britain and *A Clockwork Orange?* This country and *A Clockwork Orange* have always had a special relationship.

Perhaps understandably so – the clothes, language and drugs of Alex and his friends were directly inspired by the emergence of the early British youth cults. The rest of the world considers it a serious film by one of the greatest directors of the last thirty years. But here it has been demonised, portrayed as a danger to society and made a scapegoat for all our ills. The Fleet Street clippings of twenty years ago are full of cases of rape, murder and mayhem where it was pointed out that the defendants had seen *A Clockwork Orange* – as if that explained everything.

'We must stamp out this horrible trend which has been inspired by this wretched film,' said Judge Desmond Bailey, sending a sixteen-year-old boy to Borstal for beating up a younger boy while wearing white overalls and a black bowler hat. 'We appreciate that what you did was inspired by that wicked film, but that does not mean you are not blameworthy.'

It is, of course, impossible to say how much, if any, violence was inspired by *A Clockwork Orange*. Certainly a few terrible crimes were committed with Kubrick's symphony of violence ringing in the heads of the perpetrators (in Lancashire in 1973, for example, a seventeen-year-old Dutch girl was raped by a gang chanting 'Singin' in the Rain') but whether these crimes would have been committed without the prompting of *A Clockwork Orange* is another question. The critics of *A Clockwork Orange* have acted as though the film introduced evil into the world.

Anthony Burgess was a teacher in Malaya and Borneo from 1954 to 1960. During World War II his wife had been raped in London by four American deserters. When he returned to Britain there were still Teddy Boys on the streets, and later he and his wife witnessed the first battle between Mods and Rockers on the Brighton seafront. It is said that the expatriate who returns home after a long absence sees his country with the eyes of a time-traveller. *A Clockwork Orange* was set in the future, but in young Alex every British youth who ever wore the uniform of a teenage tribe could glimpse his own reflection. I was in my mid-teens twenty years ago and all my friends felt that here was a film about us. What a triumph for a British film!

The major difference between Burgess's novel and Kubrick's film is that in the book the reader was screened from the unfolding horrors by the barrier of language. Alex narrates his tale in Nadsat – Burgess's brilliant combination of Cockney rhyming slang and corrupted Russian (the book was written in 1962 when it still seemed as if the Reds could win the Cold War). So we hear that Alex and his three Droogs start the evening by tolchocking some starry veck, indulge in lashings of the old ultraviolence and then subject a devotchka with horror show groodies to the old in-out. But in the film, although the Nadsat is still there and although it is all as stylised as *Blade Runner*, you see the victims' faces and hear their screams.

'A film,' noted Burgess, 'is not made of words.' When people talk of *A Clockwork Orange* they usually think of the mayhem in the film's first fifteen minutes. But beatings, rape and murder are only the start of our story. Alex quickly winds up in jail after killing the woman with the XXL-phallic sculpture, where he volunteers to be brainwashed so that every thought of violence literally makes him sick. He does not want to be good. He wants to be *free*.

So with his eyes clipped open, Alex is pumped full of the appropriate medication and forced to watch scenes of Nazis marching and Droogs gang-banging while his beloved classical music plays in the background. This results in an ironic side effect to his treatment that he really objects to – not only can't he stand the thought of hurting someone, he also can't bear to listen to 'lovely, lovely Ludwig'.

The transformation of Alex from free-thinking psycho to politically correct robot forms the basis of both Burgess's novel and Kubrick's film. At the climax of the film he is brainwashed back to his old rotten ways by a government facing a storm of bad publicity for its authoritarian measures. Alex ends *A Clockwork Orange* triumphant, fantasising about some of the old in-out.

'I was cured all right!' he rejoices.

But for most of the film, Alex is a prisoner. And although *A Clockwork Orange* is relentlessly amoral, he gets more punishment for his crimes than any villain ever did. He is beaten in the cells by the police (including a young Steven Berkoff), he is subjected to radical aversion therapy, he is assaulted by his former victims and nearly drowned in a water trough by his former friends. Despite the Droog rampant you always see in stills, for most of the film Alex is in civvies, whimpering and crying and wiping snot from his nose. Alex is only part of a gang at the start – for most of the action he is horribly alone. But when the film was released, all anyone seemed to notice was the old ultraviolence in the first fifteen minutes.

It was this part of the film that made the judges and tabloid editors foam at the mouth. And it was the opening scenes of Alex on the rampage with his Droogs that touched a peculiarly resonant chord in British adolescents. *A Clockwork Orange* is the most tribal of films. The violence is ritualised, the dress code is rigorous, the cult is king. It seems appropriate that it should have become the ultimate cult film.

More than two decades after its release, *A Clockwork Orange* still seems like the most controversial film of the last thirty years. How tame the fuss around *Reservoir Dogs* seems next

to the uproar caused by *A Clockwork Orange*! How paltry is
the impact of *Hard Boiled* next to Kubrick's bloody rhapsody!
What an anti-climax are the antics of all the big screen tough
guys after a night on the tiles with little Alex!

The film continues to inspire great passions. Even now *A
Clockwork Orange* is unfairly held up in some quarters as a byword
for contemporary violence. That was one of the reasons why I
wanted to make a documentary about it for Channel 4's arts
series *Without Walls*, looking beyond the hysteria and hyperbole
that has surrounded the film and hopefully shedding light on
its dark legend. Because the documentary used clips from *A
Clockwork Orange*, Warner Bros. brought and were granted an
injunction preventing Channel 4 screening the programme,
though the injunction was overturned by the Court of Appeal.
Channel 4 argued that our use of clips was justified under
Section 30 of the 1988 Copyright Act which allows the use of
extracts for legitimate review and criticism. The programme was
eventually transmitted three weeks later than planned. It was
called *Forbidden Fruit*. What else *could* it be called? *A Clockwork
Orange* remains British cinema's missing masterpiece.

And yet, just a ferry ride away, they are selling videotapes of *A
Clockwork Orange* at the giant record megastore FNCA Musique
at Place de la Bastille, Paris. And funnily enough, there are no
records of copycat violence.

Time to reconsider, Mr Kubrick, brother?

This article first appeared in *Empire* magazine, 1995.

The Banning of Boy Meets Girl

by TOM DEWE MATHEWS

Contrary to popular belief, not many violent films are officially banned in Britain. What actually happens when newspapers demand a celluloid sacrifice is that a film's release into the cinema or on to video is quietly postponed by the censor. Such was the case with *Reservoir Dogs, Henry: Portrait of a Serial Killer, Natural Born Killers* and *The Bad Lieutenant.* Indeed many of the most controversial films of recent times have been cast by the British censor into a video or cinematic limbo before being given a belated certificate when the original press furore has finally died down. Occasionally, when a film's absence is noted by curious commentators an explanation is sought from the censor. More often, though, any delay will be imposed without much commotion by common consent between film distributors and the British Board of Film Classification.

Such public indifference to a film's whereabouts can partly be explained by the film industry and film censor's mutual dependency on secrecy. For any exposure of this partnership would – and occasionally does – bring down opprobrium and ridicule upon both censor and censored. The power of such a vetting system can therefore be measured by its current ability to withstand examination, and for that reason the censorship of British cinema still remains covert. Today, although it is possible to find out if a film has been censored in Britain, the BBFC is not obliged to reveal what has been cut and, even more importantly, why.

If covert censorship encourages public indifference to a film's whereabouts then the quality of what is actually publicly refused by the BBFC tends to encourage critical indifference. Because out of the thirty-nine films which make up the BBFC's banned video list nearly all come under such titles as *Tied and Tickled No 4* or *Head Girls at St Winifred's*, the critical fraternity tends, therefore, to ignore their exclusion from Britain's home screens. Recently, however, this select, if undistinctive, group of movies has been joined by a more serious film about violence which attempts, in the words of its director, 'to open a moral trap-door under its audience'.

In September 1995 Ray Brady's *Boy Meets Girl* was officially refused a video certificate by the BBFC. Along with his rejection slip, the third-year film student also received a two-page letter from the head censor detailing the reasons for the film's refusal. This note not only provides a unique insight into the normally secretive workings of the BBFC, but, because the Board is a government delegated body, the document also stands as a declaration of the state's attitude towards screen violence in Britain.

The plot of *Boy Meets Girl* is stark. An American woman picks up a man in a bar, dopes him, ties him up to a dentist's chair and tortures him. A masked woman who is filming his reactions on video then reveals that she has killed the American because 'she was enjoying [the violence] too much'. His potential liberator, however, does not release him. Instead she taunts, tortures and even performs surgery on him. With the 'boy's' death the camera pans round to a neat row of skulls, and reveals that he was merely the latest in a long line of victims. Finally, another tied-up victim – a woman – appears. And the process recommences.

Director Ray Brady knew that *Boy Meets Girl* would provoke the BBFC. Part of his intention when making the film was to 'attack the BBFC's censorship of screen violence'. But he didn't want – and neither could he afford – to make a film which sensationalised violence. His movie, by contrast, would be aimed at just the sort of film which 'cuts off consequence from action by breaking violence down to its barest components

188 and then blowing it all up with hot stylised air'. So he would 'show a build-up to violence, the violence itself and then the aftermath, the consequences, the psychosis, the trauma'. The first-time director released his £50,000 film, however, in the wake of the Bulger moral panic and the effects of that particular newspaper scare soon made themselves felt.

Even before *Boy Meets Girl* had been completed the BBFC had been shown a rough cut version by the film's distributors, Metro Tartan. Within a week the Board told the distributors that the film 'would never receive a video certificate in this country'. Although this was informal advice, Metro Tartan, in turn, informed Brady that 'No video equals no deal.' Now in sole possession of a film nobody could see, Brady realised that his only hope of gaining any sort of release for *Boy Meets Girl* lay in a direct approach to the head censor, James Ferman.

In the spring of 1995 at the BBFC's offices overlooking Soho Square, the head censor astonished Brady with an early indication of the BBFC's attitude towards screen violence. He expressed surprise that anyone should want to depict violence that wasn't entertaining. Receiving no reply, the BBFC's director went on to make another remark which should have given Brady pause for thought – since it showed him precisely how to carry out Ferman's wishes. 'Why can't you end your film,' the director suggested, 'with the police breaking in?' Brady was flabbergasted.

Then, presumably in an attempt to find a less surgical solution, the American-born censor proposed a deal to the ingenue director. The BBFC would grant him an uncut '18' film certificate and, depending on audience reaction in the cinema, they might grant a video classification. (This is a traditional BBFC formula for dealing with controversial films when the Board isn't sure of the public's response.) But when Brady managed to secure two London cinema showings for his film, nobody from the BBFC attended. Apparently, Ferman now felt that it should be his decision rather than a general audience's. Then Brady received the BBFC's letter.

It began with a reminder of the current law on video classification. As he read, Brady must have realised that his cause was
already in doubt. 'As you know,' Ferman wrote, 'the Criminal
Justice and Public Act 1994 laid down an additional test . . .'
That test used to be 'the likelihood of a video work being viewed
in the home'. But from now on, according to Ferman, it would
also contain the clause 'the likelihood of underage viewers'
coming into contact with a 'potentially harmful' video. Such
an all-encompassing bill has made criminals of many parents.
But more practically, it has, in the name of children, given the
BBFC the power to censor adults; and more directly it provided
Ferman with the legal means to ban *Boy Meets Girl*. For once he
had established his legal responsibility to take 'special regard' of
videos, Ferman merely had to couple Brady's film to the current
bill for his (written) word to become law.

He started out by listing Brady's visual transgressions. 'This
video,' he writes, 'focuses unrelentingly on the process of
torture, mental as well as physical, including mutilation, sexual
violation and evisceration, all in full view of the camera.' However, Ferman's judgement has subsequently been questioned by
some of his own censors on the Board. David Blewitt, who saw
the film before he left the BBFC at the end of 1994, holds the
opposite view. 'The torture cannot be described as unrelenting,'
says the ex-examiner, 'since Brady never allows the viewer to
become involved. He denies the viewer the luxury of emotional
involvement. He constantly employs distancing devices – such
as looking through a video camera or breaking up the scenes
with title cards. So you get a caption describing the violence
which is then shown in the next scene.' Blewitt concludes that,
'At times, the film is like a slide show.'

Blewitt also believes that Ferman's account of the film's violence
is false. 'Nearly all the more extreme forms of torture take place off-
camera. What you actually see is nothing compared to a run-of-the
mill action adventure movie. Part of that has to do with Brady's
budget. But mostly it's because the gore simply isn't there.'

190   But once Ferman had shackled Brady's film to the contravention of a law he was forced to move into less certain territory. For the head censor now had to make a case against the film's violence. In other words he had to become a film critic. At this point, Ferman could, by way of cultural criticism, have asked why the serial killer is female when – with the notable exception of Rosemary West – this sort of murderer is so rare in real life. But instead he chose to attack the film's treatment of its protagonists. 'The black comedy tone,' he noted, 'prevents our empathising with the characters or identifying with their human failings; but nor is there that compensating sense of dread at the realisation of our own vulnerability which the best horror films provide.'

Black comedy has been a particular bugbear of the British Board of Film Classification ever since the genre cropped up in movies some thirty years ago. The moral ambiguity of black humour, and the way in which it allows an audience to laugh at a victim's predicament has always confused the censor. (And, as a result, the bawdy, black comedies of John Waters and Russ Meyer have either been banned and/or heavily cut on both film and video in Britain.) The 'best horror films', on the other hand, prompt our sympathy for the victim. The kind of empathy that Ferman is referring to here is exemplified by the horror film *Friday the 13th* – which the BBFC released uncut in 1980. For Ferman the violence in this prototype provoked a specific response from the audience which, from then on, the BBFC would be looking for.

'The murders were so far-fetched,' commented Ferman in a magazine interview at the time of the film's release, 'with knife blades coming up through beds into somebody, that it was clearly unreal. The nice thing about fantasy,' he added, 'is all the time you can keep reminding yourself, I can't get hurt, no one's going to get hurt, it's just make believe.' On the other hand, 'If you present it [violence] realistically, it impinges on your feelings, you haven't got that suspension of disbelief.'

But Ray Brady did want to suspend disbelief. Far from pulling the audience along on a victim's fantastic, never-ending flight from pyrotechnical violence, his hero is caught and – ultimately – killed. There is no escape. The villain is not apprehended. There is no retribution. The refusal to yield to patterns and predictabilities might sound closer to everyday reality than the usual stalk 'n' slash cycle of video-fodder; nevertheless Brady's lack of moral closure, his lack of differentiation in his treatment of 'good guys' and 'bad guys' contravenes one of the BBFC's oldest unspoken rules.

Just over eighty years ago, the BBFC's Secretary T.P.O'Connor was called upon to explain the BBFC's blanket ban on the newly popular genre of 'propaganda' films – which usually contained a social message about either white slavery, birth control or sexual diseases. 'We exist mainly, almost exclusively, for the cinema theatre alone,' O'Connor stated, 'for the amusement of the public and for the profit of the proprietor or owner of the film. I would not bring educational films under our Board, as I think they are entirely outside our skill. They are for the educational authorities to decide and not for us.' Needless to say, 'educational' films are now submitted to the BBFC. But the belief that films should entertain rather than provoke questions is still confirmed by British censors.

In 1972, for instance, Mark Patterson, the chairman of the GLC's Viewing Committee, remarked that 'In the context of violent times my committee has to consider the wide, general political and social implications of films, particularly those which reflect anarchy and do not provide answers.' And more recently, this view that cinema should be the site of entertainment and not social comment can be found in James Ferman's initial words to Ray Brady when he asked the director why the violence in his film had not been designed to amuse the public.

Having walked along an alternative path to that of the censor, Brady was then informed by Ferman of the BBFC's preferred moral order. 'With a subject like rape or torture, the validity of the treatment has normally depended on the extent to which

192   the film adopts a humane and compassionate viewpoint that aligns itself with the victim rather than the aggressor.'

Leaving aside a cineaste's question of whether a film should be from somebody's – or anybody's – point of view, Ferman seemed to be implying that Brady does not make up the audience's mind for them. According to the censor, it seems, 'mindless violence' has to have a mind.

However, screen violence must do even more than that, since it must lead the audience to the right moral conclusion through sympathy for the victim and his plight. Brady's film flouts that unwritten rule: 'for most of the film, the male victim is unsympathetic.' Even worse, Ferman detected an element of initial sympathy for the female torturer. 'The validity of the film,' says Ferman, 'rests on the supposition that one is watching a feminist piece in which torture is merely a narrative device for exploring unacceptable behaviour.'

Here, unwittingly or not, Brady transgressed one of modern censorship's main reasons for being. For the head censor has not only famously declared himself to be 'a feminist before women were', but also, according to another ex-examiner, Rosemary Stark, 'a better feminist than women are'. A gratuitous use of male violence towards women can, therefore, be a reason in itself for refusing a film. In his first full year as head of the Board, in 1976, Ferman banned fifteen films for their 'unwarranted depiction' of rape and violence against women.

In *Boy Meets Girl*, though, the use of female violence against men might be acceptable – perhaps – Ferman believed, as 'an extreme form of righting a wrong'. But the head censor immediately turned tack and declared that this theme 'is a red herring [in the film]. So, too, is the idea that the torturer might be motivated by a desire to turn the table on society's victimisers.'

Yet even more disastrously for Brady, his film had mixed the apparently sacrosanct theme of feminism with a shot of dreaded black humour. In order to understand how the Board reacts to such combustible ingredients it is worth taking a swift look at the BBFC's censorship of John Waters's 1978 film, *Desperate Living* – which remained banned for nearly ten years.

At the time, the BBFC conceded that certain filmgoers would be amused by Waters's film, 'perhaps as a holiday from a world where standards really matter'; but the censor's overall verdict was that *Desperate Living* was 'a coarse, mocking, deliberately vulgar' film in which 'disgust and decadence are rampant'. When the gay mother, Mole, wins a lottery and has a penis transplant, only to cut it off because her girlfriend Muffy is less than enthusiastic, the Board sniffed that 'lesbian love is grossly parodied'; as for the sequence in which Peggy Gravel encourages her spherically-shaped black maid Grizelda to squat on her husband, Mort, and smother him to death, this was merely a confirmation of Waters's 'cynical contempt for current values'.

Unbelievably, such po-faced piety still governs the BBFC's outlook towards films that feature either black comedy and sex or black comedy and violence. Waters's most famous film, *Pink Flamingos* – from 1973 – still has over three minutes cut out of its video version and only one of Russ Meyer's films (*Beyond the Valley of the Dolls*) has been passed by the BBFC for video release.

Back in his letter to Ray Brady, Ferman stated that, having failed to demonstrate a suitable motivation for his characters – which would then induce the right response from the audience – Ray Brady had therefore opened himself up to the accusation that his film might provoke the wrong response. 'We are confronted,' noted Ferman, 'with the obscene consequences of violence on the assumption that such violence will not be experienced as pleasurable.' Once again, however, Ferman's fellow examiners were not of the same opinion. David Blewitt denies Ferman's argument that *Boy Meets Girl* will incite women to acts of vengeful butchery. 'As a censor, you ask yourself, Is this violence justified? I, along with three of my ex-colleagues, do not believe that *Boy Meets Girl* sets out to present violence to the audience as pleasurable.'

Ferman's letter, however, continues to construct a chain of cinematic circumstance around Brady. The film-maker has refused to provide 'a coherent moral justification or context' and therefore there is 'the risk of confirming sadistic tastes or reinforcing sadistic impulses'. This, says Ferman, in a reference to the Criminal Justice Bill, 'is crucial to any consideration of harm to potential viewers or, through their behaviour, to society'.

In spite of endless debate, any proof that violent behaviour can be triggered by the screen has yet to be discovered by psychologists, social researchers or censors. James Ferman himself, who has not been tardy in his search for decisive proof, admitted in a national newspaper interview that 'Social science is an inexact discipline and human behaviour is too multi-factorial. It's nature, nurture; it's what happened to us this morning; it's how much we've had to drink.'

Legislators, however, continue either to avoid this inconvenient truth, or fudge the issue. When he introduced the Criminal Justice Bill in May 1994, the Home Office Minister, Lord Ferrers, declared, 'Although there may be no evidence that videos cause crime, of course they affect people. Films affect people.' As a censor, Ferman has to make the same hurried, rearranged assumption, because only then can he make the film fit the potential crime. As a result of these verbal gymnastics *Boy Meets Girl* is indicted for carrying 'the very real risk that it could have a corrosive effect on the values and/or behaviour of certain potential viewers'.

The belief that 'a minority' of any screen audience is incapable of making an ethical choice is the bedrock upon which Britain's film censorship exists. The BBFC only has to suggest – and not even necessarily on paper – that a film contains the sort of violence that could, in the words of Margaret Ford, the deputy director of the Board, 'be imitated by those with eggshell skulls' for it to be either officially rejected or for its release on either film and/or video to be 'postponed'.

But if any film can be so easily sidelined, why, then, was *Boy Meets Girl* selected for such specific, open exclusion? More famous films like *Reservoir Dogs* might have had their video release delayed by the censor, but Quentin Tarantino's thriller avoided any accountability from the censor by never being offically banned. Even Michael Winner's salacious film *Dirty Weekend*, which deals with the same subject as *Boy Meets Girl*, has never won the dubious distinction of an outright video ban. Also, a blood-spatterless, low-budget film like Ray Brady's was unlikely to have gained a wide horror video audience. And anyway the head censor generally prefers to delay the release of controversial films within the quiet confines of a tacit informal agreement with their distributor. He does not need to call upon the law.

The bald answer is that Ray Brady was easy to pick off. As one ex-censor asks, 'Who's ever heard of Ray Brady? He's a nobody. He's not mega-bucks. He's not even cult movie bucks. Nobody is going to fight for him. He doesn't have a distributor or a production company behind him. So he's easy for Ferman to push over.' But even more importantly for the BBFC, Ray Brady is a useful scapegoat.

For the banning of *Boy Meets Girl* is, in fact, a message to other independent young film-makers who depend upon the British market. The message is, don't make a film in which the audience can identify with the killer as well as his victim. Also don't make a film in which the audience is acted upon by being forced to acknowledge its role in the fulfilment of a wish it barely knew it had: that it can be both victimiser and victim. In short, don't implicate the audience in its desire for violence and ask, 'Why are you watching this?' Because, if you do, your film will fall outside the state's sanction. Or, as James Ferman puts it at the end of his letter to Ray Brady, 'On those grounds, your video certificate is refused.' As for Ray Brady, he received the letter, he got the message. He now works in television.

Speaking Up For Corpses

JOAN SMITH

When Kathryn Bigelow's millennial fantasy *Strange Days* was released in Britain in the spring of 1996, it received damning reviews. The film's most outspoken critic was Paul Gambaccini, presenter of the BBC Radio 4 arts programme *Kaleidoscope*, who announced on air that he had refused to interview Bigelow – the first time a *Kaleidoscope* presenter had made such a stand – because he would have been able to do nothing but insult her. Gambaccini's hostility is at first sight puzzling, given that the movie is not especially violent, certainly no more so than contemporaneous releases like *Seven*. Nothing in it comes anywhere near the sadistic torture scenes in Scorsese's *Casino* or the prolonged mutilation of a cop in Tarantino's *Reservoir Dogs*; visually stylish and stylised in a way that recalls *Blade Runner* (and set, like that movie, in a futuristic version of Los Angeles), Bigelow's film gradually exposes a romantic sensibility which simultaneously envisions humanity trembling on the brink of moral chaos and capable of redemption. Ralph Fiennes plays Lenny Nero, a disgraced ex-cop who now makes a living selling 'playback' – black market tapes which offer the punter the chance to experience other people's feelings along with sound and vision. What Lenny's customers want is sex, excitement, and the occasional out-of-the way thrill such as vicariously taking part in an armed robbery; *Strange Days* opens with a noisy, confused sequence as a gang of incompetent criminals raid a Thai restaurant and run into a police ambush. The whole episode, recorded on playback by one of the robbers and seen entirely through his eyes, ends abruptly when he falls to his death during a roof-top chase.

Furious with the dealer who is trying to sell him the tape after acquiring it illegally from a paramedic, Lenny pulls the playback rig from his head and exclaims: 'What the fuck is this? Goddamit! You know I don't deal in snuff!' Yet the pivotal incident in the film, and the sequence Gambaccini cited in defence of his decision not to interview Bigelow, is a so-called 'snuff' scene. A prowler, wired up to a playback machine, uses it to record his rape and murder of a prostitute, a friend of Lenny's called Iris. What's more, after incapacitating Iris with an electric stun-gun, the prowler connects *her* to the machine, forcing her to experience his excitement as he violates her. Here is part of the scene, taken from James Cameron's screenplay:

> Iris can now see herself as the Wearer sees her . . . wide-eyed with terror, white-lipped, weeping. Helpless. And she can feel what he feels.
>
> The wearer's hand goes back into the fanny-pack and pulls out something else. A black athletic headband. We slip it over her hear head, down over her eyes. A blindfold. Now she can only see what the Wearer sees.
>
> And also from the bag we pull . . .
>
> A yellow plastic object. With our thumb we extend the five inch
> blade of the razor knife. It is the type with the tipc that can be broken off by segments when they get dull. It extends with an ominous clicking sound.

It's the standard Hollywood slice-and-dice scenario, familiar from movies like *Jagged Edge* and virtually the whole of Brian de Palma's *ouevre*, but with a significant difference. In *Strange Days*, the audience sees everything from the point of view of

198   the rapist, actually *becomes* the rapist: '*We* put the knife up to her throat, and she whimpers, afraid to cry out, and then *we* draw the flat side of the blade down across her body as if to tease her with the prospect of her death' [my italics]. Even more dramatically Lenny Nero, who has been sent the tape anonymously, is forced when he plays it to feel the killer's excitement *and* the woman's terror:

> Lenny is feeling the stalker's exhiliration, pounding heart, flushed skin, panting breath, and Lenny knows that Iris is feeling the same thing, overlaid with her own senses ... so the excitement and terror merge into one thing, one overwhelming wave of dread sensation.

Lenny goes to pieces as the tape rolls. The screenplay describes him looking as though he has been 'gut kicked', gasping for breath and vomiting the contents of his stomach in a shop doorway. 'It is the worst thing he has ever experienced', the script explains, 'sharing that horrible intimacy of rape and murder with another ... so sick, so psychotically scopophiliac'.

Actually, this isn't a precise description of what's just happened; scopophilia – Freud's preferred term for voyeurism – describes the male viewer's *habitual* position when watching scenes of sexual violence on film involving women. What is ground-breaking and transgressive about *Strange Days* is the way it imposes, however fleetingly, not just collusion with the rapist but the sensation of female terror on that half of the audience which is used to regarding it from a safe distance. For women, this sense of horrified empathy at the cinema is depressingly routine; for men, it is startlingly unusual, so much so that it is hardly surprising that Gambaccini, and other male critics, reacted so violently to the film.

This is not the only way in which *Strange Days* breaks with convention. In a movie which makes an attempt, however muddled, to challenge gender stereotypes, the men are long-haired and dishevelled while the female lead, Angela Bassett as a chauffeur/bodyguard, is resourceful and resilient; Bassett grows in stature as the male characters, from Fiennes to Michael Wincott as a sinister rock music impresario, fall apart. This is not to argue that *Strange Days* is a great movie, although I think it is under-rated. What it does confront, however, and in an innovative way, is the problem of point-of-view. Most film-makers, if they think about it consciously at all, would probably regard John Berger's famous dictum in *Ways of Seeing* as prescriptive rather than descriptive: men watch women and women watch themselves being looked at (or, in the case of Hollywood cinema, people in their image being raped and murdered). That is how life is, so why shouldn't movies reflect it? And even if you want to do something more complicated and challenging, how do you make an audience, half of it composed of people who do not share women's vulnerability to sexual predators, identify with the female victim's experience?

Strange Days is not the first Hollywood film to address this conundrum. In 1988 Jonathan Kaplan made a botched attempt to persuade filmgoers to see things from a woman's point of view in his film *The Accused*, in which Jodie Foster won an Oscar for her performance as a young working-class woman gang-raped over a pinball machine. Almost everything that could go wrong with the movie did, from its degeneration into a conventional courtroom drama – a sympathetic female district attorney, played by Kelly McGillis, decides to prosecute the onlookers when the chief culprits dodge a charge of rape – to a spectacular misunderstanding of the function of female fear in pornographic discourse. The producers, fresh from their sensational success with *Fatal Attraction*, defended their graphic rape scene on the grounds that, by focussing on Foster's terror, it forced the audience to recognise the horror of sexual violence. These were people, all too obviously, who had never read a word of de Sade's *The Misfortunes of Virtue*, where the heroine's fear

200 and pleas for help are generally the prelude to some further atrocity:

> 'O sirs!' I cried, holding my arms out to them, 'have mercy on an unfortunate creature whose fate is more to be pitied than you can think. Few have suffered calamities equal to mine. I beg you, do not allow the predicament in which you discovered me to start suspicions of me in your mind, for my situation is the result of misfortune and not of any wrongs that I have done. Do not increase the sum of the ills which lie heavy upon me, but on the contrary, I beseech you, kindly furnish me with some means of escaping the rigours by which I am pursued'.

This entreaty, far from softening the hearts of the young aristocrats to whom it is addressed, leads them to take further advantage of the heroine by tying her to a tree, stripping her and threatening to slash her buttocks with their hunting-knives. There are men for whom female terror, experienced at a safe distance, carries an erotic charge: what Kathryn Bigelow tries to do in *Strange Days*, with some degree of success judging by the furious reaction to it, is to introduce a new possibility – identification – into a spectrum of male responses which normally runs from (at best) distaste for sexual violence against women on screen to (at worst) vicarious enjoyment of it.

The reason why this question of point-of-view matters, and it does, is not that violence on screen translates directly into real-life attacks on women. During the Yorkshire Ripper murders in the late 1970s, women in the north of England picketed cinemas showing the Brian de Palma movie *Dressed To Kill*, in which Angie Dickinson is slashed to death in a lift. The film, in some ways a re-run of *Psycho*, was undoubtedly in bad taste; the most pernicious thing about it, just like the earlier movie, was the way in which it identified the killer's feminine side – Michael Caine dressed up as a woman to commit his crimes, as did Tony

Perkins in *Psycho* – as the murderous part of his personality. In the almost frantic atmosphere of fear and distrust which pervaded northern cities at that time, with the death toil of women rising and the police apparently powerless to apprehend the killer, the connection between screen violence and violence against real women was, for many people, too seductive too resist. That remains true today, with a parliamentary committee claiming in a recent report that there are now more than a thousand academic studies which establish a 'causal connection' between watching violent material in the cinema or on video and what happens in real life. Dame Jill Knight, Tory chair of the Family and Child Protection Group, said: 'There is clear evidence to show that screen sex and violence does have links with crime, and that it does harm children. More and more people want to see something done. Now we have to work out the nuts and bolts'. According to a recent article in the *Sunday Times* (23 June 1996), opinion polls show that 71 per cent of British people agree with her, and believe that freedom of expression has gone too far.

This is an old, not to say ancient, argument which predates the invention of modern electronic media by hundreds of years. The case that certain types of entertainment have a direct and malign influence on how people behave in real life was articulated by St Augustine in the late fourth century AD, when he described the effect on a young friend of his, Alypius, who was taken against his will to a gladiatorial contest:

> When he arrived at the arena, the place was seething with the lust for cruelty. They found seats as best they could and Alypius shut his eyes tightly, determined to have nothing to do with these atrocities. If only he had closed his ears as well! For an incident in the fight drew a great roar from the crowd, and this thrilled him so deeply that he could not restrain his curiosity. Whatever had caused the uproar, he was confident that, if he saw it, he would find it repulsive

and remain master of himself. So he opened his eyes, and his soul was stabbed with a wound more deadly than any which the gladiator, whom he was so anxious to see, had received in his body. He fell, and fell more pitifully than the man whose fall had drawn that roar of excitement from the crowd . . .

When he saw the blood, it was as though he had drunk a deep draught of savage passion. Instead of turning away, he fixed his eyes upon the scene and drank in all its frenzy, unaware of what he was doing. He revelled in the wickedness of the fighting and was drunk with the fascination of bloodshed. He was no longer the man who had come to the arena, but simply one of the crowd which he had joined, a fit companion for the friends who had brought him.

Need I say more? He watched and cheered and grew hot with excitement, and when he left the arena, he carried away with him a diseased mind which would leave him no peace until he came again, no longer simply together with friends who had dragged him there, but at their head, leading new sheep to the slaughter. (*Confessions*, Book VI, Section 8)

For Augustine, the case was made: exposure to violence corrupts those who see it, no matter how innocent they are to begin with. Yet there is no evidence to suggest that Augustine's friend went on to perpetrate violent acts himself; like a spectator at a modern-day boxing match, which is perhaps the nearest equivalent to a gladiatorial contest, he simply went back for more. As Professor James Twitchell suggests in his book *Preposterous Violence*, it seems likely that these bloody contests 'reflect and even predict the wishes and responses of those in the coliseum stands' rather than creating them. Even the much-vaunted studies 'proving' the link between screen violence and criminal acts turn out, when you look at them more closely, to establish something rather different: that violent offenders, like many law-abiding citizens, enjoy recreational violence at the cinema and in the comfort of their own homes. Who can say which came first? Rapists and murderers are as much in need of a scapegoat as anyone else, indeed more so, and they are not insulated from this debate; they know that blaming *I Spit on your Grave* or *The Silence of the Lambs* or *Reservoir Dogs* for their crimes will be music to a defence lawyer's ears (as is the schizophrenia defence unsuccessfully adopted at his trial by Peter Sutcliffe, the Yorkshire Ripper). Taking the argument one step further, it may even be the case that watching violent fictions *reduces* the need, in some individuals, to commit violent acts: can we really justify the claim that attending a performance of the *Oresteia* or *Titus Andronicus* is cathartic but watching a film like Oliver Stone's *Natural Born Killers*, whose moral didacticism is equally overt, inevitably leads to murder?

It seems likely that an audience's reponse to screen violence is far more complex, and diverse, than this model of straightforward imitation suggests. What is more important, in a sense, is the cultural message conveyed by movies in which the male leads wade to their destiny through the corpses of butchered women. Two points are worth noting here: that celluloid violence against women, as opposed to male-on-male violence, is almost without exception sexual, and that the contest is always unequal. The atmosphere in movies like *Pulp Fiction* or the pyrotechnic John Travolta vehicle *Broken Arrow* is cartoon-like, so much so that they would easily translate to action comics with the words 'pow!' and 'splat!' standing in for the soundtrack; compared with the chilling torture and murder scene which opens *Jagged Edge*, both films could fairly claim to come under the heading good clean fun. Nor is it obvious, even in an extreme example of the cops-and-robbers *genre* like *Reservoir Dogs*, which of the characters is going to die and which will survive: the mortally-wounded undercover cop takes out the psychopath who has tortured the captive policeman and, in what looks like a deliberately ironic twist, the sole survivor of the bungled heist is the least conventionally 'masculine' of the

204 robbers, which is to say the only homosexual character. Events are not, in these films, pre-ordained in the way that they are for a certain type of female character in a standard Hollywood thriller; the audience knows, as soon as it sees Page Forrester asleep in bed in *Jagged Edge* or the actress Nancy Allen in *Blow Out* or Iris running panic-stricken down the escalator in *Strange Days*, that her fate is sealed. It also recognises, because of the visual code which marks them out as disposable (rich bitch/cheap hooker) that it should not get emotionally involved with these women, ensuring that their deaths are a thrilling but not too painful part of the entertainment package.

What is different about *Strange Days* is that Iris, although her character is coded in exactly this way – tight, low-cut dresses, wildly unstable behaviour – becomes a real person for Lenny Nero, and for the audience, at the moment of her death. Male viewers are not permitted to maintain the customary safe distance from which they observe the process which turns these women into corpses: instead, they are forced through Lenny's reaction to realise what Iris is suffering. There is a parallel here with *In The Cut*, Susanna Moore's controversial novel set in downtown New York, except that Moore addresses the question of point-of-view even more directly by making the narrator herself the victim of a serial killer; neither woman is saved, but in each case the reader/viewer is forced to recognise sexual violence as something more than a thriller cliché. It is hardly a coincidence that the novel has prompted similar furious reactions to the film, specifically the accusation that women should not be dirtying their hands like this. There is something illogical about this response, for it is precisely these women – the victims of serial rapists and killers – whose voices are silenced first in real life and second by the authors and directors who find their attackers endlessly fascinating. Men, it seems, can bump off as many women as they like in novels and on screen. What will not be tolerated is women speaking up for corpses.

The Movies, Me and Violence

HARRY MCCALLION

It has become fashionable to link cinema violence with the growing trends of violent activity in society in general. Is there a link? Have the films I watched over the years affected me?

When I was growing up, in the back streets of Glasgow, I saw very little in the way of films. For those that have not read my autobiography (*Killing Zone*) suffice it to say that my early life was more concerned with such fundamental matters as survival and getting enough to eat, than with more pleasant pastimes.

It was only when I joined the army, at seventeen, that I started my love affair with the movies that lasts until the present time. (In fact I'm writing my next novel in the hope that someone will make a movie out of it.) For someone who had grown up without a father figure the film world provided me with my early heroes: John Wayne, straight as an arrow, you could almost believe his tongue would shrivel up if he told a lie; Humphrey Bogart, hard as nails, irresistible to women.

The cinema also helped to perpetuate my own self-image. I had joined the Parachute Regiment, the best of the best. We saw ourselves as modern-day samurai. Assault infantry whose life expectancy on the battlefield, pitted against hordes of advancing Russian tanks, would be measured in days, not weeks. I remember on a wet Saturday afternoon I, along with about two hundred other Paras in various states of sobriety, crowded into a small picture hall in Aldershot to watch Alan Ladd in *The Red*

206 *Beret*. In those days you could get into the cinema for half price if you wore uniform, something no self-respecting Para would ever do, but two young engineers did turn up in full No. 2 uniform and sat at the very front of the cinema.

For those who have not seen the film, there is a scene were Alan Ladd walks past a group of other soldiers who laugh at his new red beret. Taking off his beret he advances on them to deal out retribution with the immortal words, 'nobody laughs at the red beret'. A spontaneous roar from two hundred drunken Paras, nearly bringing the roof down, and the two young engineers wilted visibly in their front seats.

Violence in those early movies was sanitised. Big John would take a .45 slug in the shoulder, role over, light a cigarette, then calmly shoot the bad guy in the black hat, who in turn would clutch at a faint spot of red on his shirt and die with little or no fuss. Even the dozens of German soldiers shot by Alan Ladd in *The Red Beret* died with hardly a grunt between them. I soon learned that real life was infinitely worse than anything the cinema could then portray.

The first man I ever saw shot was a petrol bomber, shot during the internment riots on August 9th, 1971. He was hit in the spine, the shock of the 7.62 full-jacketed round, travelling at nearly twice the speed of sound, lifting his entire body into the air. It was an incredible thing to see, I can still replay the scene in my mind all these years later. One minute the youth was running at full stretch, the next it was as if a giant invisible hand had suddenly whipped away his legs. He hit the ground rolling, over and over, screaming in a high-pitched, almost childlike voice. I would never look at a John Wayne movie in the same way again.

The reaction of the man who shot him, a vicious little Scots soldier called Matt, was also interesting. On the movies my heroes had always expressed sadness when they had been called upon to end the life of some dastardly villain. Some were even sick, or cried with regret. Matt's face took on a look of unsurpassed glee. He threw a clenched fist into the air and said softly, 'got him!'

We were, of course, paratroopers. We had been trained and expected to kill: a popular 2nd Battalion T-shirt had the logo 'Happiness is a Confirmed Kill'. It had been hammered into us during training, at the para depot in Browning Barracks, Aldershot. We would be lined up after gruelling five- or ten-mile runs and made to repeat, 'for the right to kill we must suffer', over and over again. It was brainwashing of the crudest, and most effective, kind.

Mercy was not a quality that was prized or even expected. Towards the end of my training I took part in a simulated ambush on a party of terrorists. One was left alive and I was sent forward to 'interrogate' him. Once I had obtained the information I crawled back to my position and was asked by the supervising major what I was going to do with the prisoner. I hesitated, he kicked me in the ribs and screamed, 'you kill him, kill him, we'll have no squeamishness here'.

We lived in a macho culture of violence that no film director of the Seventies would have been allowed to portray, even if he wanted to. When we were not in action in Ulster, we fought other soldiers, or other paratroopers, in brutal no-holds-barred fist fights. Considering how strong and fit we were, it amazes me today that none of us was killed; still, more often than not I would wake up on Saturday morning with my face stuck to the pillow with blood.

It quickly became apparent to me that the movies, which I had taken as an example of how people and life should be, were horribly wrong. The weak were never protected, but preyed upon and exploited, both in my world and on the streets of Ulster, where the IRA blew the kneecaps off petty thieves and joyriders and the heads off anybody who challenged their authority.

Even the moral message of films of the time, the sanctity of marriage, the portrayal of women as objects of desire that had

208   to be wooed and respected, was hopelessly out of tune with the reality I inhabited. Every married man slept around, when we were abroad they were the first into the whorehouses. Casual sex was the norm, not the exception. The women who came into our pubs could often outdrink us, outswear us and sometimes even outfight us. This was years before the guardians of morality started to claim that the film world was corrupting society. If Mary Whitehouse had spent a Saturday night in Aldershot she would have had a heart attack.

By the middle of the 1970s a had stopped watching war films altogether, they were so bland and unrealistic compared to screaming nightmares I had witnessed on the streets of Ulster. I still watched Big John, fighting off the Indians and riding into the sunset, but without any sense of reality. Besides it was as good a way as any to fill in the time between afternoon and evening pub opening.

Some might argue that is the true function of films, to allow you to escape from reality; personally I felt then, and do now, that the cinema must provoke people and make them think. You can't do that if films are so sanitised they lose the ability to shock. In fact, I believe this actually encourages violence. People see Big John shooting the guns out of the robbers' hands, or the bad guys dying with so little fuss, and think that gun battles can be safe, maybe even fun. In Ulster I saw my friends die, blown to bits by IRA bombs, saw IRA men screaming as our bullets ripped away their stomachs and knew the reality, felt all the hatred, pain and fear, and knew there was nothing funny about gun battles.

Times were changing, and directors like Sam Peckinpah started to produce films that portrayed something of the reality of my world. One of these was *The Wild Bunch*. Although produced in 1969 I did not see it until late 1975; it was to have a profound effect on me. The closing scene, where William Holden leads four men into a hopeless gun battle against overwhelming odds, mesmerised me. The violence was so graphic, I think I actually stopped breathing as I watched the slow motion destruction of the four men and dozens of the opposition. One thought was uppermost in my mind, 'what a way to go'.

Frustrated at not being able to get to grips with the IRA in Ulster, I had been thinking about going to Africa, to fight in a real war. *The Wild Bunch* only fuelled that desire. The reader will have to understand that I was very young and had more than a passing death wish: I never expected to live beyond thirty. The self-imposed moral guardians of society might argue that my reaction proves that the cinema does influence people to imitate violence, and they are right, up to a point.

If I had never seen *The Wild Bunch*, I would still have gone to Africa and still have killed with the abandon and relish that I did. I was conditioned by my life to do that and, thankfully, mentally and physically equipped to survive. I was impressionable, but strong-willed and intelligent. Someone less strong-willed and intelligent might not have survived; in fact I saw several friends, lured by promises of adventure and money, killed or executed as mercenaries in Angola before I left.

I can only remember seeing one film while I was in Africa and I was marched to see it in full uniform. It was the South African premiere of *A Bridge too Far*. It took all my will-power to hold back the tears as I watched my battalion (2 Para) being slowly decimated on the bridge at Arnhem. God, I felt so homesick.

I was now a member of the South African Special Forces, the renowned Reconnaissance Commandos, known as 'The Recces' to South Africans. They held the same mystique and glamour in the Republic of South Africa as the SAS does now in Britain, and they earned it. Nothing I had ever seen on a cinema screen came even close to matching the reality of my life at that time. We killed, bled and some of us died, fighting tooth and nail with irregular black guerrilla groups and their Cuban supporters, behind the front lines in countries all over southern Africa. When I came back to the UK after two and a half years with them I was a changed man, mentally stronger and fitter and probably even more violent than when I left the Parachute Regiment.

Within five days of returning to the UK I was back in the British Army and in Hereford on selection for the Special Air Service. The rigours of SAS selection apart, it was good to be back in the UK and good to be going to the cinema regularly. It was now 1980 and I noticed a big difference in the films on offer. Graphic sex and violence seemed to be the order of the day, films like *Death Wish II* spared the audience nothing and for the first time I saw violence on the screen that mirrored some of my own experiences.

After I passed SAS selection, I did a short tour in Ulster, then joined the Anti-Terrorist Team. It was a fantastic experience, spending hours in the 'Killing House', a specialist indoor range, perfecting our shooting and close-quarter combat drills. One weekend we went down to Hythe in Kent to do some sniper training. The local cinema was showing *Who Dares Wins* and nearly the entire SAS Anti-Terrorist Team trooped down to watch it. We sat in embarrassed silence as the actors portrayed attitudes and drills that had as much in common with the real SAS as chalk with cheese. Around us the civilians cheered on their heroes dressed in black, unaware that the real thing was sitting next to them. Embarrassed and bored out of their minds.

It was about this time that I started to educate myself, taking my 'A' levels. When I wasn't abroad or in some foreign country I attended the cinema regularly, now as a genuine leisure activity and not a way to fill in the time until the pubs opened. I suppose because I was studying at the time I was more keenly aware of the debate about violence and the cinema. I felt then, as I do now, that the supporters of more censorship miss the point completely. Violence, however graphically portrayed, does not in itself promote more violence. What promotes violence is the message that it works, or is the only answer.

In the films of my early youth, the villains were always caught, or killed. Now, in series like the *Death Wish* and *Dirty Harry* films, not to mention *Rambo*, it was hard to see who the villains were. In these movies politicians and police were either corrupt or incompetent, a trend copied by British film-makers in such films as *The Long Good Friday*. This is the real danger of the cinema, suggesting an easy, violent answer to their grievances, real or imagined, for the more unstable members of our society.

It was only a matter of time before there were copycats and on a subway in New York a commuter shot three youths, one of whom had threatened him with a screwdriver. I shook my head in wonder, blamed it on American society, safe in the knowledge that it would never happen over here: we were British after all. By 1985 my own life was reaching a turning point. I had decided to leave the SAS and join the Royal Ulster Constabulary, for reasons I have never fully understood myself – perhaps I just needed a change.

I found the RUC a stimulating challenge, especially after I was posted to Tennant Street RUC station, then reputed to be the busiest police station in Europe. On one side the station was bounded by the republican Ardoyne and on the other the fiercely loyalist Shankill Road. Sectarian killings were commonplace, by both sides. I lost count of the numbers of, mostly innocent, people that died in my three years there.

Bad as our problems were, the English police forces were about to face an even worse one. On a dull afternoon I reported to Tennant Street CID office for a two-month attachment. The room was strangely silent as I walked in, everybody grouped around the television set. I pushed my way to the front; an English town was on fire, bodies strewn everywhere. Thoughts of a terrorist attack flashed through my mind but I was wrong, the town was Hungerford. One lone deranged gunman had run amok, dressed like Rambo.

I had seen the film starring Sylvester Stallone and read the book, *First Blood*, it was based on. I had thought the book

212   excellent, the film almost laughable. Yet in the aftermath of the slaughter at Hungerford many blamed the film for instigating the violence. That violence instigates violence, copycat violence, is beyond reasonable argument, as the RUC were about to witness.

In the small border town of Belleek two plainclothes RUC officers from the RUC protection team were escorting a VIP. As they waited outside for their charge a combat-clothed figure stepped up behind them armed with an automatic shotgun. He opened fire, injuring one of the officers. The other pulled his gun and rolled out of the car to confront what he thought was an IRA assassination team. The man dropped the shotgun; later he would tell investigating CID officers that 'he wanted his body count to be greater than Hungerford'.

I had to leave the RUC in 1992, due to injuries I received in a car crash. I still return at regular intervals, to keep in touch with the many friends I still have on the force. The last film I saw in Belfast was *Patriot Games*, starring Harrison Ford. I was in good company, several members of the RUC's elite E4A surveillance team. The film started off well then deteriorated rapidly. By the middle there were groans of disbelief all around the cinema. It was worse than watching *Who Dares Wins*. Even the civilians around us, knowledgeable in the ways of the IRA and security forces after almost twenty years of violence, were embarrassed.

Recently I watched a television interview with a director famed for his graphic portrayal of cinema violence. His interviewer asked if he felt any personal responsibility for some of the acts of violence that had been inspired by his films. His answer was unequivocal, he did not. He believed that people who imitated acts of violence they saw on film were flawed individuals who would carry out those same acts, irrespective of what they had seen.

Today as a barrister at law, I spend most of my life surrounded by people who have committed the most appalling crimes imaginable. In the summer of 1995 I was marshall to a high court judge at the Old Bailey. While I was there I observed a trial; two young men, one eighteen, the other twenty-one, had kicked a man to death and stolen twenty pounds off him. They had followed the unfortunate man from a cashpoint machine believing he had more money on him. They became known as the cashpoint killers.

One of their backgrounds had been very similar to mine, born in the backstreets of Glasgow, deprived childhood. As I listened to his barrister I felt a cold hand on my heart; if along my life I had turned left instead of right that could have been me. The cause of his downward spiral to oblivion was deprivation and the hopelessness of poverty – I doubt if he had ever been in a cinema in his life.

So have the films I have watched over the years affected me? On balance I would say yes. But no more so than the poverty, deprivation and violence of my childhood and early manhood. The reasons for violence in society are myriad and some violence seems to need no reason at all.

I still go to the cinema regularly. My taste in films has changed and whenever I see graphic violence portrayed, I tend to view it with dispassion, the same way I read any brief that is sent to me. I see *The Wild Bunch* is to be re-released this month. I must go and see it again, and perhaps in it an echo of what I used to be.

Role Models

RODERICK ANSCOMBE

Violence is difficult to bring into focus. At least, that was my experience in maximum security. My first assault occurred at the hands of an ex-priest whose compulsions I was trying to treat. He was reluctant to expand on his symptoms, and those he had described did not fit easily into the established diagnostic categories. So when he approached me in his slightly diffident manner, asking courteously, 'Dr Anscombe, may I have a word with you?' I was glad of the opportunity to hear any information which would shed more light on his condition. He had spoken so quietly that I had difficulty hearing him, and so it was natural for me to lean forward, towards him, with my head inclined slightly to one side, perfectly set up for the right jab which he promptly delivered to the middle of my face. Gotcha!

When I say 'right jab', I am extrapolating from our respective positions. I don't remember. I remember the suddenly intent expression which came to his face, but the movement of his hand and the landing of the blow are lost to me. This blank is filled in by assumptions of what must have happened, by knowledge rather than experience. I am sure that this brief amnesia was not the result of a concussion. It wasn't a hard punch, and I was pleased, for the sake of my standing in that macho environment, that I didn't bleed excessively or go down. When the sergeant joshed me with a 'He got you good, doc,' I still had the presence of mind to insist that I'd suffered nothing more than a technical eight count.

The experience of violence as a blur is very common in both victims and perpetrators. The majority of violent incidents take everyone concerned by surprise. Most violence isn't planned. It surges out of strong emotion, and it happens very quickly. By the time we might have been ready for it, it's over. Even when the attack doesn't have the blitz quality of a single, decisive blow or a gunshot, the assailant is often submerged in the self-sustaining emotion of the violence. Fifty stab wounds to the body is not an uncommon finding at autopsy. Subsequently, the murderer may have no idea that he inflicted so much damage: he lost himself in the action.

I have been struck by how many murderers don't remember the moment of death. It's true that most of them had been sent to the facility where I worked in the hope of laying the groundwork for a verdict of not guilty by reason of insanity, and so they had reason to simulate amnesia; but many of those with nothing to gain by presenting themselves in this way could not recall the crucial seconds. This is particularly true of crimes of passion, in which the murderer has killed the woman he loved. The event, at its centre, is too intense to experience. It is as if the emotional overload causes the fuses to blow.

Because violence is extraordinarily rapid, time feels compressed. Time is distorted: too much of vital significance is occurring too quickly. Subjectively, more happens than ought to fit into a couple of seconds. The mind can't keep up. Experience falls behind. Events proceed without us. The shower scene in *Psycho* catches this quality of the victim's experience of sudden, unexpected violence with its fragmentation of viewpoints, flashes of the knife poised high above the victim, blows which begin but do not land.

The opposite of blurring is violence which is drawn out in slow motion, depicted in hallucinatory clarity, in expanded time. In *The Wild Bunch*, Sam Peckinpah depicts a gun battle in which bullets rip through men and throw them about like puppets in an extended, forensically correct ballet of death. This depiction of violence allows you to see, for example, the exact backward thrust a .45 slug exerts on the upper body before its explosive exit below the shoulder blade.

My second assault was a Peckinpah-like experience. The unit I worked on housed four men who were judged to be the most dangerous psychiatric patients in Massachusetts. They had attacked staff and other patients persistently and unpredictably, and they required special security arrangements. They were all psychotic, but they were not emotionally inaccessible. I decided that since medication had largely failed to improve their situation, I would try to establish a bridge to reality by forming a relationship with one of these men, Jack, by walking with him and engaging him in conversation if I could. To begin with, we paced up and down the unit's corridor. Later we circled the prison campus which was enclosed on four sides by buildings or wire, visible at all times to the guards in the watch tower.

I anticipated assault. It was by no means a certainty – I thought I had a good chance of evading it – but it was a distinct possibility that I'd rehearsed many times in my imagination. When Jack blinked three times, let out a cry, and lunged out of his chair, hands outstretched, for my throat, something like 'Holy shit – this is It!' went through my mind.

I don't believe that your whole life flashes before you at such times, but the mind does cover a lot of ground. It's as if consciousness is turbo-charged. When I thought, 'This is It!' the It included an awareness that the chance of Jack killing me before the officers arrived was real but very small (with the reality predominant), a plan to block and parry to buy time, a recollection of the psychiatrist who resided, brain damaged following a patient assault, in a nearby nursing home, a technical question about the seams in the human face, and a glimmer of perverse vanity in the thought that a discreet mutilation along the lines of Edward Fox's ineffably noble Hugh in *The Go-Between* might play nicely on a book tour. These components of It were not fully unpacked, to be sure, and perhaps it is not entirely correct to say that I experienced all this, but rather that I recorded impressions which later, articulated, would seem like experience.

It was all, however, very clear. The experience had an odd, hyper-real quality. As Jack came out of his chair, I was in motion too. I jumped to my feet, assumed the defensive stance, and noted the signs which supported a diagnosis of temporal lobe epilepsy, an explanation of Jack's sudden assaults which I'd been considering for some time. There seemed time to do all these things. Time had slowed. It was elastic, like chewing gum drawn out between the teeth.

The Peckinpah experience of violence attenuates the victim's terror to a level which allows his mind to continue functioning. The participant meets the situation as a problem-solver, rather than as a passive victim. Because it has been rehearsed, the experience drops into a net which waits to catch it. But rarely does the victim experience violence in this hyper-real mode – it depends on anticipation, and generally a person will not be a victim if he can anticipate the danger he may meet.

The Peckinpah experience is the perpetrator's prerogative, since he can stalk his victim, choose his moment, and stage-manage his kill. While the blurred, overwhelming experience of violence is well represented on the screen, it is the second kind of experience, the experience of violence which is anticipated and practised, the extended moment, which I will concentrate on here, because it is most commonly depicted without its crucial elements. It is a species of violence which remains endlessly fascinating and seems never to go out of fashion. The anticipation of violence, the planning of violence, and the rehearsal of violence are, of course, the hallmarks of the serial murderer – men like Count Dracula, Norman Bates and Hannibal Lecter.

We see these men gloat, brood, plot, choreograph their kills.

218 But the It, the meaning which the experience of murder has for them, is strangely missing from the picture. These are serial murderers who have, to greater or lesser degrees, been psychologically sanitised. Juxtaposed against the careers of real men who have been motivated by blood lust, their actions seem anaemic. They lack the sharp tang of reality.

In *Dracula*, for example, the missing element is filled in with a supernatural account of the count's need for blood. But although we know that Dracula requires blood for his continued existence, it is clear from the gleam in Bela Lugosi's eyes as he approaches his sleeping victims that he is about to indulge an intense pleasure. This is not the act of a hungry beast of prey about to slake his thirst. That is a motivation we could forgive. Dracula's turning in fear and revulsion from the crucifix tells us that his is an evil appetite. For much of the film his face is properly other-worldly; he displays little indication of human feeling. Only as he closes on his victim, as he comes close to satisfying his urge, does his otherwise impassive mien show the outlines of desire, and we can imagine his deep, thrilling pleasure, even if we never actually witness the voluptuous moment when his teeth enter the tender young neck of his victim.

Better that we don't, for the vampire's bite is not a pretty picture. Bela Lugosi's count leaves twin puncture marks on the side of the victims' necks, and we must assume that his canines are fashioned like hypodermic syringes which can puncture the blood vessel and siphon off the precious stuff. The teeth are so incredibly sharp that they leave neat wounds which are scarcely visible. They are also remarkably clean, since the count's victims do not suffer from the infections for which bite injuries are notorious. These teeth turn out to be complicated structures: since his victims are enabled to join the undead by a transfusion of the count's blood, we must wonder whether these hollow needles are provided with a system of valves to allow for a two-way flow. The fragility of this wonder of biological engineering is troubling. If the count's teeth are slender enough to slip into an artery with such ease that the victim barely stirs in her sleep, it's hard to believe that they can be very durable. Are not they liable to snap off? The consequences are both dire and undignified. An edentulous vampire is not poignant, but pathetic.

The reality of the bite is considerably less than suave. It's hardly the kind of thing a chap would want to attempt in white tie. First, the skin of the neck is supple and elastic; this means that it is hard to puncture, because it gives around the point of the tooth. The skin, and the moderately meaty sterno-mastoid muscle beneath it, must be penetrated by a combination of chewing and tearing. And having accomplished this feat, the would-be vampire must deal with the carotid artery. This is no easy matter, either: imagine biting into a small garden hose.

The bite is not a simple matter of mastication. Clearly, the perpetrator must be motivated by the most intense desire in order to carry it through, for beyond the extreme physical demands of such an act, lies a unique viciousness. To a large extent, we live in our heads; if we had to say where the 'I' is, it would be somewhere an inch or two behind the eyes. That is where people feel themselves to be centred. Measured from this centre, the murderer rarely comes closer than eighteen inches to his victim, as he would, for instance, in strangulation, the preferred method of serial murderers. No homicide brings the perpetrator so close to the victim as the vampire's bite. At the moment of death, as his lips feel the pulse ebb and stall, the centre of the count's being is pressed as close to that of his victim as it could conceivably be. It is this intimacy, far more than the bloody exertions of getting to blood, which makes the vampire's bite the ultimate kill.

Dracula spares us the gruesome physical reality of the vampire's bite, but more importantly, it evades the extraordinary emotional reality of the act. The missing element in *Dracula*, replaced with supernatural mumbo-jumbo, is cruelty. Perhaps no man better exemplifies the disparity between crime scene and film screen than Peter Kürten, the vampire of Düsseldorf.

By coincidence, Kürten was executed in 1931, the same year in which *Dracula*, starring Bela Lugosi, was released. Such was the panic that his attacks caused in Düsseldorf that the trial received enormous publicity, and the public around the world followed the proceedings in the newspapers, with books telling Kürten's story selling on both sides of the Atlantic. The murders he committed appeared to be random, because his victims ranged from young girls to a man in his forties, and because his choice of weapon and method of attack varied, and this stymied the police in their investigations and prolonged Kürten's murder spree. It was not until after he was finally arrested that the common thread in these attacks, his delight in blood, became evident.

Kürten himself was a small, unprepossessing man who was a natty dresser. He bears some resemblance to Peter Lorre, who played the character he inspired in Fritz Lang's *M*, a film which captures the city's climate of hysteria. Kürten was in his mid-forties at the time of the murders, but wore rouge and powder to make himself look younger. Although he had no real friends, he had a remarkable charm which enabled him to get young women to accompany him to unfrequented places, even at the height of the terror. In this respect, he resembles Bela Lugosi's count, whose hypnotic gaze makes women surrender themselves to his will. Children, fatally, trusted Kürten and would gladly run errands for him while he took care of the younger sibling they were supposed to watch.

Like the count, Peter Kürten was obsessed with blood. He hit many of his nine murder victims on the side of the head with a hammer to see the blood spurt from the ruptured artery. Once, walking in a park, frustrated because he had been unable to find a victim to his liking, he cut the head off a swan and drank its blood instead. His motivation was not supernatural, but it is almost as difficult to understand. During his frequent stretches in prison he whiled away the hours in the darkness of solitary confinement in daydreams – such erotic fantasies as causing the deaths of thousands of people by tampering with a town's water supply, or the mass murder of schoolchildren by delivering boxes of poisoned chocolates to them (also in solitary confinement, Hannibal Lecter muses in a similar vein in *Manhunter*, the predecessor to *The Silence of the Lambs*).

It is hard to comprehend in anything more than a detached, clinical way, the blend of eroticism and cruelty which Kürten shares with so many serial killers. Twenty-six years before the murders in Düsseldorf, for example, Kürten raped and killed a young girl in a bedroom over an inn; a few days later, he returned in order to enjoy a glass of beer and, from behind a newspaper, to listen to the shocked voices of the locals as they consoled the innkeeper for his tragic loss. He delighted in setting fire to barns and hay ricks so that he could watch the anguish on the farmers' faces as the results of their labour were consumed in flames. Once he attacked a man and a woman with a hammer, coming to spontaneous orgasm at the sight of their blood. For a real vampire, these are the blunt facts of life.

Norman Bates, the motel owner of *Psycho*, behaves in many respects like a serial sex killer, except that we are told by a handy psychiatrist in the penultimate scene that the man is, well, psycho. If Norman wants to dress up in women's clothes and have imaginary conversations with his mother, that's his business, but the chances are a jury won't buy it. The jury in the trial of Richard Chase, the vampire of Sacramento, didn't hesitate to condemn him to death in 1979, even though he was clearly schizophrenic, and I think that Norman would get short shrift too.

Norman's problem in going for an insanity plea, like Chase's, is that the sex shows through. Norman's *modus operandi* meets many of the FBI's criteria for an organised lust murderer. The assault takes place at a time and place which he judges will give him the best chance of evading detection. He gains

222 the victim's confidence by socialising before the assault. He selects his victim on the basis of her sexual attractiveness to him, but also because he has determined that she is running from something and is therefore less likely to be missed. He controls the crime scene (he even has a peep hole from his office through which he can observe the victim and so pick his opportunity). He brings a weapon to the crime scene, rather than making do with whatever comes to hand in the immediate environment. He cleans the crime scene thoroughly (almost). Norman is practised and prepared (we are told he might be able to help the authorities in regard to a couple of other young women who went missing) and makes sure his victim takes cabin number one, which has the peep hole. Most amateurs are under-powered in their choice of blades, but not Norman, who wields an impressive eight inches. Although an assault in the shower has practical implications in making the clean-up easier (stains are a major problem with a knife attack in one's own home or place of business), it also reveals the sexual motivation for Norman's attack, since he specifically chooses a time when his victim is naked. Like a number of serial killers who like to feel the presence of their victims nearby, he disposes of the cars and luggage belonging to the victims handily in the swamp. Norman, in his isolation and his awkwardness around still-living women, fits the profile of a socially inadequate type of serial killer. In reality, the missing element of this profile is Norman's sexual gratification with the still-warm corpse, a denouement yet too pungent for 1960 audiences.

Norman's mother bears a striking resemblance to Mrs Gein. During her life, Ed Gein's harsh, moralistic mother prevented him from having anything to do with women. After she died, Ed Gein killed over a dozen women and preserved various parts so that they would always be with him. When Gein was arrested in 1957, police found furniture which had been made from arms and legs and upholstered in human skin. In a manner echoed by Buffalo Bill, Hannibal Lecter's colleague in *The Silence of the*

Lambs, Gein made masks of his victims' faces, and body coverings from their skin and genitals, in order to invest himself with the appearance of a woman, as if he could, by placing himself inside a woman, take on her qualities.

Ed Gein was also a cannibal à la Hannibal Lecter (clearly, if Gein hadn't existed, Hollywood would have had to invent him). In the beginning, he stole bodies from graves, scanning local newspapers for funerals, then driving to the cemetery at dead of night to dig up the corpse. Later, he turned to murder as a means of acquiring female flesh. Lecter's cannibalism is treated in *The Silence of the Lambs* with a wry humour. It is difficult to know what else to do with it. Cannibalism is so grotesque that even cannibals make jokes about eating people. Ed Kemper, a serial murderer sentenced to life imprisonment in 1973, liked to feel the presence of his victims nearby and so planted several of the heads of young women whose bodies he had eaten in the flowerbed, facing his own and his mother's bedroom: 'People look up to you, Mom,' he told her.

The ghoulish, nervous humour fills in for the context that cannibalism lacks. Cannibalism is about possessing a person, and it can't be understood without reference to the defining moment in which the murderer brings the victim under his total control. Eating the body parts of the victim is a way of evoking them and savouring the memory of the incident in which they were acquired. Cannibalism is an act of evocation quite like Proust's remembrance prompted by a piece of madeleine dipped in tea.

The evocation of memory is essential to the organised serial killer, because his exquisite moment is so brief – it is not Peckinpah enough. The violent episode is carefully set up, not only so that it will conform to his fantasy, but also so that he will remember what happened. Serial murderers do not kill in the frenzy depicted in *Psycho.* A man with Norman Bates's experience would not rush his fifth kill. He has taken a lot of risks and worked very hard for this moment. The serial

224 killer wants to control the situation, to slow the course of events to a pace that allows him to register the act of violence in all its richness of detail.

Thirty sadistic criminals who had been responsible for the deaths of 187 known victims (and an estimated 300) described to FBI agents how they went about their business. Almost all of them were unemotional and detached during the commission of their crimes. These were not men who acted in a frenzy of knife thrusts, or who gave themselves up to their emotions as they enacted their violent fantasies. These were sex crimes, not crimes of passion. The men were not spontaneous, and they did not wish to be surprised either by their victims or by themselves. They already knew what they wanted, and they wanted the experience to be clear, and for the moment to stretch out.

This may explain why the reciprocal influence, the effect of screen violence on sex killers, is less than their influence on the fictional depiction of violence. Apart from sadistic pornography, screen violence is generally too tame for the very specialised tastes of serial killers. When screen violence does influence murderers, it misleads them. On the screen, for example, a single knife thrust to the chest is generally sufficient to get the job done: the victim gasps, her eyes pierce those of the murderer in silent accusation, then slowly glaze – end of life. The reality is more prolonged. From a dramatic perspective, victims do not die so neatly on cue. To begin with, the average murderer may miss the heart and major arteries with his first few thrusts. When his knife does enter the heart, death is by no means instantaneous, since there are reports of people with heart lacerations running several yards before expiring. Agonal events such as epileptic seizures, occurring as the victim passes irretrievably towards death, may give the illusion of animation or even of struggle. Whereas in screen violence the victim goes quietly and quickly, the reality of a stabbing is that she is liable to thrash around, twitch and generally show (misleading) signs of life even after the body has been pierced several times. This is surely confusing to the murderer schooled in the TV way of death. He thrusts in the knife just as he has been taught, but on the surface at least, nothing happens. Of course, if he cared to wait a few minutes, all movement would eventually cease. Instead, we see overkill – scores of stab wounds – in a victim who apparently will not die.

Some sadists say that the most important element in a killing is the total control of another human being, not the infliction of pain, which is only a proxy for control. The serial murderer's objective is to enact a fantasy which embodies his particular interpretation of control. Often serial murderers have elaborate scripts which they require their victims to act out in their last minutes alive. For many men, memory alone does not suffice, and they record the killing and the violence leading up to it on video tape, or on a tape recorder, or in photographs, or in diary entries complete with diagrams, so that they can relive the moment with the utmost clarity. Films, mementos and meat represent the end-point of the Peckinpah experience: violence slowed to a stop in a physical record, the essence of violence savoured through the evocative power of tissue. For Hannibal Lecter, what could be more beguiling than to ensnare a pretty FBI agent as his instrument of reminiscence?

These points of contact between screen and crime scene are moves in a flirtation with evil. Men who arrange Peckinpah experiences of violence are evil. What could be more evil than taking the life of a human being for the sake of an orgasm – her life, versus his seven seconds? I believe that our fascination with these men has to do with our perplexity about evil. Serial killers are men who have placed themselves outside society. They are predators who disregard the law in their pursuit of pleasure. More essentially, they have put aside kindness and fellow-feeling. They have broken the essential bonds which hold society together. In this sense, serial murderers exist at the extreme edge of human nature, and they prompt basic

226   questions. Are serial murderers sick – victims of pathological childhoods or mental illness? Are they monsters – freakish anomalies outside our range of behaviour and feeling, beyond our ken? Or are they – the worst case scenario – like us? And if they are like us, how do you get from us to them? Under different circumstances, following a different path, am I capable of acquiring a human being for my pleasure?

The Silence of the Lambs comes close to the depiction of evil, but cries off with humour when the going gets hot. To my mind, the evasive *Dracula* and the extenuating *Psycho* are not violent enough – deficient not in the depiction of the physical movement of murder, but in the portrayal of the cruelty which is the soul of violence. No doubt more films will come which will approach closer to the heart of the matter, and we are certain to view more violence of the extended moment, because the theme is timeless, because it is endlessly entertaining, and because we have a need for killing of better quality.

Natural Bred Killers

JOHN GRISHAM

The town of Hernando, Mississippi, has 5,000 people, more or less, and is the seat of government for De Soto County. It is peaceful and quiet, with an old courthouse in the centre of the square. Memphis is only fifteen minutes away to the north, straight up Interstate 55. To the west is Tunica County, booming with casino fever.

For ten years I was a lawyer in Southaven, a suburb to the north, and the Hernando courthouse was my hangout. I tried many cases in the main courtroom. I drank coffee with the courthouse regulars, visited my clients in the nearby jail.

It was in the courthouse that I first met Bill Savage. I did not know much about him back then, just that he was soft-spoken, exceedingly polite, always ready with a smile and a warm greeting. In 1983, when I first announced my intention to seek office in the state legislature, Mr Savage stopped me in the second-floor rotunda of the courthouse and offered me his encouragement and good wishes.

A few months later, on election night as the votes were tallied and the results announced to a rowdy throng camped on the courthouse lawn, it became apparent that I would win my race. Mr Savage found me and expressed his congratulations. 'The people have trusted you,' he said. 'Don't let them down.'

He was active in local affairs, a devout Christian and solid citizen who believed in public service and was always ready

228 to volunteer. For thirty years he worked as the manager of a cotton gin two miles outside Hernando on a highway that is heavily used by gamblers anxious to reach Tunica County.

At about 5 p.m. on March 7, 1995, someone entered Bill Savage's office next to the gin, shot him twice in the head at point-blank range and took his wallet, which contained a few credit cards and $200.

There were no witnesses. Nobody heard gunshots. His body was discovered later by an insurance salesman making a routine call.

It had to be a simple robbery. Why else would anybody want to murder Bill Savage?

The townspeople were stunned. Life in the shadow of Memphis had numbed many to the idea of random violence, but here was one of their own, a man who, as he went about his daily affairs, was killed in his office just two miles from the courthouse.

The next day in Ponchatoula, Louisiana, 300 miles south and again just off Interstate 55, Patsy Byers was working the late shift at a convenience store. She was thirty-five, a happily married mother of three, including an eighteen-year-old who was about to graduate from high school. Patsy had never worked outside the home before, but had taken the job to earn a few extra dollars to help with the bills.

At about midnight, a young woman entered the convenience store and walked to a rack where she grabbed three chocolate bars. As she approached the checkout counter, Patsy Byers noticed the chocolate, but not the .38. The young woman thrust it forward, pulled the trigger and shot Patsy in the throat.

The bullet instantly severed Patsy's spinal cord and she fell to the floor bleeding. The young woman screamed and fled the store, leaving Patsy paralysed under the cash register.

The girl returned. She'd forgotten the part about the robbery. When she saw Patsy she said: 'Oh, you're not dead yet.'

Patsy began to plead. 'Don't kill me,' she kept saying to the girl, who stepped over her and tried in vain to open the cash register. She asked Patsy how to open it. Patsy explained it as best she could. The girl fled with $105, leaving Patsy, once again, to die.

But Patsy did not die, though she will be a quadriplegic for the rest of her life.

The shooting and robbery were captured on the store's surveillance camera and the ideo was soon broadcast on the local news. Several full facial shots of the girl were shown.

The girl, however, vanished.

Authorities in Louisiana had no knowledge of the murder of Bill Savage, and authorities in Mississippi had no knowledge of the shooting of Patsy Byers and neither state had reason to suspect the two shootings were committed by the same people.

The crimes, it was clear, were not committed by sophisticated criminals. Soon two youths began bragging about their exploits. And then an anonymous informant whispered to officials in Louisiana that a certain young woman in Oklahoma was involved in the shooting of Patsy Byers.

The young woman was Sarah Edmondson, nineteen, the daughter of a state court judge in Muskogee, Oklahoma. Her uncle is the attorney-general of Oklahoma. Her grandfather once served as a congressman, and her great-uncle was governor and then later a US senator. Sarah Edmondson was arrested on June 2, 1995, at her parents' home, and suddenly the pieces fell into place.

Sarah and her boyfriend, Benjamin Darras, eighteen, had drifted south in early March. The reason for the journey had not been made clear. At any rate, they stumbled through Hernando on March 7 and stayed just long enough, Sarah says, to kill and rob Bill Savage. Then they raced deeper south until they ran out of money. They decided to pull another heist. This is when Patsy Byers met them.

Though Sarah and Ben have different socio-economic backgrounds, they made a suitable match. Sarah, a member of one

230   of Oklahoma's most prominent political families, began using drugs and alcohol at thirteen. At fourteen she was locked up for psychiatric treatment. She had admitted to a history of serious drug abuse. She managed to finish high school with honours, but then dropped out of college.

Ben's family is far less prominent. His father was an alcoholic who divorced Ben's mother twice, then committed suicide. Ben, too, has a history of drug abuse and psychiatric treatment. He dropped out of high school. Somewhere along the way he met Sarah, and for a while they lived that great American romance of young, troubled, mindless drifters surviving on love.

Once they were arrested, lawyers got involved and the love affair came to a rapid end. Sarah blames Ben for the killing of Bill Savage. Ben blames Sarah for the shooting of Patsy Byers. It appears Sarah will also attempt to blame Ben for somehow controlling her in such a manner that she had no choice but to rob the store and shoot Patsy Byers.

It should be noted here that neither Ben nor Sarah has yet been tried for any of these crimes. They have not been found guilty of anything, yet.

On January 24, 1996, during a preliminary hearing in Louisiana, Sarah testified under oath about the events leading up to both crimes. It is from this reported testimony that the public first heard the appalling details of both crimes.

According to Sarah, she and Ben decided to travel to Memphis to see the Grateful Dead. They packed tinned food and blankets and left on the morning of March 6. Sarah also packed her father's .38, just in case Ben happened to attack her for some reason. Shortly before leaving Oklahoma, they watched the Oliver Stone film *Natural Born Killers*.

For those fortunate enough to have missed *Natural Born Killers*, it is the repulsive story of two mindless young lovers, Mickey (Woody Harrelson) and Mallory (Juliette Lewis), who blaze their way across the south-west, killing everything in their path while becoming famous. According to the script, they indiscriminately kill fifty-two people before they are caught. It seems like many more. Then they manage to kill at least fifty more as they escape from prison. They free themselves, have children, and are last seen happily cruising down the highway.

Ben loved *Natural Born Killers*, and as they drove to Memphis he spoke openly of killing people, randomly, just like Mickey spoke to Mallory. He mentioned the idea of seizing upon a remote farmhouse, murdering all its occupants, then moving on to the next slaughter. Just like Mickey and Mallory.

They left Memphis after learning the concert was still a few days away, and headed south. Between Memphis and Hernando, Ben again talked of finding an isolated farmhouse and killing a bunch of people. Sarah said it sounded like he was fantasising from the film. They left Interstate 55, drove through Hernando and on to the highway leading to the cotton gin where Bill Savage was working in his office.

Ben was quite anxious to kill someone, she says. He professed a sudden hatred for farmers. This was the place where they would kill, he said. Ben told her to act 'angelic', and then they went inside.

Ben asked Bill Savage for directions to Interstate 55. As he gave directions he walked round the desk towards Ben, at which point Ben removed the .38 and shot Mr Savage in the head. 'He threw up his hands and made a horrible sound,' she testified. There was a brief struggle between the two men that ended when Ben shot Mr Savage a second time.

Sarah claims to have been so shocked by Ben's actions that she started to run outside; then, after a quick second thought, she decided to stand by her man. Together they rummaged through Mr Savage's pockets and took his wallet.

Back in the car, Ben removed the credit cards from the wallet, threw the driver's licence out of the window, and found two $100 bills. According to Sarah, 'Ben mocked the noise the man made when Ben shot him. Ben was laughing about what

232 happened and said the feeling of killing was powerful.' The Mickey character in *Natural Born Killers* felt much the same way. He sneered and laughed a lot when he killed people, and then he sneered and laughed some more after he killed them. He felt powerful. Murder for Mickey was the ultimate thrill. It was glorious. Murder was a mystical experience, nothing to be ashamed of and certainly nothing to be remorseful about. In fact, remorse was a sign of weakness. Mickey was, after all, a self-described 'natural born killer'. And Mickey encouraged Mallory to kill.

Ben encouraged Sarah.

After the murder of Mr Savage, he and Sarah drove to New Orleans where they roamed the streets of the French Quarter. Ben repeatedly assured Sarah that he felt no aftershocks from committing the murder. He felt fine. Just like Mickey. He pressed her repeatedly to kill someone herself. 'It's your turn,' he kept saying. And: 'We're partners.'

Sarah, as might be expected, claims she was completely repulsed by Ben's demands that she slay the next person. She claims that she considered killing herself as an alternative to surrendering to Ben's demands that she shed blood. But Sarah did not kill herself. Instead she and Ben drove to Ponchatoula.

According to Sarah, she did not want to rob the store, and she certainly did not wish to shoot anyone. But they were out of money and, just like Mickey and Mallory, robbery was the most convenient way to survive. Ben selected the store and, through some yet-to-be-determined variety of coercion, forced her out of the car and into the shop with the gun. It was, after all, her turn to kill.

In *Natural Born Killers* we are expected to believe that Mickey and Mallory are tormented by demons and that they are forced to commit many of their heinous murders not because they are brainless young idiots, but because evil forces propel them. They both suffered through horrible, dysfunctional childhoods, their parents were abusive, etc. Demons have them in their clutches and haunt them and stalk them, and make them slaughter fifty-two people.

This demonic theme, so as not to be missed by even the simplest viewer, recurs, it seems, every five minutes in the film.

Guess what Sarah Edmondson saw when she approached the checkout stand and looked at Patsy Byers? She did not see a thirty-five-year-old woman next to the cash register. No.

She saw a 'demon'. And so she shot it. Then she ran from the store. Ben, waiting in the car, asked where the money was. Sarah said she forgot to take the money. Ben insisted she return to the store and rob the cash register.

We can trust the judicial systems of both Mississippi and Louisiana to deal effectively with the aftermath of the Sarah and Ben romance. Bar a fluke, Sarah will spend the rest of her life behind bars in a miserable prison and Ben will be sent to death row, where he will endure an indescribable hell before facing execution. Their families will never be the same.

Patsy Byers is a quadriplegic for life, confined to a wheelchair, faced with enormous medical bills, unable to hug her children or do any one of a million things she did before she met Sarah Edmondson.

A question remains: are there other players in this tragic episode? Can fault be shared? I think so.

Troubled as they were, Ben and Sarah had no history of violence. Their crime spree was totally out of character. They were confused, disturbed, shiftless, mindless – the adjectives can be heaped on with shovels – but they had never hurt anyone before. Before, that is, they saw a movie. A horrific movie that glamorised casual mayhem and bloodlust. A move made with the intent of glorifying random murder.

Oliver Stone has said that *Natural Born Killers* was meant to be a satire on our culture's appetite for violence and the media's craving for it. But Oliver Stone always takes the high ground in

234   defending his dreadful movies. A satire is supposed to make fun of whatever it is attacking. But there is no humour in *Natural Born Killers*. It is a relentlessly bloody story designed to shock us and to numb us further to the senselessness of reckless murder. The film was not made with the intent of stimulating morally depraved young people to commit similar crimes, but such a result can hardly be a surprise.

Oliver Stone is saying that murder is cool and fun, murder is a high, a rush, murder is a drug to be used at will. The more you kill, the cooler you are. You can be famous and become a media darling with your face on magazine covers. You will not be punished.

It is inconceivable to expect either Stone or the studio executives to take responsibility for the after-effects of their film. Hollywood has never done so; instead, it hides behind its standard, pious First Amendment arguments and pontificates about the necessities of artistic freedom.

It is no surprise that *Natural Born Killers* has inspired several young people to commit murder. Sadly, Ben and Sarah are not the only kids now locked away and charged with murder in copycat crimes. Since the release of the film, random killings have been executed by several troubled young people who claim they were under its influence.

I am sure Oliver Stone would disclaim all responsibility. And he would preach a bit about how important the film is as a commentary on the media's insatiable appetite for violence. If pressed, he would probably say there are a lot of crazies out there and he can't be held responsible for what they might do. He is an *artist* and he can't be bothered with the effects of what he produces.

I can think of only two ways to curb the excessive violence of a film like *Natural Born Killers*. Both involve large sums of money – the only medium understood by Hollywood.

The first way would be a general boycott of similar films. If people refused to purchase tickets to watch such an orgy of violence as *Natural Born Killers*, then such films would not be made. Unfortunately, boycotts do not work. The viewing public is a large eclectic body and there are enough curious filmgoers to sustain a controversial work.

The second and last hope of imposing some sense of responsibility on Hollywood will come through another great American tradition, the lawsuit. Think of a film as a product, something created and brought to market, not too dissimilar from breast implants. Though the law has yet to declare movies to be products, it is only one small step away. If something goes wrong with the product, whether by design or defect, and injury ensues, then its makers are held responsible.

A case can be made that there exists a direct causal link between *Natural Born Killers* and the death of Bill Savage. Viewed another way, the question should be: would Ben have shot innocent people *but for* the movie? Nothing in his troubled past indicates violent propensities. But once he saw the movie, he fantasised about killing and his fantasies drove him to his crime.

The notion of holding film-makers and studios legally responsible for their products has always been met with guffaws from the industry.

But the laughing will soon stop. It will take only one large verdict against the likes of Oliver Stone, and his production company, and perhaps the screenwriter, and the studio itself, and then the party will be over. The verdict will come from the heartland, far away from southern California, in some small courtroom with no cameras. A jury will finally say enough is enough; that the demons placed in Sarah Edmondson's mind were not solely of her making.

Once a precedent is set, the litigation will become contagious and the money will become enormous. Hollywood will suddenly discover a desire to rein itself in. Sadly, the families of Bill Savage and Patsy Byers can only mourn and try to pick up the

236   pieces, and wonder why such a wretched film was allowed to
be made.

from the spring 1996 issue of *The Oxford American.*

Don't Sue the Messenger

OLIVER STONE

The hunt for witches to explain society's ills is ancient in our blood, but unholy for that none the less. The difference is that now we do not blame the village hag and her black cat but the writer, photographer and film-maker. Increasingly indicted by art and fearful of technology, our society scours them for scapegoats, in the process ignoring Shakespeare, who reminds us that artists do not invent nature but merely hold it up to a mirror. That the mirror now is electronic, widescreen or cyberspace is all the more intimidating to the unschooled and the more tempting to the lawyers.

John Grisham predictably draws upon the superstition about the magical power of pictures to conjure up the undead spectre of censorship. Too sophisticated to clamour for government intervention, he calls instead for civil action. Victims of crime should, he declares, rise up against the purveyors of culture high and low and demand retribution, thereby 'sending a message' about the mood of the popular mind. And so we arrive at yet another, more modern, more typically American superstition: that the lawsuit is the answer to everything. Fall victim to a crime acted out in films and all you have to do is haul the director into court. Has your father been brutalised? Sue Oedipus and call Hamlet as a witness. Do you hate your mother? Blame Medea and Joan Crawford. Has your lawyer-husband been unfaithful? Slap a summons on Grisham since, after all, he wrote *The Firm*.

238   Grisham is at pains to insist that before seeing my film *Natural Born Killers,* accused murderers Ben Darras, eighteen, and Sarah Edmondson, nineteen, had 'never hurt anyone'. But, even by Grisham's admission, Darras and Edmondson are deeply disturbed young people with histories of drug and/or alcohol abuse and psychiatric treatment. Darras's alcoholic father divorced his mother twice, then committed suicide. Grisham mentions it as if it was only a matter of time until they showed their anger.

It is likely that, whether they had seen *Natural Born Killers, The Green Berets* or a *Tom and Jerry* cartoon the night before their first crime, Darras and Edmondson would have behaved in exactly the way they did.

It is equally clear that the specific identity of the victim was irrelevant. 'Ben was quite anxious to kill someone,' Grisham states and Edmondson was ready to help. At the crucial moment when the carefully twisted springs of their psyches finally uncoiled, as they were bound to do, not I nor Newt Gingrich nor Father Flanagan of Boys Town could or did influence them.

Did *Natural Born Killers* have an impact on members of its audience? Undoubtedly. Did it move some to a heightened sensitivity towards violence? It did, some. Does it reveal a truth about the media's obsession with the senseless sensations? Ask O.J. Simpson. But did it drive Darras and Edmondson to commit two murders? No. If they are guilty, perhaps a negligent or abusive upbringing, combined with defects in their psyches, did. Parent, school and peers shape children from their earliest days, not films. Once grown and gone horribly wrong, those children must answer for their actions, not Hollywood directors. An elementary principle of our civilisation is that people are responsible for their own actions. If Dan Whyte, the killer of San Francisco supervisor Harvey Milk and Mayor George Moscone, could claim that 'Twinkies made me do it', what's next? 'A movie made me do it' perhaps?

A recent survey showed that the average teenager spends 15,000 hours a year watching television, compared with 11,000 hours a year in school. According to the study, most programmes contain violence and half of these violent acts do not depict the victim's injuries or pain. Astonishingly, only 16 per cent of all programmes show the long-term effects of violence while, for three-quarters of the time, the perpetrators of violence on television go unpunished. Is it possible that 15,000 hours of mostly violent television programming might have had slightly more effect on these two youngsters than two hours of *Natural Born Killers?*

Grisham points to 'several' anonymous youths who claim to have committed crimes under the influence, 'to some degree', of my film. Leaving aside the self-serving vagueness of this statement, we might ask: how many thousands of murders have been committed under the influence of alcohol? Yet Grisham does not call for the breweries and distilleries to be shut down by lawsuits. How many homicidal lunatics have purchased guns? Yet he mounts no campaign to close the weapons factories.

It gives me a shiver of fear when an influential lawyer and writer argues, as Grisham does, that a particular work of art *should never have been allowed to be made.* Strangle art in its infancy, he suggests, and society will be a better place. One might more persuasively argue that cold-blooded murderers should be strangled in their infancy. Yet, as with human infants, we can never know the outcome of nascent art and so both must be protected and nurtured precisely for society's sake. For it is only a small step from silencing art to silencing artists, and then to silencing those who support them and so on until, while we may one day live in a lawyer's paradise, we will surely find ourselves in a human hell.

from *LA Weekly* magazine, 1996.

Parade of Violence

A FILM CRITIC

We came out of *The Blue Dahlia*, two of us, both disappointed and angry, and my friend, a big man, shouted at the top of his voice: 'More and more murders! Bigger and better beatings-up! By all means break your toe kicking the hero in the head. Corpses littered all over the place, never mind who does the shooting so long as they're dead!'

The speaker was taken by passers-by for a Fascist advocating his creed; his qualifying remark: 'That's what the Hollywood producers seem to be saying nowadays,' was lost in the general outcry.

How right he was, however. Gone completely the sophisticated and adult attitude of American film melodramas such as *Laura*, *The Maltese Falcon*, *Mask of Dimitrios*, etc.; instead we have the purposeless parade of violence for its own sake: physical violence unrelated to any known form of life and apparently catering for a supposed audience of sadistic schoolchildren.

Start off with *The Blue Dahlia* itself, a film which has been praised by critics who should certainly know better, unless they have themselves become punch-drunk with watching the hallucinated antics of the slap-happy puppets on the screen.

Here was an opportunity missed: a good cast, Alan Ladd, Veronica Lake, William Bendix, Howard da Silva, Doris Dowling; Raymond Chandler was apparently given a free hand to do the script and dialogue. One expected something outstanding, and what does one get? Conventional characters and story, conventional neurotic war-torn hero (Ladd), conventional psychopathic pal (Bendix), conventional night-club racketeer (da Costa), conventional wise-cracking dreary lost-girl wife of racketeer (Lake), bound for conventional happy ending with Ladd after racketeer has been ironed out in conventional gun battle during which his henchmen are also accidentally shot to death. This high rate of mortality continues throughout the film and nobody could care less: the whole picture is made incomprehensible for much of its length by bad cutting and, I am sorry to say, by bad scripting; the director seems determined to equal in savagery the beatings-up in *The Glass Key*: a gangster does indeed break his toe by kicking Alan Ladd too hard, and Ladd afterwards stamps on the broken toe of his aggressor when this has just been withdrawn from a mustard bath.

In another picture of the same kind, *The Dark Corner*, there is more stamping: this time on thumbs; Mark Stevens, a new star attempting unsuccessfully to emulate Bogart, smashes William Bendix's thumb with a paperweight; later his own thumb is stamped on by Bendix when he is laid out in turn. Even bigger and better beatings-up, but one of the features of this type of film is that everyone recovers from the most savage pasting with incredible speed and few ill effects: although it is true that in *The Dark Corner* Bendix fails to recover after being thrown from the thirty-third floor of a skyscraper by Clifton Webb.

Yes, Clifton Webb, so admirable in *Laura*, is on the scene again: typed, alas, as an art-dealer with a fund of malicious epigrams and a cuckolded devotion to a young wife with a Laura hair-do; this time it takes six bullets, fired by the wife, to dispatch him, after which the wife, for whose lover's death he has been responsible, throws the empty gun in his dead face.

Tough, what? Never mind: we're tough too. Tough enough to take, also, Dick Powell bashing his enemy's face to a pulp in *Cornered*: this, in my opinion, a much better show despite its slowness in getting to the point: the direction more lively than

242   the dull long-shot-to-medium-shot-to-close-up technique of the two films previously discussed.

In *Cornered*, too, we have Walter Slezak, plump, obsequious and untrustworthy, in soiled white ducks and a character-part; it is uncertain up to the date of writing whether he or Vincent Price will finally occupy the place left vacant by the death of Laird Cregar: Slezak is fatter of course, but Vincent Price has a good, deep, soft toneless voice, almost equal to that of the master himself (Cregar was once billed as Hollywood's super-soft-silky-voiced-slaughter-man).

Cornered takes place, if I remember rightly, in the Argentine; Lisbon is the scene of *The Conspirators*, in which the complete cast of *The Mask of Dimitrios*, with the exception of Faye Emerson and the addition of Paul Henreid, assembled under the direction of Jean Negulesco in an attempt to repeat the success of his former fine melodrama; a resounding failure resulted instead, despite the presence of Sidney Greenstreet, Peter Lorre, Victor Francen, Joseph Calleia and Eduardo Ciannelli: these last two, curiously enough, cast as chiefs of police, instead of as gangsters or spies. The story was completely altered from Frederic Prokosch's novel; this in fact resembled the plot of *Cornered*: a man hunting down his enemy, a traitor and murderer, in the labyrinths of a neutral city.

After *The Conspirators*, Jean Negulesco had another go with *Three Strangers*, which had a good story by John Huston, director of *The Maltese Falcon*; the film, with Greenstreet and Lorre to act in it, suffered a little from its scene being laid in London and the usual irritating errors entailed thereby; but here at least violence was cut to a minimum: a copper (designated in the dialogue as a Bobby, to make it more English) murdered off-stage, an informer knifed in a train, a woman's head bashed in by Greenstreet with the Chinese idol that has caused all the trouble.

Not in any way an outstanding film, but there *is* at any rate an attempt at characterisation – the drunkard, the embezzling solicitor, the horrible nymphomaniac spiderwoman (excellently played by Geraldine Fitzgerald); the characters are a cut above the conventional marionettes of *The Blue Dahlia* and *The Dark Corner.*

Film critics also went crazy over *The Spiral Staircase*, a film directed by Robert Siodmak from the novel by Ethel Lina White. I attended the performance of this with a pleasant feeling of expectation, remembering the director's splendid piece of work in his first American picture, *Phantom Lady*; also it seemed that I was to be transported back to the film-world of my childhood, the atmosphere of Pearl White and the silent serials: lonely girl terrorised by mysterious killer in dark house miles from anywhere, a crippled malignant woman upstairs, night pressing closer to the windows, shots of gloved hands and glaring eyes: the whole *Cat and the Canary* set brought up-to-date in fact, with additions from Freud.

I was disappointed. *The Spiral Staircase* had the distinction of being one of the few thrillers in the middle of which I almost went to sleep. The heroine was dumb, and played by an actress whose name I cannot even remember, but whom the critics raved over: I found her dumb in more senses than one, and her acting negligible. Of course the murderer is a maniac (there is a maniac concealed in every Siodmak film); he finally corners the dumb girl on the landing and prepares to do her in, but unfortunately his preparations take too long and there is time for his paralysed stepmother, who has suddenly recovered the use of her legs, to shoot him from the top of the stairs. Whereupon the heroine, in turn, miraculously recovers the power of speech and is able to telephone the police.

The moral of the film seems to be, get yourself assaulted by a madman and, if you're afflicted in any way, you're bound to snap out of it on the dot: a curious theory vaguely reminiscent of the conditions obtaining in certain army psychiatric hospitals, where sergeant-majors themselves on the borders of lunacy are allowed to shout at the patients, presumably

244 with the idea that neurosis can be cured on the word of command.

The critics, oddly enough, gave bad notices to *The Unseen*, another Ethel Lina White adaptation, which I found, personally, far superior to *The Spiral Staircase*. Here again a lonely girl is trapped in a house where a murderous maniac prowls by night; but a new turn of the screw is given (for by no means the first time, it is true, *vide* James) by the fact that the children of the household are being corrupted into co-operation with the murderer. The little boy of seven is in love with the former governess, who bribes him with silver dollars to let the killer into the house at night, and also to lure her successor to the dark alley where he lies in wait.

Finally the maniac is unmasked and, about to draw his gun and iron everybody out, is forestalled by the little boy who says: 'Here, take your money back. You're a bad man, you kill people,' and shoves the dollars into the pocket containing the pistol. The murderer then gives himself meekly up to the waiting detectives: a conclusion, I think, much more original and satisfying than the penultimate scenes of *The Spiral Staircase*.

The script, by the way, was by Raymond Chandler, who did a much better job on it than he did on his own film, *The Blue Dahlia*.

Such films as *The Unseen* and *The Spiral Staircase* are, of course, not to be taken seriously, even with the present literary trend in England and France (Mervyn Peake and Julien Gracq) to read symbolical meanings into books which derive directly from the House of Usher and the Castle of Otranto.

Let us return from the modern horror-fairy tale to a realistic vision of the world with two films by Fritz Lang: *The Woman in the Window* and *Scarlet Street*: both featuring the same team, Edward G. Robinson, Joan Bennett and Dan Duryea, in practically the same parts; in both Edward G. starts off as a typical stuffy American citizen coming home a bit tight from a bachelor reunion; Joan Bennett crosses his path and trouble starts immediately; the stage is set for Dan Duryea to stroll on in his straw hat, as a pimp or blackmailer.

The Woman in the Window contains a stabbing with scissors and turns out to be a dream; *Scarlet Street* has a stabbing too, but done with a palette-knife and through Joan Bennett's bedclothes: this time it isn't a dream, though the wrong man is hanged and Robinson remains haunted for the rest of his life by the whispering voices of the dead sordid couple; therefore the film caused a scandal in America and was considered by critics over here as highly adult, despite the fact that it bears the same relation to, say, *Destiny* that *No Orchids for Miss Blandish* does to *Sanctuary* by William Faulkner.

Fritz Lang, however, always brings with him some of his cold German-intellectual quality: a feeling for the squalor and menace of a great city which has a parallel in novels like *Auto da Fé* by Elias Canetti. The city with its dark streets is a trap for the unwary (he is usually middle-aged and a professor); stark horror lies in wait round its corners, ready to pounce out at any moment; repression from within and circumstance from without, combine to drive the scissors home and the victim out of his mind. I must say, though, that I consider Robinson miscast in these roles as Little Man; I prefer to see him as Little Cæsar.

Otto Preminger, director of *Laura*, is also, one supposes, of German or Austrian origin; his film, *Fallen Angel*, has much of Lang's quality: this time the dark streets are those of a small town whose English equivalent would be perhaps Littlehampton, and the trap closes round Dana Andrews as a bird of passage who lives on his wits. The bait is Linda Darnell, a waitress on the make and with her hair down; soon she and Dana Andrews are seen kissing in huge close-ups. But Darnell wants money and marriage: Andrews, in order to raise the ready, is obliged to make love to a rich girl who plays the organ in the Methodist church and regularly attends the congregation. Naturally it's not long before Darnell gets bumped off and Andrews is accused of the murder and forced to flee. The rich girl follows him into

246 exile: all comes right in the end and a sadistic detective, who draws on a glove over his knuckle-duster, proves to be finally responsible for the crime.

I preferred *Fallen Angel*, both for direction, acting and story, to *Scarlet Street*, because in it a moral problem has been posed: not a problem of sexual morals (those in *Fallen Angel* are on the whole far looser and the scenes of love-making genuinely erotic), but a problem in which sin and the sense of sin is considered important; the rich church-going girl throws over her principles to stand by her dubious husband, who has married her in the first place in order to give her money to another girl; but her devotion does bring him to heel and back into the fold, in the sort of happy ending unknown to the world of *The Blue Dahlia* and *The Dark Corner*, where sexual morals are far stricter and a genuine moral code is simply non-existent.

That, I think, is the secret of success and failure in all these thrillers: the absence of any moral standard by which the characters can be judged, other than a sexual one: and this is always rigidly enforced; though violence is *de rigueur* in *The Dark Corner* and the wife of the villain may be allowed a lover, dreary Lucille Ball, as the heroine, is consistently hard to get outside of marriage, and her teasing technique is regarded as admirable; whereas when Linda Darnell tries the same tactics in *Fallen Angel* she is represented as evil and self-seeking. The rich organ-playing girl doesn't act hard to get; she is only too ready to give herself to Dana Andrews, to take the chance of securing his love that way; yet this is not shown as reprehensible either; in *The Dark Corner* it would, however, be extremely reprehensible if Lucille Ball were to succumb to the advances of her neurotic private-detective employer; the theme of secretary eventually marrying boss is glamourised and made savoury to satisfy the tawdry suburban typists who only a year ago were determinedly pursuing G.I. Joe up and down London Town.

Scarlet Street is naturally more sophisticated, but here again there is no contrast between good and evil; the victimised hen-pecked cashier, who does a spot of painting in his spare time, is not 'good', but merely a crashing bore; and a picture of pure evil, as represented by Bennett and Duryea, fails to convince, as pure evil always does; even Hitler had ideals, even if they were perverted, and Lucifer himself was once an angel of the Host.

Nor am I particularly enthralled by a blackmailer feeling a sudden lech for a woman when she has just attempted to poison him (*Woman in the Window*); although I am sure that to a Central European mind it would seem the acme of sophistication: I am reminded of the Viennese girl saying of the scene in *Laura* when Waldo Lydecker was about to shoot his protégé to prevent her from belonging to anyone else: 'Now he should drop the gun and they should make love,' and all the Café Royal film-people acclaiming her acumen.

No, it is time that film directors, scriptwriters and critics grew up and realised that a cinematic world of violence and corruption without contrast or code of moral values does not make for distinction and certainly not for art; such a world may well be considered existentialist, but existentialism is at least based on a philosophy and I would sooner read Albert Camus than see Alan Ladd booted once more in the boko.

The two best films I have left to the last: they are too well known (I hope) to be discussed at length; I refer to *The Lost Weekend* and *The Southerner*. These, too, are films of violence, but in one the violence is spiritual and in the other political and social: these qualities at once place them on a different plane. Don Birnam in *The Lost Weekend* is driving himself mad with drink; the family in *The Southerner* are being driven mad by their environment and by catastrophes of nature which they attribute, humbly, to God's will.

Birnam has no talent; no amount of persuasion on the part of the director or his girlfriend in the film will persuade me that he has any; he can't write, so he seeks illusion in soaking it up instead: his proposed regeneration at the end doesn't

248   convince me either, any more than I believe that the Southern
       family will build up their life again after the flood and the final
       disaster; but at any rate a ray of hope has been shown and the
       optimism of man asserted itself: an optimism surely less foolish
       than that which presupposes that the possession of Lucille Ball
       or Veronica Lake will make the world we live in any less violent,
       treacherous and cruel.

                              From *Penguin New Writing 30*, 1947

Biographies

Karl French is the co-author of *The French Brothers' Film Quiz Book* and the editor of *The Collected Marx Brothers' Screenplays*.

Martin Amis's novels include *The Rachel Papers, Money, London Fields* and *The Information*.

Michael Medved is a film critic for the *New York Post*, co-author of *The Golden Turkey Awards* and sole author of seven books including *Hollywood vs. America*.

Camille Paglia is the author of *Sexual Personae, Sex and American Culture* and *Vamps and Tramps*.

Mary Whitehouse is the Founder and President Emeritus of the National Viewers' and Listeners' Association.

Poppy Z. Brite novels include *Lost Souls, Swamp Foetus, Drawing Blood* and *Exquisite Corpse*.

Will Self is the author of *The Quantity Theory of Insanity*, shortlisted for the 1992 John Llewellyn Rhys Memorial Prize and winner of the 1993 Geoffrey Faber Memorial Prize, *Cock & Bull, My Idea of Fun, Grey Area* and *Junk Mail*.

Nicci Gerrard is a journalist whose co-written first novel, *The Memory Game*, will be published in 1997.

Alexander Walker is the film critic for the *London Evening Standard*. The subjects of his biographies range from Elizabeth Taylor to Stanley Kubrick.

Ptolemy Tompkins is the son of Peter Tompkins, the author of *The Secret Life of Plants*, and his autobiography will be published in 1997.

250 **John Waters** is a writer and director. His films include *Female Trouble*, *Pink Flamingoes* and *Serial Mom*.

Kim Newman is a film critic, horror novelist and author of *Nightmare Movies*.

Nigel Andrews is a film critic of the *Financial Times* and the author of *True Myths – The Life and Times of Arnold Schwarzenegger.*

David Thomson is a film critic and author of *The Biographical Dictionary of Cinema, Suspects, Showman: The Life of David O. Selznick* which won the BFI Prize for Film Book of the Year, *Rosebud: The Life of Orson Wells*, and *4-2.*

Jason Jacobs is a lecturer in film and television studies at the University of Warwick and is currently completing a book on the history of television drama.

Pauline Kael was the film critic of *The New Yorker* for more than twelve years until her recent retirement.

Tony Parsons is a columnist for the *Daily Mirror*, hosts Channel 4's *Big Mouth* and regularly contributes to BBC2's *Late Review*. He has written four novels and two non-fiction books and has twice won the PPA Magazine writer of the Year Award. In honour of Stanley Kubrick's ultraviolent masterpiece, *A Clockwork Orange*, he always wears orange socks.

Tom Dewe Mathews is the author of *Censored*, a history of British censorship.

Joan Smith is a journalist and the author of *Misogynies* and the *Loretta Lawson* series of novels. An anthology about food, *Hungry for You*, will be published by Chatto & Windus in November 1996 and she is currently working on a new collection of essays *Different for Girls.*

Harry McCallion a qualified barrister has served in the Paras, the South African Special Forces, the SAS and the RUC. His best-selling autobiography *Killing Zone* was published in 1995.

Roderick Anscombe is an assistant clinical professor at Harvard Medical School who has worked extensively with the criminally insane. He is the author of the novels, *The Secret Life of Laszlo, Count Dracula* and *Shank.*

John Grisham is one of the most successful novelists in the world. His novels include *The Firm, The Client* and *The Pelican Brief.*

Oliver Stone wrote the screenplay for *Midnight Express* and has directed films which include *Platoon, Wall Street, JFK, Nixon* and *Natural Born Killers.*